Developing Educationally Meaningful and Legally Sound IEPs

Special Education Law, Policy, and Practice

Series Editors: Mitchell Yell, PhD, University of South Carolina, and
David Bateman, PhD, Shippensburg University of Pennsylvania

The *Special Education Law, Policy, and Practice* series highlights current trends and legal issues in the education of students with disabilities. The books in this series link legal requirements with evidence-based instruction and highlight practical applications for working with students with disabilities. The titles in the *Special Education Law, Policy, and Practice* series are not only designed to be required textbooks for general education and special education preservice teacher education programs but are also designed for practicing teachers, education administrators, principals, school counselors, school psychologists, parents, and others interested in improving the lives of students with disabilities. The *Special Education Law, Policy, and Practice* series is committed to research-based practices working to provide appropriate and meaningful educational programming for students with disabilities and their families.

Titles in Series

The Essentials of Special Education Law by Andrew M. Markelz
and David F. Bateman
Special Education Law Annual Review 2020 by David F. Bateman, Mitchell L. Yell,
and Kevin P. Brady
Developing Educationally Meaningful and Legally Sound IEPs by Mitchell L. Yell,
David F. Bateman, and James G. Shriner
Sexuality Education for Students with Disabilities by Thomas Gibbon,
Elizabeth Harkins Monaco, and David F. Bateman

Developing Educationally Meaningful and Legally Sound IEPs

Mitchell L. Yell
University of South Carolina

David F. Bateman
Shippensburg University

James G. Shriner
University of Illinois at Urbana-Champaign

ROWMAN & LITTLEFIELD
Lanham • Boulder • New York • London

Acquisitions Editor: Mark Kerr
Assistant Editor: Courtney Packard
Sales and Marketing Inquiries: textbooks@rowman.com

Credits and acknowledgments for material borrowed from other sources, and reproduced with permission, appear on the appropriate pages within the text.
Published by Rowman & Littlefield
An imprint of The Rowman & Littlefield Publishing Group, Inc.
4501 Forbes Boulevard, Suite 200, Lanham, Maryland 20706
www.rowman.com

6 Tinworth Street, London SE11 5AL, United Kingdom

British Library Cataloguing in Publication Information Available

Library of Congress Cataloging-in-Publication Data

Names: Yell, Mitchell L., author. | Bateman, David, author. | Shriner, James G., author.
Title: Developing educationally meaningful and legally sound IEPs / Mitchell L. Yell, University of South Carolina, David F. Bateman, Shippensburg University, James G. Shriner, University of Illinois at Urbana-Champaign.
Description: Lanham, Maryland : Rowman & Littlefield, [2022] | Series: Special education law, policy, and practice | Includes bibliographical references and index.
Identifiers: LCCN 2021018318 (print) | LCCN 2021018319 (ebook) | ISBN 9781538138007 (cloth) | ISBN 9781538138014 (paperback) | ISBN 9781538138021 (epub)
Subjects: LCSH: Individualized education programs. | Education—Parent participation. | Students with disabilities—Services for. | School improvement programs.
Classification: LCC LC4019 .Y45 2022 (print) | LCC LC4019 (ebook) | DDC 371.9/046—dc23
LC record available at https://lccn.loc.gov/2021018318
LC ebook record available at https://lccn.loc.gov/2021018319

♾️™ The paper used in this publication meets the minimum requirements of American National Standard for Information Sciences—Permanence of Paper for Printed Library Materials, ANSI/NISO Z39.48-1992.

Brief Contents

List of Illustrations   xiii

Introduction   1

1 A Brief History of Free Appropriate Public Education and
   Individualized Education Programs   5

2 The Courts and Free Appropriate Public Education   15

3 Foundations – IEP Development: Procedural, Substantive,
   and Implementation Requirements   25

4 The IEP Process and Components: Ensuring Meaningful
   Parental Participation and Conducting the IEP Meeting   43

5 The IEP Process and Components: Conducting
   Assessments and Crafting Present Levels of Academic
   Achievement and Functional Performance Statements
   (with Dawn Rowe)   67

6 The IEP Process and Components: Developing Measurable
   Annual Goals and Monitoring Student Progress   93

7 The IEP Process and Components: Developing Special
   Education Services, Related Services, and Supplementary
   Aids and Services (with Paula Chan)   113

8 Determining Placement   135

Epilogue   151

Resources   155

Appendix A: IEP: Frequently Asked Questions   157

Appendix B: Schedules for IEP Development   167

Appendix C: Tips for Virtual IEP Meetings   173

Appendix D: Determining if an Aide Is Needed   177

Appendix E: Behavioral Aide Levels of Supports Form   181

Appendix F: Instructional Aide Levels of Supports Form   191

Appendix G: Health Aide Levels of Supports Form   197

Appendix H: Questions Related to Transportation for Students   203

References   211

Index   219

About the Author   227

Contents

List of Illustrations   xiii

Introduction   **1**

**1 A Brief History of Free Appropriate Public Education and
    Individualized Education Programs**   **5**

Compulsory Attendance Laws and the Exclusion of Children with Disabilities
from Education   5

Brown v. Board of Education (1954)   7

Advocacy for Students with Disabilities after the *Brown* Ruling   8

*Pennsylvania Association for Retarded Children v. Commonwealth
of Pennsylvania* (1972)   9

Mills v. Board of Education (1972)   9

Subsequent Developments in the States   10

Federal Involvement in Special Education   10

    The Nondiscrimination Path: Section 504 of the Rehabilitation Act   11

    The Educational Grant Path: Education for All Handicapped Children Act   12

Summary   13

2 The Courts and Free Appropriate Public Education   **15**

*Board of Education of the Hendrick Hudson Central School District
v. Rowley* (1982)   16

    Facts of the Case   16

A Split in the Circuit Courts over FAPE   19

Endrew F. v. Douglas County School District (2017)   20

    Facts of the Case   20

    The Due Process Hearing   21

    The US District Court   21

    The US Court of Appeals for the Tenth Circuit   22

    US Supreme Court   22

    The Ruling of the US District Court on Remand   23

Summary   23

3 **Foundations – IEP Development: Procedural, Substantive, and Implementation Requirements** 25

The Dimensions of FAPE: Procedures, Substance, and Implementation 26

The Procedural Dimension 26

Child Find 26

Evaluation 28

The Individualized Education Program 29

Parental Participation 32

Placement 33

Summary of the Procedural Dimension of FAPE 34

The Substantive Dimension 34

The Four IEP Content Questions 35

The Internal Consistency of the IEP 39

Summary of the Substantive Dimension of FAPE 40

The Implementation Dimension 40

Summary of the Implementation Dimension of FAPE 41

Summary 41

4 **The IEP Process and Components: Ensuring Meaningful Parental Participation and Conducting the IEP Meeting** 43

The IDEA and Parental Participation 44

Who Is a Parent under the IDEA? 44

Parental Rights 45

Conducting the IEP Meeting 50

Tips for Ensuring Meaningful Parental Involvement in the IEP Process 51

Talking Points and Assurances to Share with Parents 52

Parent Expectations 53

Parental Involvement in Developing the Present Levels, Goals, Services, and the Progress Monitoring System 53

Specific Steps for Ensuring Meaningful Parental Involvement 54

Meeting Leadership and Agendas 55

The Individualized Education Program Team 57

Mandatory School-Based Members 57

Others with Knowledge about the Child or Special Expertise 61

Consideration of Special Factors in IEP Development 62

Summary 65

5 **The IEP Process and Components: Conducting Assessments and Crafting Present Levels of Academic Achievement and Functional Performance Statements (with Dawn Rowe)**   **67**

Assessment   68

Assessment Requirements in the IDEA   68

Assessment in the Special Education Process   70

Assessment for Instructional Planning   73

Assessment for Progress Monitoring   74

Assessment for Accountability   75

Additional Issues in Assessment   77

Identification of Students with Learning Disabilities   77

Transition Assessment   78

Compliance and Better Practices PLAAFP Statements   82

What Do Better Practices PLAAFP Statements Mean for IEP Teams?   83

Practices That IEP Teams Should Avoid When Writing PLAAFP Statements   86

Summary of Better Practices PLAAFP Statements   91

6 **The IEP Process and Components: Developing Measurable Annual Goals and Monitoring Student Progress**   **93**

A Method for Ensuring That Annual IEP Goals Are Measurable   94

Additional Elements of Goals   98

Identifying High-Quality Measurable Annual IEP Goals   100

Practices That IEP Teams Should Avoid in Crafting Annual Goals   104

Developing Short-Term Objectives   105

Using Goals to Monitor Student Progress   106

How to Monitor a Student's Progress toward the Annual IEP Goals   107

Characteristics of Progress Monitoring   107

When and How to Analyze the Progress Data   108

When and How to Report the Student's Progress to His or Her Parents   110

Practices IEP Teams Should Avoid in Measuring Student Progress   110

Summary of Better Practice IEP Annual Goals and Measurement   111

7 **The IEP Process and Components: Developing Special Education Services, Related Services, and Supplementary Aids and Services (with Paula Chan)**   **113**

Specially Designed Instruction and Peer-Reviewed Research   114

Specially Designed Instruction: Special Education Services   117

    Beginning Date, Duration, Frequency, and Location   118

    Service Delivery Models   118

Specially Designed Instruction: Related Services   120

    Determining Eligibility for Related Services   120

    Processes for Determining Related Services   121

    General Strategies for IEP Teams   122

    General Tips for Working with Related Service Providers   122

Specially Designed Instruction: Supplementary Aids and Services   122

    What Does This Mean?   124

    Step 1: Observe the Needs of the Student in the General
    Education Classroom   124

    Step 2: Identify Barriers   124

    Specially Designed Instruction: Program Modifications and Support for
    School Personnel   125

Transition Services   127

    What Is Transition?   127

    What Is Included in Transition Planning?   127

    Who Should Participate in Transition Planning?   128

    The Domains of Adulthood to Consider   129

    Developing Post-School Goals   129

    Planning for Transition Services or Activities   129

    Transition in Practice   129

    Summary of Transition Services   130

Extended School Year Services   130

    Requirements of ESY Services   131

    Limits to ESY Services   131

    Summary of ESY Services   132

Ensuring That Services Are Delivered with Fidelity   132

Summary   134

8 Determining Placement   **135**

What Is a Placement Decision and Who Makes It?   136

Placement and Least Restrictive Environment   137

    Continuum of Alternative Placements   139

    What Are Supplementary Aids and Services?   140

    Case Law and Least Restrictive Environment   140

The *Roncker* Test   141

The *Daniel* Test   141

The *Rachel H.* Test   142

Summary of the Judicial Tests   143

General Education Class vs. General Education Curriculum   143

Determining Student Placement   144

Practices to Follow When Determining Student Placement   145

Practices to Avoid When Determining Student Placement   147

Steps in Determining Student Placement   148

Summary of Determining Placements   150

Epilogue   **151**

Resources (with Amelia Blanton)   155

Appendix A: FAQs on IEPs   157

Appendix B: Schedules for IEP Development   167

Appendix C: Tips for Virtual IEP Meetings   173

Appendix D: Determining if an Aide Is Needed   177

Appendix E: Behavioral Aide Levels of Supports Form   181

Appendix F: Instructional Aide Levels of Supports Form   191

Appendix G: Health Aide Levels of Supports Form   197

Appendix H: Questions Related to Transportation for Students   203

References   211

Index   219

About the Authors   227

List of Illustrations

Figure 3.1	Internal Consistency of an IEP	39
Figure 5.1	Student Data Graph	75
Figure 6.1	Example of Progress Monitoring Graph	108
Figure 8.1	Placement Determination Flowchart	149
Table 4.1	Suggestions to Ensure Meaningful Parent Involvement	47
Table 5.1	Initial Assessment, Selected Requirements	69
Table 5.2	Components of Better Practices PLAAFP Statement	82
Table 5.3	Structure of PLAAFP Summary Statements	84
Table 5.4	Test Questions for PLAAFP Statement	84
Table 5.5	PLAAFP Test Questions	87
Table 5.6	PLAAFP Test Questions Example for Rosie	88
Table 5.7	PLAAFP Test Questions for James	89
Table 5.8	PLAAFP Test Questions for Tyler	90
Table 5.9	Practices to Follow and Practices to Avoid	91
Table 6.1	Depiction of the Requirements of a Better Practices Measurable Annual Goal	98
Table 6.2	Test Questions for Well-Written Annual Measurable Goals	101
Table 6.3	Goal Assessment Form	102
Table 6.4	Goal Test Questions and Sample Goals Example 1	102
Table 6.5	Goal Test Questions and Sample Goals Example 2	102
Table 6.6	Goal Test Questions and Sample Goals Example 3	103
Table 6.7	Goal Test Questions and Sample Goals Example 4	103
Table 6.8	Goal Test Questions and Sample Goals Example 5	104
Table 6.9	Characteristics of Better Practices Data Collection	108
Table 6.10	Example of Progress Monitoring Form	109
Table 6.11	Practices to Follow and Practices to Avoid in Writing Measurable Annual Goals and Monitoring Student Progress	111
Table 7.1	Websites with Peer-Reviewed Interventions	116
Table 7.2	Characteristics of Better Practice IEP Services	118
Table 7.3	Nonexhaustive List of Related Services	120
Table 7.4	Implementation Checklist Example—Teacher	133
Table 7.5	Implementation Checklist Example—Counselor	133
Table 7.6	Practices to Follow and Practices to Avoid	134
Table 8.1	Practices to Follow and Practices to Avoid	150

Textbox 3.1   Child Find: Red Flags That Indicate That District Personnel
Knew or Should Have Known   27

Textbox 3.2   Procedural Requirements of the Initial Evaluation
and Re-evaluation   29

Textbox 3.3   Required Members of an IEP Team   30

Textbox 3.4   Required Components of an IEP   31

Textbox 4.1   Parental Procedural Rights under the IDEA   45

Textbox 4.2   Sample IEP Team Meeting Agenda   55

Textbox 5.1   Present Levels of Academic Achievement and Functional
Performance Test Questions   86

Textbox 6.1   Goal Test Questions and Sample Goals   102

Textbox 8.1   The Continuum of Alternative Placements (IDEA Regulations,
34 CFR § 300.115, 2006)   139

Textbox 8.2   Factors to Consider in Determining Student Placement   144

Textbox 9.1   IEP Process and Content Checklist   152

INTRODUCTION

> *The Individualized Education Program is the heart of the Education for All Handicapped Children Act as we wrote it and intended it to be carried out. (Senator Robert Stafford, 1978, p. 72)*

In the early 1970s, only one out of five students with disabilities were educated in America's public schools. More than 1 million students with disabilities were refused admission to public schools and over 3.5 million students with disabilities were admitted to public schools but received only limited educational services or received an education not appropriate to their needs (Zettel & Ballard, 1982). Given the challenges faced by students with disabilities in their efforts to access educational services, the US Congress passed legislation ensuring the educational rights of all students with disabilities.

In 1975, the Education for All Handicapped Children Act (EAHCA; renamed the Individuals with Disabilities Education Act [IDEA] in 1990) was enacted to guarantee eligible students with disabilities the right to receive a free appropriate public education (FAPE) in public schools. The Congressional authors of the EAHCA believed this goal was best accomplished by individualizing a student's education. The vehicle by which Congress attempted to ensure students with disabilities would receive an individualized and appropriate education was through collaboration between school personnel and a student's parents (Stafford, 1978).

Senator Robert Stafford from Vermont was one of the Congressional sponsors of the EAHCA. In 1978, Senator Stafford wrote an article for the *Vermont Law Review* in which he noted that the very essence of special education was to improve the quality of lives of students with disabilities and that the way the law could meet this goal was by ensuring students received an appropriate education that met their unique educational needs. The way Congress decided to accomplish this policy objective was by mandating an Individualized Education Program (IEP) for eligible students with disabilities in which their individualized

1

needs were assessed and then addressed through a program of special education and related services. Stafford wrote about how the Congressional authors of the EAHCA made the clear assumption that better IEPs would lead to measurable results for students who were eligible for special education services under the law. Thus, the IEP would be the roadmap for improving the lives of students with disabilities.

Although IEPs have been the linchpin of students' special education programs for more than 30 years, they have not yet met the expectations that Congress originally intended when it mandated IEPs (IDEA, 2004). Frequently, IEPs are fraught with legal errors (Bateman, 2017; Huefner, 2006), and far too often IEPs are neither individualized nor educationally meaningful (Bateman, 2017; Yell, 2019). Moreover, often (a) assessments are not aligned with the annual goals in an IEP (Bateman, 2017; Yell, 2019), (b) unmeasurable goals are included in the IEP (Bateman, 2017; Bateman & Herr, 2013; Shriner, et al., 2013), and (c) data are not collected to monitor student progress (Bateman, 2017; Bateman & Linden, 2012; Yell & Busch, 2012). The problems school-based teams have with IEP development led Bateman and Linden (2012) to observe:

> Sadly, most IEPs are horrendously burdensome to teachers and nearly useless to parents and children. Far from being a creative, flexible, data-based, and individualized application of the best educational interventions to a child, the typical IEP is empty . . . many, if not most goals and objectives couldn't be measured if one tried, and all too often no effort is made to actually assess the child's progress toward the goal. (p. 63)

In the 2017 Supreme Court ruling in *Endrew F. v. Douglas County School District*, the chief justice of the Court, John Roberts, wrote, "the essential function of an IEP is to set out a plan for pursuing academic and functional advancement" (*Endrew F.*, 2017, p. 998). In this case, the High Court ruled "to meet its substantive obligations under the IDEA a school must offer an IEP reasonably calculated to enable a child to make progress appropriate in light of the child's circumstances" (*Endrew F.*, 2017, p. 1002). Unfortunately, the problems school districts often have with IEPs now are as true as they were over 20 years ago, when Bradley and Danielson (2001) observed that many school personnel and parents lack the resources, training, and supports necessary to craft educationally meaningful and legally sound IEPs.

In this book, we present a framework and process for collaboratively developing educationally meaningful and legally sound IEPs enabling eligible students to make progress. Because educators must collaboratively develop IEPs that are meaningful and enable students to make progress while, at the same time, being legally sound, we propose a method of IEP development that is legally sound and relies on "better practices." Using better practices in IEP may go beyond what the law actually requires, but the use of such practices will enable special educators to meet the legal requirements while developing and implementing special education programs that enable students to make progress in light of their unique educational needs. Although we are not offering legal advice, we believe the better practices we propose will assist special educators to develop and implement IEPs.

In *Rutland South Supervisory Union*, a due process hearing officer wrote:

The IEP can be viewed as an intricate puzzle that has been pieced together by the combined efforts of teachers, parents, school staff and other professionals whose sole purpose is to create an educational program from which a (student with a disability) can benefit. How the puzzle is constructed is crucial. Missing pieces jeopardize the whole picture. (p. 153)

Because IEP development is a process, we encourage the reader to continue to come back to the book and review the process, the resources, and the framework. Our hope is that this book will help you to assemble your intricate puzzle in an educationally meaningful and legally correct manner.

CHAPTER 1

A Brief History of Free Appropriate Public Education and Individualized Education Programs

The development of laws requiring students with disabilities receive a free appropriate public education (FAPE) in conformity with their individualized education programs (IEPs) has shown a steady progression in the courts and federal and state legislature since the early-to-mid-twentieth century. The early court rulings and legislation involved issues of access to public education, whereas the issues addressed in recent years have involved issues of accountability for results and student progress. In this chapter we provide a brief history of the development of FAPE and IEPs.

Compulsory Attendance Laws and the Exclusion of Children with Disabilities from Education

Since the enactment of the first compulsory school attendance laws in the middle-to-late 1800s, education in the public schools has been viewed as a birthright and an absolute necessity to maintain a viable democracy (Levine & Wexler, 1981). Unfortunately, children and youth with disabilities were often not included in this crucial effort to have an educated populace. In fact, despite the presence of compulsory school attendance law mandating that children of certain ages were required to receive an education, state and school officials were often free to exclude students with disabilities solely because of the presence of a disability or, in some cases, the perception that a child had a disability. For example, according to a state law in Ohio

> The superintendent of schools of the district in which the child resides may excuse him from attendance for any part of the remainder of the current school year upon satisfactory showing of either of the following facts: (1) that his bodily or mental condition does not permit his attendance at school during such period. (Ohio Revised Code Annotated, p. 1972)

As Handel (1975) aptly wrote, "Laws such as this very often result(ed) in the compulsory *non*-attendance for the handicapped child, and neither the handicapped child nor his parents had a statutory right to demand (educational) placement" (Handel, 1975, p. 351). The reasoning behind policies and law excluding students with disabilities was often that "the handicapped cannot learn, their presence in school will negatively affect the learning of normal children, these children make non-handicapped children and adults feel uncomfortable, the cost of their education is too great, and the teachers and facilities are in short supply" (Weintraub & Abeson, 1972, pp. 1057–1058).

There were many ways in which children and youth with disabilities were denied educational opportunities (Handel, 1975). Many students with disabilities, estimated at over 1,000,000, were simply denied admission to public schools (Weintraub & Abeson, 1972). Additionally, approximately 3,500,000 students who were admitted were denied anything close to the special educational programming that they needed (Weintraub & Abeson, 1972). As chief justice of the US Supreme Court William Rehnquist wrote years later, these children were "left to fend for themselves in classrooms designed for education of their nonhandicapped peers" (*Board of Education v. Rowley*, 1982, p. 191).

Regrettably, courts often upheld these efforts to exclude students with disabilities from a public education. For example, in 1919 the Wisconsin Supreme Court took a case, *Beattie v. Board of Education* (1919), which involved a young student, Merritt "Bud" Beattie, who had cerebral palsy. Merritt Beattie had attended public school until the fifth grade and had done well in his classes. In fact, he was reported to have been very bright and had been taught to read and write at a very early age (*Beattie v. Board of Education* 1919; Blakely, 1979). However, Merritt's cerebral palsy caused drooling, facial contortions, and speech problems. School officials claimed this condition nauseated the teachers and other students, required too much teacher time, and negatively affected school discipline and progress. School officials expelled the student from school and suggested he attend a day school for students who were deaf. Merritt's parents brought a lawsuit asking that the school be required to reinstate Merritt. In a jury trial, the parents prevailed and the school was required to allow Merritt to enter the sixth grade. The school appealed the ruling to the Wisconsin Supreme Court, which overturned the decision and ruled school officials could exclude Merritt Beattie. One is tempted to think that such court rulings were in the distant past, but that would not be true. For example, in 1958 the Supreme Court of Illinois, in *Department of Public Welfare v. Haas*, held that Illinois' existing compulsory attendance legislation did not require the state to provide a free public education for a boy described as "mentally deficient or feeble minded" (p. 212). According to the Illinois Supreme Court

> Existing legislation does not require the state to provide a free educational program, as a part of the common school system, for the feeble minded or mentally deficient children who, because of limited intelligence, are unable to receive a good common school education. Under the circumstances, this constitutional mandate has no application. (p. 212)

Similarly, in 1969 North Carolina made it a crime for parents to persist in forcing the attendance of a child with disabilities after the child's exclusion from public school (Weber, 2008).

As a result of the poor educational programming their children with special needs were receiving, and in many cases their children's outright exclusion from schools, parents banded together to advocate for their children's education rights and to work for change. For example, in 1933, five mothers of children with intellectual disabilities formed the Cuyahoga County Ohio Council for the Retarded Child (Levine & Wexler, 1981; Winzer, 1993) and in 1922 faculty and students at Teachers College, Columbia University, in New York, founded the Council for Exceptional Children (Kode, 2016). Similar types of advocacy groups formed of parents and educators were established throughout the nation during the 1930s and 1940s. These organizations served as a means to provide educational programming for their children, offered means to unite and make change locally, and provided an avenue of support for parents (Yell, 2019). These local organizations led the way for national organizations, such as the Council for Exceptional Children, which is currently the leading organization advocating on behalf of the education of children and youth with disabilities. The progress made in educating children and youth with disabilities can be attributed to the success of parents as advocates for their children. These groups worked tirelessly to push local school boards, administrators, and legislators to provide appropriate educational programming for their children. In his book addressing the beginnings of federal special education legislation, Martin (2013) noted the importance of parents. Martin wrote that

> I quickly came to admire (parent's) knowledge and untiring advocacy. I realized that parents had provided the energy and will to create special education programs wherever they occurred. They had petitioned school administrators, school board members, state officials, state legislators, and increasingly, federal legislators and administrators. It became apparent to me that there would be little, if any, special education if the parent had not created it directly or through political persuasion. (Martin, 2013, p. 22)

The efforts of these groups met with mixed success. Then in 1954, the US Supreme Court issued a ruling in a momentous court case that was to change the landscape of American education. That seminal ruling was, of course, *Brown v. Board of Education* (1954).

Brown v. Board of Education (1954)

Brown v. Board of Education (hereinafter *Brown*) was a case heard by the US Supreme Court. *Brown* was actually five cases that had been consolidated by the Supreme Court into one case. The five cases were *Briggs v. Elliott* (1952), filed in South Carolina; *Brown v. Board of Education of Topeka* (1952), filed in Kansas; *Davis v. County School Board of Prince Edward County* (1952), filed in Virginia; *Gebhart v. Belton* (1952), filed in Delaware; and *Bolling v. Sharpe* (1954), filed in Washington, DC. When the rulings in these cases were appealed to the US Supreme Court, the High Court consolidated the cases and used the name of the most well-known, *Brown v. Board of Education of Topeka*, to address the separate but equal doctrine in public schools.

The case was heard by the Supreme Court in 1953. The chief justice at the time was Fred M. Vinson who believed the doctrine of separate but equal, set in *Plessy v. Ferguson* (1896), should be upheld. After the oral arguments were finished, the attorney for the defendants remarked he believed the defendants would win the case (Lennon, 2007). The Supreme Court justices, however, were unable to come to a decision, so Associate Justice Felix Frankfurter asked that the case be reheard. A hearing was set to take place at the beginning of the next term. Prior to the beginning of the new term, Chief Justice Vinson died. President Dwight Eisenhower nominated the former governor of California, Earl Warren, to be the next chief justice. Thus, Warren was the chief justice of the US Supreme Court during the rehearing of *Brown* and in the eventual decision in the case.

Chief Justice Earl Warren guided the court to a unanimous decision in *Brown*, overturning *Plessy*. In the opinion, Warren wrote, "in the field of public education the doctrine of separate but equal has no place. Segregated schools are inherently unequal" (*Brown*, p. 495). The Court ruled that because of segregation in the schools, the plaintiffs were being "deprived of the equal protection of the laws guaranteed by the 14th Amendment" (*Brown*, p. 495). Chief Justice Warren also wrote:

> Today, education is perhaps the most important function of state and local governments. . . . In these days, it is doubtful that any child may reasonably be expected to succeed in life if he is denied the opportunity of an education. Such an opportunity, where the state has undertaken to provide it, is a right that must be available to all on equal terms. (*Brown*, p. 493)

The ruling in *Brown* was a major victory for the civil rights movement and became a foundation for further civil rights action and changes in education. The ruling made it clear that state-required or state-sanctioned segregation solely on the basis of a person's unchangeable characteristics, such as race, was unconstitutional because it violated the equal protection and due process clauses of the US Constitution. Additionally, many people believed the *Brown* ruling could be used to affirm the rights of another segregated group of children: children and youth with disabilities (Weintraub & Abeson, 1972).

Advocacy for Students with Disabilities after the *Brown* Ruling

One of the first persons to comment on the applicability of the *Brown* ruling to persons with disabilities was Dr. Gunnar Dybwad, the executive director of the National Association of Parents and Friends of Mentally Retarded Children (now the Arc). Dr. Dywad believed the *Brown* decision had great implications for children with disabilities and their families because these children often had no access to public education (Gilhool, 2011). Attorneys such as Thomas Gilhool and Stanley Herr collaborated with parent advocacy groups to begin filing lawsuits against school districts that excluded children with disabilities using the *Brown* ruling as a basis for their complaints (Gilhool, 2011).

Pennsylvania Association for Retarded Children v. Commonwealth of Pennsylvania (1972)

Pennsylvania Association for Retarded Children v. Commonwealth of Pennsylvania (1972; hereinafter *PARC*) was a class-action lawsuit filed by the Pennsylvania Association for Retarded Children and the parents of 13 students with intellectual disabilities on behalf of all children, ages 6 to 21, with intellectual disabilities, then referred to as mental retardation. Pennsylvania had a law that allowed public school districts to exclude children who were found to be "uneducable or untrainable" (*PARC v. Commonwealth of Pennsylvania*, 1972, p. 280). PARC hired Thomas Gilhool to represent the organization in a class-action lawsuit against Pennsylvania's exclusionary law. Officials at the PARC organization knew Thomas Gilhool had been involved in the civil rights movement in the late 1950s and 1960s (Gilhool, 2011). In the case, Gilhool based his arguments on the *Brown* decision, asserting that if the court should find for the African American children, then states could no longer segregate on the basis of sex, age, or disabilities (Gilhool, 2011). The case ended with a judicially approved consent decree. The court noted that the willingness of officials for the State of Pennsylvania to negotiate reflected "an intelligent response to overwhelming evidence against their position" (*PARC v. Commonwealth of Pennsylvania*, 1972, p. 290). According to the consent decree, the existing law restricting education to the class of students of ages 6 to 21 was unconstitutional. The consent decree also required that Pennsylvania was responsible for providing free public education to all children. The quality of the education and training given to the children with disabilities had to match that of the education and training given to general education students.

A few months after this decision, a lawsuit was filed against the Board of Education of Washington, DC, that went further than the *PARC* (1972) decision in noting that the students with disabilities were entitled to a specialized education under the equal protection and due process clauses of the US Constitution. The case was *Mills v. Board of Education* (1972).

Mills v. Board of Education (1972)

Mills v. Board of Education (hereinafter Mills, 1972) was a class-action suit brought on behalf of seven children who were labeled as emotionally disturbed, mentally retarded, having behavioral problems, and hyperactive, and who were excluded from participating in public education by the Washington, DC Board of Education. The class represented was all children and youth of school age in Washington, DC, who had been excluded from public schools because of their disability. The plaintiffs asserted the practice of denying students with disabilities from a public education without due process of law was unconstitutional. The plaintiffs had asked for preliminary injunctive relief in which the DC Board of Education would (a) admit the named children to school immediately; (b) provide lists of all children who remained excluded from public school; and (c) initiate outreach to these students, which was estimated at 18,000 students (Mills, 1972). The day that the hearing was to begin, attorneys for the DC Board of Education sought a postponement of the hearing. When the judge in the case, Joseph Waddy, denied the request, the defendants immediately agreed to the terms of the requested relief (Herr, 1972a). Judge Waddy granted summary judgment for the plaintiffs. In addition to ordering all of the plaintiffs' requests, Judge Waddy also ordered the Board of Education to provide procedural mechanisms that would ensure parents could act to enforce their children's rights. Many of the rights for students with disabilities announced in the *Mills* consent decree were later enshrined in special education law.

Subsequent Developments in the States

The *PARC* and *Mills* decisions were followed by similar cases throughout the country. In the 2.5 years following the *PARC* and *Mills* decisions, 46 right-to-education cases were filed on behalf of children with disabilities in 28 states (Zettel & Ballard, 1982). The outcomes of these cases were consistent with the outcomes of *Mills* and *PARC* (Yell, 2019). Moreover, by the early 1970s, many states had passed laws requiring students with disabilities receive a public education. Unfortunately, these laws varied substantially and resulted in uneven attempts to provide education to students. Despite the successes in these cases and state legislatures, many students with disabilities continued to be denied an appropriate public education (Zettel & Ballard, 1982). These problems led many to advocate for the passage of federal laws to bring an end to these uneven efforts to provide appropriate educational programming to students with disabilities. As Martin (2013) noted,

> In local school programs, children were frequently subjected to substandard services in poor facilities. Parents reported classes in basements, janitor's rooms, condemned buildings, and similar sites. Children were often placed in classes inappropriate for their needs . . . (Programs) were frequently trained teachers, and instructors generally had to create their own curriculum and materials . . . not a single state even pretended to educate all its children with disabilities. Even states that had mandatory laws did not enforce them. (Martin, 2013, pp. 30–31)

These problems led many to advocate for the passage of federal laws to bring an end to these uneven efforts to provide appropriate educational programming to students with disabilities.

Federal Involvement in Special Education

The Elementary and Secondary Education Act (ESEA) of 1965 was the first federal effort to provide federal financial aid to the schools (Martin, 2013). The ESEA provided money to states to improve educational opportunities for disadvantaged children, including students with disabilities. The following year an amendment to this act, Title VI of the ESEA, added funding for grants for pilot programs to develop promising programs for children with disabilities. In 1970, Title VI of the ESEA was replaced by the Education of the Handicapped Act (EHA), which was to become the framework for subsequent special education legislation. The purpose of the EHA was to provide funding to states to initiate, expand, or improve education programming for students with disabilities. The EHA also provided funding for grants to colleges and universities to prepare teachers of students with disabilities and development money for regional resource centers. Colker (2013) asserted that despite not containing any substantive rights for students with disabilities, the EHA was, nonetheless, an important first step in legislating special education programming for students with disabilities.

The passage of free-standing federal legislation regarding the education of students with disabilities that provided funding but no actual educational rights led advocates and persons in Congress to advocate for the passage of federal legislation with teeth. The passage of this legislation took two paths to ensuring the educational rights of students with disabilities: nondiscrimination and an educational grant program (Martin, et al., 1996).

The Nondiscrimination Path: Section 504 of the Rehabilitation Act

Following two vetoes of the Rehabilitation Act by President Nixon, the principal authors of the law, Representatives Charles Vanik of Ohio and Senator Hubert Humphry of Minnesota, made changes to the Act. Congress passed and President Nixon signed the Rehabilitation Act in 1973. The Rehabilitation Act provided for federally assisted rehabilitation programs for persons with disabilities. A brief section of the Rehabilitation Act, Section 504, prohibited discrimination against persons with disabilities.

This nondiscrimination aspect of the Rehabilitation Act was modeled on Title IV of the Civil Rights Act of 1964, which prohibited discrimination based on race, color, and national origin in programs receiving federal financial assistance. Section 504 required that

> No otherwise qualified individual with a disability in the United States . . . shall, solely by reason of his or her disability, be excluded from the participation in, be denied the benefits of, or be subjected to discrimination under any program or any activity receiving federal financial assistance. (Section 504, 29 U.S.C. § 794[a])

According to Senator Hubert Humphrey "[Section 504] is the civil rights declaration of the handicapped. It was greeted with great hope and satisfaction by Americans who have had the distress of physical or mental handicaps compounded by thoughtless or callous discrimination" (*Congressional Record*, April 26, 1977, p. 12,216).

With respect to schools and students with disabilities, discrimination occurs when students are excluded from participation or receive inferior or different treatment because they have a disability. It was believed by advocates that this nondiscrimination path would ensure that students with disabilities would receive an appropriate education. It soon became obvious that because of certain issues with Section 504, including the lack of federal regulations, funding, and a mechanism to monitor compliance with the law, school district officials virtually ignored Section 504 (Martin et al., 1996). It became obvious to many advocates for students with disabilities that the most effective path to ensuring appropriate educational programming lies in the second pathway: an educational grant program.

The Educational Grant Path: Education for All Handicapped Children Act

In 1975, Congress passed the Education for All Handicapped Children Act (EAHCA)[1]. Factors such as the (a) judicial rulings finding constitutional requirements for educating children and youth with disabilities in public schools, (b) awareness of the poorly met needs of students with disabilities, and (c) inability of states to provide educational opportunities for students with disabilities were among the important factors that led to the enactment of the EAHCA (Jones, 1975). As Senator Harrison Williams, the chief sponsor of the EACA, asserted, "it is time that Congress took strong and forceful action. It is time for Congress to assure equal protection of the laws and to provide to all handicapped children their right to education" (*Congressional Record*, 1975, remarks of Senator Williams). The EAHCA was a bipartisan effort that passed by overwhelming margins in the House and Senate. The EAHCA, however, was not without its critics (Martin et al., 1996). President Ford believed Congress had overpromised the amount of funding to be provided and the law would infringe on state perogatives. Nonetheless, President Ford signed the bill into law.

The EAHCA required all eligible students with disabilities be provided a FAPE. The EAHCA accomplished this by providing a funding mechanism to assist states by funding the excess costs in providing a FAPE to students with disabilities. To receive these funds, state officials had to submit plans to the federal government ensuring the state would identify, evaluate, and provide a FAPE to all eligible students with disabilities in conformity with the requirements of the EAHCA.

Under the EAHCA, federal funding would flow from the federal government to state education agencies (SEAs) and then to local education agencies (LEAs) within the state. The LEAs (i.e., local school districts), in turn, had to have programs meeting the state requirements (Yell, 2019). By 1985, all states had complied with the requirements of the provisions of the EAHCA. Thus, the EAHCA represented a federal commitment to students with disabilities both in the educational rights of eligible students, which were enforceable in the courts, and as a fiscal partnership with the states (Stafford, 1978). Unfortunately, the federal funding promise in terms of the federal share, which was set to rise to 40% of the average per-pupil expenditure for students in the respective states, was never met. Instead, the federal funding to the states was usually about 15% of the average per-pupil expenditure.

The fundamental premise of the EAHCA was that all eligible students with disabilities would be provided with a FAPE. The definition of FAPE in the EAHCA was as follows:

(A) are provided at public expense, under public supervision and direction, and without charge,

(B) meet standards of the state educational agency,

---

[1] The name of the EAHCA was changed to the Individuals with Disabilities Education Act (IDEA) in 1990. In chapter 1 whenever referring to the law and historical events prior to 1990 we will use the EAHCA.

(C) include an appropriate preschool, elementary, or secondary school education in the state involved, and

(D) are provided in conformity with the individualized education programs . . . (IDEA, 20 U.S.C. § 1401 (a)(18), 2006).

According to Senator Robert Stafford (1978), "We in Congress did not attempt to define 'appropriate' in the law but instead we established a base-line mechanism, a written document called the Individualized Education Program (IEP)" (Stafford, 1978, p. 75). Thus, the IEP, developed collaboratively between a student's parents and school personnel, was the basis for determining if the educational program offered to a student with disabilities was appropriate for that student. (Martin, 2013). According to Martin (2013), the IEP was, in fact, the "operational definition" of appropriate for a given student (Martin, 2013, p. 2635). The IEP was, in the words of Senator Stafford, "the central part of this Act as we wrote it and intended it to be carried out" (Stafford, 1978, p. 79).

Congressional authors of the EAHCA included a number of procedural safeguards in the law which were meant to ensure that a student's parents were involved in the development of their child's program of special education (see chapter 3). The Congressional authors also recognized that disputes would occur regarding a student's special education program in his or her IEP, so they included resolution mechanisms whereby parents, and sometimes school districts, could request a review by an impartial due process hearing officer. Following a due process hearing, either party may appeal part or all of a decision to state or federal court.

Congress specified that the IEP would be the means by which an appropriate program for an eligible student with disabilities would be developed and implemented. Nonetheless, interpreting what the standard of appropriateness should be was difficult. As Martin et al. (1996) noted, "Neither the statutory language of the (EAHCA) nor the regulations interpreting the (EAHCA) . . . specify in detail what constitutes an appropriate education" (p. 34). It would be up to the courts, and especially the US Supreme Court, to clarify how IEP teams could ensure the special education programs they develop and implement provide students with an appropriate education. In the next chapter we address court interpretations of the FAPE requirement of the IDEA.

Summary

By the early 1900s, all of the states had compulsory education laws; however, the exclusion of children with disabilities was still widely practiced. The civil rights movement, specifically the US Supreme Court's decision in *Brown v. Board of Education* (1954), provided the impetus for subsequent legislation and litigation granting students with disabilities the right to an education. These efforts, led by the efforts of parents of children with disabilities and their advocates, resulted in laws, such as Section 504 of the Rehabilitation Act of

1973 and the EAHCA of 1975. These laws ensured the rights of students with disabilities to receive appropriate individualized instruction in public schools and led to uniformity in programming for children and youth with disabilities among the states. The history of special education law can be characterized as a movement to ensure access to education to one that seeks to ensure quality of educational programming.

CHAPTER 2

The Courts and Free Appropriate Public Education

When parents and school personnel cannot agree on certain aspects of a child's special education program, the IDEA includes a dispute resolution system, which can be used to settle their differences (IDEA Regulations 34 CFR § 300.140). In this system, states are required to have a procedure in which parents can file a complaint with their state's educational agency (IDEA Regulations 34 CFR § 300.151-153). If state officials determine that an investigation of the complaint is needed, the state then has 60 days to conduct an on-site investigation of the complaint.

The IDEA also includes another dispute resolution format in which a student's parents or school district personnel may request a due process hearing. In this hearing, an impartial third party (i.e., the due process hearing officer or administrative law judge) will hear both sides of the disputed issue, determine the facts of the case, compare the facts to the requirements of the IDEA, and issue a ruling to settle the dispute. Following the hearing, the losing party may appeal any or all of the hearing officer's decision to state or federal court. Since the enactment of the EAHCA in 1975, there have been many rulings from US District Courts and the US Circuit Courts of Appeals. Some special education cases have been heard in the highest court in the United States: the US Supreme Court. All these cases began with disagreements regarding the IEP, which then proceeded to a due process hearing, and eventually wound up in federal court.

The American legal system relies heavily on court rulings to interpret federal law. Special education is a litigious area, which has resulted in many court decisions, the results of which are often referred to as case law. Case law represents a body of law created by judicial decisions rather than legislation or regulation, and involves precedents and authority created by the judicial rulings (Yell, 2019). Of this body of case law, no court decisions create greater and more wide-ranging precedent than do decisions of the US Supreme Court.

There are many matters in which special education cases have occurred, and a body of case law has formed, such as FAPE, least restrictive environment, and discipline. By far the most frequent area in which court rulings in special education have been issued has been whether or not a student's special education conferred a FAPE. It is especially important, therefore, that special education administrators and teachers understand what the courts have told us about providing a FAPE to students with disabilities, which occurs in the IEP development process. Our purpose in this chapter is to review the two major rulings by the US Supreme Court clarifying FAPE. We also address additional rulings by the High Court on issues of importance to special education administrators and teachers when developing students' IEPs. We begin with the first special education case heard by the US Supreme Court.

Board of Education of the Hendrick Hudson Central School District v. Rowley (1982)

In 1982, the Supreme Court issued a ruling in *Board of Education of the Hendrick Hudson Central School District v. Rowley* (hereinafter *Rowley*, 1982). This seminal case was the first special education case heard by Supreme Court, and it addressed the central issue in special education: What constitutes a FAPE for a given student? In the following sections, we present the facts of the case, the rulings by the hearing officer, the ruling by the US District Court, the ruling of the US Court of Appeals for the Second Circuit, and the ruling by the Supreme Court.

Facts of the Case

The case involved Amy Rowley, a student eligible for special education and related services due to her needs related to her being deaf. Shortly after it was medically confirmed that Amy was deaf, the EAHCA became law. Amy's parents were enthused because this new law requiring a FAPE for eligible students with disabilities meant that Amy would be able to attend the local public school, Furnace Woods Elementary School, rather than attending a regional school for deaf and blind students (*Rowley*, 2008). When her parents contacted the principal of Furnace Woods School, he and the faculty indicated that they were willing to provide the services that Amy would need.

The year before she was to start school, the principal, faculty, and parents agreed to place her in a general education kindergarten class and discuss the supports necessary for Amy to receive an appropriate education. The school personnel and Amy's parents agreed to a number of accommodations and supports, including (a) training in sign language for the school administrators and some faculty; (b) installing a teletypewriter in the principal's office so Amy could communicate with her parents, who were also deaf; (c) providing the services of a speech and language pathologist; and (d) having Amy's teachers use an FM hearing system. Amy's parents were satisfied with these services but also requested that Amy have a sign language interpreter assigned to her class. Although the principal was agreeable to this service, district officials were wary of assigning a full-time interpreter (*Rowley*, 2008). The school principal agreed to provide Amy with a sign language interpreter in the classroom for a trial period toward the end of her kindergarten year. The trial period ended early because the interpreter pointed out Amy did not need his services and was frightened by his being in her class. The interpreter also pointed out his conclusions applied strictly to the class in which he was providing his services and did not apply to other classes or to subsequent academic years (Smith, 1996).

When Amy entered first grade, her IEP team provided for continuation of her regular class placement with the use the FM hearing aid, daily one-hour instruction by a tutor for the deaf, and three hours of speech therapy a week. Her parents agreed to these provisions and again requested a sign language interpreter in all of Amy's academic classes. Because of the failed trial period with the sign language interpreter and Amy's academic and social progress, school officials refused her parents' request for an interpreter. Amy's parent objected and brought the case before a hearing officer.

The Due Process Decision Subsequently, the hearing officer denied the request for a sign language interpreter because Amy was "achieving educationally, academically, and socially" without the sign language interpreter. Amy's parents appealed to the New York State Commissioner of Education, who also denied the request by upholding the decision of the hearing officer. Her parents then filed an appeal in the US District Court for the Southern District of New York.

The US District Court When Amy's parents appealed the decision of the hearing officer and State Commissioner of Education to the US District Court, the court noted Amy had an IQ of 122, performed above average academically in class, was well-adjusted, had many friends among her peers, and interacted well with her teachers. Observers in Amy's classes, however, noted she also appeared isolated at times and her interactions with her peers were generally superficial. Moreover, the results from auditory speech discrimination tests indicated Amy could only identify 59% of the words spoken to her when she was using her hearing aids and her lip reading skills. They also noted that when Amy's classrooms were noisy, when more than one person was speaking at a time, and when her peers failed to face Amy when they talked to her, then this was likely to result in Amy understanding substantially less than 100% of what was spoken. According to the court, because Amy understood considerably less of what was going on in class, she was not learning or performing as well academically as she would have if she was not deaf.

The court determined the FAPE mandate of the law required that "each handicapped child be given an opportunity to achieve his full potential commensurate with the opportunity provided to other children" (*Rowley*, 1980, p. 534). The court ruled that even though evidence established Amy was receiving an adequate education, district officials failed to consider "the importance of comparing her performance to that of nonhandicapped students of similar intellectual caliber and comparable energy and initiative" (*Rowley*, 1980, p. 534). The court ruled that by not providing Amy with a sign language interpreter, the school district had failed to provide Amy with a FAPE.

The US Court of Appeals for the Second Circuit The school district filed an appeal with the US Court of Appeals for the Second Circuit. The appellate court affirmed the district court's ruling finding in favor of the parents in a two-to-one ruling. Two of the judges agreed with the district court judge that Amy was entitled to a sign language interpreter for all her academic subjects to enable her to have equal educational opportunity under the FAPE standard of the IDEA, then the EAHCA. The court acknowledged that the lower court's opinion was well reasoned and adequately supported the decision for providing an interpreter for Amy. The court also noted the narrow scope of the decision: "the evidence upon which our decision rests is concerned with a particular child, her atypical family, her upbringing and training since birth, and her classroom experience. In short, our decision is limited to the unique facts of this case and is not intended as an authority beyond this case" (*Rowley*, 1980, p. 948). One of the appellate court judges wrote a dissent, believing the district court judge had incorrectly interpreted the FAPE mandate of the law. The Henrick Hudson School District then exercised its final appeal, called filing a petition for certiorari, to the court of last resort, the US Supreme Court.

The US Supreme Court The appeal was granted and on March 23, 1982, oral arguments were made in the first special education case to be argued before the High Court, and the first one where an attorney who was deaf used captioning to make the case. In a six-to-three ruling, the Supreme Court reversed the ruling of the lower courts and concluded Amy was receiving educational benefits sufficient to meet the FAPE requirement of the act without providing a sign language interpreter. According to the majority opinion, written by Chief Justice William Rehnquist, the FAPE-related requirements of the EAHCA are satisfied "when the state provides personalized instruction with sufficient support services to permit the handicapped child to benefit educationally from that instruction" (*Rowley*, 1982, p. 177).

Chief Justice Rehnquist further observed that FAPE "consists of educational instruction specially designed to meet the unique needs of the handicapped child supported by such services as are necessary to permit the child 'to benefit' from the instruction" (*Rowley*, 1982, pp. 188–189). The Court further noted Congress had intended to bring "previously excluded handicapped children" into the public school system and developed procedures for schools to ensure an individualized instruction. Thus, the intent of FAPE was access.

The Supreme Court also noted that the EAHCA did not include "any substantive standard prescribing the level of education to be accorded handicapped children," nor did the law require school districts to maximize each child's potential "commensurate with the opportunity provided other children" (*Rowley*, 1982, p. 198). Because Congressional intent was to make public education available to students with disabilities, therefore, "Congress did not impose upon the states any greater substantive educational standard than would be necessary to make such access meaningful," and "that in many instances the process of providing special education and related services to handicapped children is not guaranteed to produce any particular outcome" (*Rowley*, 1982, p. 192). Maximizing potential for children with disabilities "commensurate with the opportunity provided nonhandicapped children," therefore, was not the intent of the act and was erroneously applied by the lower courts. In fact, Justice Rehnquist wrote requiring states to "provide 'equal' educational opportunities would present an entirely unworkable standard requiring impossible measurements" (*Rowley*, 1982, p. 198).

The Court established a two-step test for determining if a school district had met the FAPE standard of the EAHCA. The test was as follows: First, has the state complied with the procedures set forth in the act? And second, is the individualized educational program developed through the act's procedures reasonably calculated to enable the child to receive educational benefits? The first part of the *Rowley* test was procedural and stressed the importance of school personnel adhering to the procedural requirements of the IDEA when determining if a school had provided a FAPE. The second part of the *Rowley* test was substantive and required courts examine a student's IEP to determine whether the IEP developed by the school was reasonably calculated to enable a student to receive educational benefits. According to the US Supreme Court, "If these requirements are met, the state has complied with the obligations imposed by Congress and the courts can require no more" (*Rowley*, 1982, p. 207).

Justice White filed a dissenting opinion in the case, joined by Justices Brennan and Marshall. In the dissent, Justice White argued the Supreme Court had misinterpreted Congressional intent. He noted that in numerous instances in the EAHCA, Congress announced the purpose of the law was to provide a full and equal educational opportunity commensurate with the educational opportunities provided to their nondisabled peers. He further noted that the High Court's definition of the educational benefits of FAPE was so low it would have been satisfied if "a deaf child such as Amy (was) to be given a teacher with a loud voice, for she would benefit from that service. The act requires more" (*Rowley*, 1982, p. 238). Following the Supreme Court's ruling in *Rowley*, FAPE cases continued to be heard at due process hearings and in the federal courts. Of course, hearing officers and judges needed to apply the *Rowley* test to the facts of each individual case. As indicated by Justice White's dissent, the educational benefit standard announced in *Rowley* resulted in different interpretations regarding what amount of educational benefit was necessary to provide a FAPE.

A Split in the Circuit Courts over FAPE

The Supreme Court did not "establish any one test for determining the adequacy of educational benefits conferred upon all children covered by the Act" (*Rowley*, 1985, p. 461), and lower courts began to adopt different standards to determine what degree of educational benefit was necessary to provide FAPE. Some courts adopted a higher standard of educational benefit, whereas many, if not most, courts used a lower standard. Courts that used a lower standard often ruled that if a school district provided some degree of educational benefit, no matter how small, the district conferred a FAPE. Circuit courts that had adopted the low standard of educational benefit included the second, fourth, seventh, eighth, tenth, and eleventh (Yell & Bateman, 2017). For example, the US Court of Appeals for the Tenth Circuit used the standard "merely more than de minimis"[1] (*Endrew F. v. Douglas County Public School District*, 2015, p. 1342) in determining if the educational benefits provided by a school district were sufficient to provide a FAPE. Two circuit courts of appeals, the third and the sixth rejected the lower standard and adopted a higher educational benefit standard to determine FAPE (Yell & Bateman, 2017).

---

[1] *De minimis* is a Latin term meaning trivial or trifling.

The different interpretations of educational benefit in the US Courts of Appeals for the various circuits made it likely that the US Supreme Court would eventually hear another FAPE case in an effort to clarify the standard. The opportunity presented itself when *Endrew F. v. Douglas County School District* (2015) was appealed to the High Court.

Endrew F. v. Douglas County School District (2017)

Thirty-five years after the Rowley decision, the Supreme Court ruled on its second FAPE case in *Endrew F. v. Douglas County School District Re-1* (2017; hereinafter *Endrew F.*). The ruling provided additional guidance on what constitutes adequate educational benefit. In the following sections, we present the facts of the case, the district court's decision, the ruling of the US Court of Appeals for the Tenth Circuit, and the ruling by the US Supreme Court. We also describe the final *Endrew F.* ruling when the case was remanded to the US District Court for the District of Colorado.

Facts of the Case

This case involved Endrew F., called Drew by his parents, a child diagnosed at the age of two with autism. Autism is a neurodevelopmental disorder that generally affects the child's social and communicative skills. Drew received special education services at Douglas County from preschool through the fourth grade. Each year, Drew's IEP addressed his educational and functional needs. By fourth grade, however, Drew's parents became dissatisfied with his progress, viewing his academic and functional progress "essentially stalled," as well as noting that his IEP goals and objectives were the same from one year to the next. Although Drew showed some progress, he exhibited behaviors that inhibited his learning, such as eloping (e.g., running away from school), dropping to the ground, climbing, making loud vocalizations, using perseverative language, and picking/scraping. He also had severe fears of commonplace things like flies, spills, and public restrooms.

When presented with the proposed IEP for his fifth-grade year, Drew's parents noted much of the IEP was the same as IEPs from previous years and enrolled him at the Firefly Autism House, a private school specializing in children with autism. At the private institution, Drew was given a behavior intervention plan addressing his most pressing behavioral problems. Within months, his behavior significantly improved and he made academic progress that had not been evident while he was attending the public school. After six months, Drew's parents met with the Douglas County School District representatives and were provided with a revised IEP. The parents did not notice any meaningful changes in the revised IEP compared to previous ones, so they continued with Drew's placement at the Firefly Autism House.

Drew's parents filed a complaint with the Colorado Department of Education seeking tuition reimbursement for Drew's private school placement, claiming the school district failed to provide him with a FAPE. The parents also argued Drew's successful educational experience at Firefly Autism House showed the school district had failed to implement an IEP designed to provide Drew substantive educational benefit.

The Due Process Hearing

Because the hearing was held in the Tenth Circuit, the administrative law judge (ALJ)[2] was required to follow the two-part FAPE as interpreted by the US Court of Appeals for the Tenth Circuit. The Tenth Circuit Court had used the *Rowley* test, but had interpreted the second part of the test as requiring a very low standard to prove that the IEP was sufficient to provide educational benefit. To meet this low standard, a school district in the Tenth Circuit had to offer a FAPE that provided educational benefits that were slightly more than *de minimis* (*Urban v. Jefferson County School District*, 1996). In denying the request for reimbursement, the ALJ noted Drew made "some measurable progress" toward the academic and functional goals in his IEPs during the time that he was enrolled in the district. The judge also noted that although the district provided minimal detail when reporting the student's progress, not having a more robust reporting did not amount to substantive denial of FAPE.

The US District Court

On appeal to the US District Court for the District of Colorado, the court affirmed the decision of ALJ denying reimbursement, concluding the Douglas County School District had provided Drew with a FAPE. The court addresses the parents' primary assertions in the following ways. First, Drew's parents asserted he had not made progress toward his goals. In addressing the lack of progress allegation, the court noted that though some of the objectives carried over from year to year with some being slightly modified, expectations increased over time and there was evidence of "a pattern of some progress on his education and functional goals" (*Endrew F.*, 2015, p. 9). Therefore, the court found evidence that showed Drew received some educational benefits and further noted that lack of progress did not mean that Drew had to make progress toward every goal.

Second, Drew's parents alleged the school district failed to provide reports on Drew's progress. In addressing this allegation, the court concluded that despite the lack of formal progress reports, there was significant informal communication with the parents, particularly related to the educational/functional objectives. Parents also received a copy of the IEPs and notations on progress at the annual review. Furthermore, three times a year Drew's progress on the IEP goals and objectives was reported and sent home on his daily take-home folder in his backpack. However, the court noted many of the quarterly reports were missing for the second and third grades.

Third, Drew's parents alleged the school district had failed to perform a behavioral assessment and develop a behavior intervention plan. In addressing this assertion, the court observed there was evidence that the district was addressing Drew's behavioral issues and that the district was in the process of reassessing his behavior intervention plan in light of Drew's escalating behavioral issues. The court also noted a functional behavioral intervention and behavior intervention plan was only required when certain disciplinary actions were taken and that a school

---

[2] Many states use ALJs to conduct and issue opinions in impartial due process hearings.

district only had to "consider" behavioral programming when the behavior interfered with learning.

The US Court of Appeals for the Tenth Circuit

On appeal to the US Court of Appeals, Tenth Circuit, the court affirmed the district court's decision concluding that (a) gaps in reporting student's progress did not deprive them of meaningful participation, (b) a BIP was not required, and (c) Drew's IEP was not substantively inadequate. In deciding the case, the court first concluded the district did not fail to provide FAPE because the district met both the procedural and substantive requirements of the act, and therefore reimbursement for the unilateral placement at Firefly was not warranted. Second, in addressing procedural challenges which allegedly impeded meaningful parental participation, the court pointed out that even in assuming a procedural violation associated with progress reporting, such deficiency did not amount to denial of FAPE. Similarly, regarding allegations for failure to address behavioral concerns, the court observed there was evidence the district attempted to address Drew's behaviors (second and fourth grade IEPs include behavior plans), and in light of recent escalating behaviors, the district was in the process of collecting data revising its behavioral interventions. Finally, on the issue of substantive violations, the court concluded there was evidence the district actively worked to address Drew's disability-related behaviors and that he made some academic progress despite his behavioral challenges. Furthermore, review of IEPs showed that the objectives and measuring criteria increased with difficulty from year to year; objectives in areas in which there was no progress remained the same. The US Court of Appeals for the Tenth Circuit determined the case was "without question a close case, but we find there are sufficient indications of Drew's past progress to find the IEP rejected by the parents substantively adequate under our prevailing standard" (*Endrew F.*, 2015, p. 1432).

US Supreme Court

In an appeal to the Supreme Court, the party filing the appeal typically asks the High Court to answer one or two specific questions. In the *Endrew F.* case, the petitioners (i.e., Drew's parents) asked the Supreme Court to answer the following question: "What is the level of educational benefit that school districts must confer on children with disabilities to provide them with a free appropriate public education guaranteed by the Individuals with Disabilities Education Act?" (Solicitor General, 2017). Oral arguments were heard on January 11, 2017, and on March 22, 2017, the US Supreme Court vacated[3] the judgment of the Court of Appeals and remanded[4] the case for further proceedings consistent with the Supreme Court's opinion. In deciding the case, the Supreme Court first observed that in order to meet the substantive requirement under IDEA, a school district must develop an "an IEP reasonably calculated to enable a child to make progress appropriate in light of the child's circumstances" (*Endrew F.*, 2017, p. 999). Furthermore,

---

[3] To set aside or annul a ruling
[4] To send a ruling back to a lower court for further action

the Court concluded that a child's "educational program must be appropriately ambitious in light of his circumstances, just as advancement from grade to grade is appropriately ambitious for most children in the regular classroom. The goals may differ, but every child should have the chance to meet challenging objectives" (*Endrew F.*, 2017, p.1000). Such a standard is "markedly more demanding than the merely more than *de minimis*" test applied by the Tenth Circuit . . . Aiming so low would be tantamount to "sitting idly . . . awaiting the time when they were old enough to drop out" (*Endrew F.*, 2017, p.1001).

The Ruling of the US District Court on Remand

On remand to the Tenth Circuit, the court of appeals vacated its decision in light of Supreme Court decision and remanded the case to the district court for further proceedings consistent with the decision. Consequently, the district court ruled "the April 2010 IEP offered to him by the district was insufficient to create an educational plan that was reasonably calculated to enable petitioner to make progress, even in light of his unique circumstances, based on the continued pattern of unambitious goals and objectives of his prior IEPs" (*Endrew F.*, 2018, p.16). Furthermore, the court observed Drew's IEP "was clearly just a continuation of the district's educational plan that had previously only resulted in minimal academic and functional progress" (*Endrew F.*, 2018, p.16). In addition, the district's failure to address Drew's behaviors clearly "impacted his ability to make progress on his educational and functional goals" (*Endrew F.*, 2018, p.17). Therefore, Drew was entitled to reimbursement for costs incurred at the private facility as well as reasonable attorneys' fees and litigation costs, which amounted to $1.3 million dollars (Aguilar, 2018).

Summary

These two seminal rulings from the US Supreme Court outlined the FAPE requirements of the IDEA. The *Rowley* decision divided the FAPE mandate into two types of obligations school personnel and IEP team members must meet. The first obligation was to fulfill the procedural requirements of the law (i.e., the first part of the *Rowley* test), and the second obligation was to develop an IEP calculated to enable a student to receive educational benefit (i.e., the second part of the *Rowley* test). Following the *Rowley* decision, rulings in various circuits of the US Courts of Appeals adopted different standards for the substantive or educational benefit part of the *Rowley* test. The US Courts of the Appeals for the Third and the Fifth Circuits used a meaningful educational benefit standard when determining whether not a student's IEP conferred a FAPE, whereas the US Courts of the Appeals for the Second, Fourth, Seventh, Eighth, Tenth, and Eleventh Circuits used a lower standard of educational benefit, variously described as some benefit, *de minimis* (trivial), or merely more than *de minimis*. The split in the circuits made it likely that the US Supreme Court would eventually hear a case to resolve the division. In other words, an *Endrew F.* type case was bound to happen. It was only a question of when. When the Supreme Court handed down its decision in *Endrew F.*, it set forth a new educational benefit standard, replacing the second part of the *Rowley* test with the new *Endrew F.* test, which is that a student's IEP should be reasonably calculated to enable the student to make with progress appropriate in light of his or her circumstances. Thus, there is a new two-part test, the *Rowley/Endrew F.* test, that hearing officers and judges will use when determining if a school district has provided a FAPE. In the next chapter, we examine what these rulings mean for IEP teams when developing a student's program of special education.

CHAPTER 3

Foundations

IEP Development: Procedural, Substantive, and Implementation Requirements

In the first chapter we noted that the Congressional authors of the EAHCA did not specify a level of achievement necessary for students to receive a FAPE; rather, they outlined the process by which a student's FAPE would be developed and implemented. In the second chapter, we explored how the United States further defined the responsibility of school district personnel to provide a FAPE under the IDEA in two rulings, *Board of Education of the Hendrick Hudson Central School District v. Rowley* (1982) and *Endrew F. v. Douglas County School District* (2017). In the *Rowley* case, the High Court found that following the procedures of the law "are not a mere formality" and that "adequate compliance with the procedures prescribed would in most cases assure much if not all of what Congress wished in the way of substantive content in an IEP" (*Rowley*, 1982, p. 177). In *Endrew F.* (2017), the High Court set forth the educational benefit standard necessary for a school district to meet the substantive FAPE requirements of the IDEA. According to these decisions, to develop IEPs that confer FAPE, we must (a) follow IDEA-required procedures when identifying, evaluating, and programming for students and (b) develop IEPs that are reasonably calculated to enable students to make progress appropriate in light of their circumstances.

The purpose of this chapter is to explain the Congressionally established elements of FAPE and how the US Supreme Court added clarity to school districts' responsibilities when developing a student's FAPE in his or her IEP. We refer to the dimensions of FAPE as procedural, substantive, and implementation.

Students' IEPs have been, and continue to be, the center of most IDEA-related disputes (Bateman, 2017) and these disputes usually involve errors in one or more of the procedural, substantive, or implementation requirements. Thus, it is important that administrators and teachers understand these requirements and how serious errors may be avoided. We next explain the three dimensions of FAPE. In chapter 8, we provide strategies for avoiding these errors and correcting them when they are made.

The Dimensions of FAPE: Procedures, Substance, and Implementation

In 1982, the US Supreme Court ruled in *Rowley* that to determine if a school district had offered FAPE, courts had to establish a school district had satisfied the procedural requirements of the EAHCA and a student's IEP was reasonably calculated to enable a student to receive educational benefit. In this ruling, the Supreme Court decision solidified the dichotomy between the procedural and substantive FAPE requirements of the IDEA and provided a framework by which courts could analyze these different types of FAPE violations (Berney & Gilsbach, 2017).

Congress further codified this procedural and substantive distinction in the 2004 amendments to the IDEA, the Individuals with Disabilities Education Improvement Act (IDEIA). According to the IDEIA, when hearing officers heard disputes about the provision of a FAPE, they were to base their decisions upon substantive grounds of whether a student received a FAPE (IDEA 20 USC § 1415 [f][3][E][i]). Thus, Congress also recognized the procedural and substantive dimensions of FAPE.

The Procedural Dimension

The procedural dimension of FAPE involves questions of "when" and "how" we accomplish IDEA-required tasks such as identifying students with disabilities, conducting evaluations, developing IEPs, and setting the timelines in which we should accomplish these tasks. These procedures are set in federal law, but certain aspects of the procedures, such as timelines, may be set in state law. When state law specifies timelines and the IDEA does not, educators must adhere to state guidelines.

The IDEA includes many procedural requirements to which school district personnel must adhere. Moreover, in the 2004 amendments to the IDEA, Congress noted that some procedural requirements are so important that if not followed the violation could result in a school district denying students a FAPE. These procedural violations included (a) impeding a student's right to a FAPE, (b) impeding a student's parents' opportunity to participate in the decision-making process regarding their child's FAPE, or (c) depriving a student of educational benefits (IDEA 20 USC § 1415 [f][3][E][ii]).

This has been referred to as "the harmless error" approach (Zirkel & Hetrick, 2017). As Osborne (2004) noted, "when deficiencies in an IEP do not compromise the student's right to [a substantively] appropriate education or the parents' right to participate in the process, the courts have let the IEP stand" (p. 16). Thus, even though districts are required to comply with all of the IDEA's procedural requirements, mistakes do not automatically lead to finding of a denial of a FAPE. Nonetheless, it is extremely important that school personnel follow the procedural requirements of the IDEA. In the following sections, we examine the procedural requirements that, if violated, may result in the denial of a student's right to a FAPE.

Child Find

School districts have an affirmative duty to identify, locate, and evaluate children with disabilities who may be in need of special education and related services residing in their jurisdiction, including children with disabilities who are (a) homeless, (b) wards of the state, and (c) attending private schools (IDEA Regulations § 300.111[a][i]). The meaning of child find has been developed thorough litigation that has established the following two crucial factors in meeting the child find obligation of the IDEA. First, a school district must evaluate a child when there is reasonable suspicion that the child is eligible for special education services (textbox 3.1 depicts a number of indicators that could lead school officials to reasonably suspect that a child may have a disability and need special education services). When a child find case is before a hearing officer or judge, they will often determine when district personnel knew or should have known the child may have had a disability and needed special education and make their decision on that basis (the so-called "KOSHK" standard; *T.B. v. Prince George's County Board of Education*, 2016). If the district personnel knew or should have known, it is very likely the school district will lose. Second, a school district must initiate the evaluation within a reasonable period of time (Zirkel, 2015). It is not permissible for school district officials to wait for a child to be referred by his or her parents; rather, child find obligations require school district officials to look for, find, refer, and evaluate students who may have a disability and need special education services.

Textbox 3.1 Child Find: Red Flags That Indicate That District Personnel Knew or Should Have Known

These red flags by themselves or in combination may be an indication that school officials should consider a referral for evaluation.
  Remember the KOSHK standard.

- Poor or declining grades or standardized test scores
- A student's 504 plan is not effective
- Failure to succeed in a school's MTSS or RTI system despite intensive interventions
- Poor peer relationships
- Excessive number of trips to school nurse
- Numerous disciplinary referrals
- Behavior problems that impede a student's learning or that of others
- Parent concerns about their child (or parent referral to special education)
- Teacher concerns about the student (or teacher referral to special education)
- Counselor concerns about the student (or counselor referral to special education)
- Diagnosis by a psychologist, therapist, or medical doctor of a disorder listed in the Diagnostic and Statistical Manual (e.g., attention deficit hyperactivity disorder, autism)
- Hospitalization for behavioral or mental health issues
- Student had a 504 plan or was in special education in a previous school

---

Adhering to the child find procedural obligations of the IDEA is a critically important procedural requirement. Clearly a student with a disability will not receive a FAPE if they are not identified as eligible. Violating child find, therefore, is a crucial procedural error that will likely lead to a violation of the IDEA.

Evaluation

Special education is based on thorough evaluation of a student's needs. That is, a student must first be determined eligible for special education services to receive programming, and the programming that a student receives is based on the instructional implications of the evaluation results. The IDEA requires school-based personnel conduct a "full and individual initial evaluation . . . before the initial provision of special education and related services" (IDEA, 20 USC § 1414[a][1][A]. Thus, an evaluation is the gateway for students to receive special education services.[1]

The first important procedural requirement in the evaluation process is that prior to conducting an evaluation for special education eligibility, school district personnel must receive informed written consent from a student's parents to do so. There are three essential components to informed consent. First, a student's parent must clearly understand to what they are consenting, which includes providing descriptions of the evaluation procedures. Second, the parents must consent in writing. Third, the parent must understand that their consent is voluntary and they can revoke consent at any time. When parents do not provide consent, school district officials may use the IDEA's mediation or due process procedures to override the lack of consent as long as this is not in conflict with state law.

After receiving consent to evaluate, the evaluation must be conducted within 60 calendar days, although states may have specific timelines that must be followed as long as they are within the 60 calendar days (34 CFR § 300.301 [c][1] [i-ii]). The 60-day time frame does not apply when a parent repeatedly fails to produce their child for the evaluation or if the student moves during the evaluation but before it has been completed (34 CFR § 300.301 [d][1-2]). The procedural requirements that school personnel (a) must obtain informed written consent before conducting an evaluation and (b) have 60 days to conduct the evaluation after receiving consent are extremely important and must be followed.

When conducting an evaluation, school personnel should gather information that will assist a student's IEP team in determining "the content of the child's individual education program" (IDEA, 20 USC § 1414[b][2][A][ii]). Additionally, the IDEA requires that IEP teams include "an individual who can interpret the instructional implications of the evaluation results" (IDEA, 20 USC § 1414 [d][1] [B][v]) on the team. Additional IDEA requirements regarding the initial evaluation and the re-evaluation are given in textbox 3.2.

Clearly, the evaluation is a crucial element of the special education process because the full and individualized evaluation leads to (a) eligibility and (b) instructional programming. The IDEA includes several procedural requirements regarding how school district personnel should conduct student evaluations. If these procedural requirements are not met, it is likely that the entire evaluation may be invalid. Therefore, because procedural violations of the evaluation results could result in an evaluation that (a) impedes a student's right to a FAPE (e.g., a

---

[1] The procedural obligations in this section only apply to evaluations for special education placement (or re-evaluations) under the IDEA. Many school districts have adopted schoolwide assessments and evaluate students for placement in a multi-tiered system of support (MTSS). Assessment/evaluation for placing students in the appropriate tier, as long as it is not specifically for special education placement, does not require permission.

Textbox 3.2 Procedural Requirements of the Initial Evaluation and Re-evaluation

- School districts personnel must conduct full and individual evaluations before the initial provision of special education.
- Initial evaluation may be initiated by school district personnel or a student's parents (school district may refuse to conduct an evaluation but issue prior written notice and notify parents of their procedural safeguards).
- The initial evaluation must be conducted within 60 days (states may have laws or regulations that mandate the evaluation must be conducted in fewer days than the IDEA; in such a situation, school district personnel must adhere to state guidelines).
  a) The time frame does not apply if the student's parents repeatedly fail or refuse to produce their child for the evaluation, or
  b) A student enrolls in another school district after the timeline has begun.
- Assessments/evaluations must consist of procedures to:
  a) Determine if a student is a student with a disability, and
  b) Determine the educational needs of the student.
- A re-evaluation should also be conducted if the school district determined if the academic or functional needs of the student warrant it or if a student's parents request it.
- A school district must ensure that a re-evaluation of each student with a disability must be conducted once every three years, unless the parents and school district officials agree that a re-evaluation is not needed.

---

student will not receive any special education and related services if he or she is not determined to be eligible because of improper evaluation) or (b) deprives a student of educational benefits (e.g., a student will not receive the appropriate special education and related services that will enable him or her to make progress if the evaluation is incomplete).

The Individualized Education Program

According to the IDEA, a student's FAPE consists of special education and related services provided in conformity with his or her IEP (IDEA 20 USC § 1401 [9] [D], 2004). After a student has been determined to be eligible for special education and related services, an IEP team must meet within 30 days to craft the IEP, which then must then be implemented as soon as possible (IDEA Regulations, 34 CFR § 300.323[c], 2006). The IDEA includes numerous procedures to which school districts must adhere in the IEP development process. These procedures include (a) timelines for IEP development, (b) composition of the IEP team, and (c) components to include in an IEP. We next address these procedural requirements.

Timelines for IEP Development. According to Lake (2014), failing to adhere to the procedural requirements will likely result in a FAPE violation because the IDEA's statutory and regulatory scheme emphasizes the importance of the IEP in conferring a FAPE. Thus, if a school district fails to develop an IEP within 30 days after a student is determined eligible for special education services, that could result in a denial of FAPE if the failure causes substantive harm to the student (see *Gerstmyer v. Howard County Public Schools*, 1994). Readers should note that states may have their own required timelines if they are not less than the timelines in the IDEA; thus, it is important to be aware of any state timelines.

Composition of the IEP Team. According to Lake (2007), "Almost nothing will foil a district's ability to provide an appropriate education to a student more completely than failing to ensure that the composition of a child's IEP team is in line with the federal requirements" (p. 41). The IDEA and regulations delineate the required participants who should be on a student's IEP team (20 USC § 1414[d][B][i-vii]). These participants are essential when developing a student's IEP. Improperly constituted IEP teams have led to rulings that a student's IEP was flawed and did not provide a FAPE (see *M.L. v. Federal Way School District*, 2005). For example, IEPs have been declared invalid because required IEP participants (a) were not present at the IEP meeting (*District of Columbia Public Schools*, 2007), (b) left the IEP meeting too early (*Board of Education of the Wappingers Central School District*, 2004), and (c) arrived late for an IEP meeting (*Board of Education of the City School District of New York*, 1996). On the other hand, a student's parents' contention that an IEP was defective because it was drafted by an improperly constituted team could be rejected if it did not lead to a substantive violation of FAPE (see *B.P. and A.P. v. New York City Department of Education*, 2012). Nonetheless, the composition of the IEP team is so important to the process of developing a student's FAPE that it is likely that a hearing officer, state educational agency, or judge may find that an IEP prepared by an invalidly composed IEP is a nullity (*Board of Education of the Monroe-Woodbury School District*, 1999). The required participants in IEP meeting are listed in textbox 3.3. Chapter 4 includes additional information on the required members of the IEP team.

Textbox 3.3 Required Members of an IEP Team

- The parents of the student
- Not less than one general education teacher of the student
- Not less than one special education teacher
- A representative of the local education agency
- A person who can interpret the instruction implications of the evaluation results. It may be a person already on the team except for the parents.
- At the discretion of the parents or school district personnel. Other persons with knowledge or special expertise about the child, including related service personnel.
- Whenever appropriate, the student
- If transition services are being discussed, the student must be invited.

The 2004 amendments to the IDEA allowed essential IEP team participants to be excused from an IEP meeting only under very specific circumstances if the parents and representatives of the school follow the agreement and consent requirements of the IDEA (IDEA Regulations, 34 CFR § 300.321[c], 2006). First, an IEP team meeting participant may be excused from part or all of an IEP meeting if the particular team member's area is not being discussed and the parents and representative of the school agree in writing that the attendance of the member is not required. Second, an IEP team meeting participant may be excused from part or all of an IEP meeting if the meeting involves discussion of the member's area of the curriculum if the parents and representative of the school agree to the excusal in writing and the particular IEP team member submits his or her input in writing prior to IEP development.

The excusal exceptions in the IDEA should be used sparingly and only in cases of emergency. According to the US Department of Education, an "IEP team that routinely excuses IEP team members from attending IEP meetings would not be in compliance with the requirements of the (IDEA), and, therefore, would be subject to the state's monitoring and enforcement provisions" (*Federal Register*, v. 71, p. 46,674, 2006d).

Components of the IEP. Because a student's IEP is the mechanism by which his or her FAPE is developed and delivered, school district personnel must ensure all the necessary components of the student's IEP are included in the document. The regulations of the IDEA specify that the following content components be included in students' IEPs: (a) present levels of academic achievement and functional performance; (b) measurable annual goals; (c) a description of how progress toward meeting goals will be measured; (d) a statement of the needed special education and related services and supplementary aids and services, based on peer-reviewed research to the extent practicable, and a statement of the program modifications or supports for school personnel; (e) an explanation of the extent, if any, to which the child will not participate with nondisabled children in the regular class and in [other] activities; (f) a statement of accommodations, if any, necessary in assessments and/or in assessment standards; and (g) the projected date, frequency, location, and duration of services and modifications (IDEA Regulations, 34 CFR § 300.320, 2006). Additionally, beginning with the first IEP after a student turns 16 years old or earlier if required by the state, the IEP must contain a transition plan that includes measurable postsecondary goals based on age-appropriate transition assessments and services that enable the student to meet these goals. In textbox 3.4, we list the required components of IEPs.

Textbox 3.4 Required Components of an IEP

- A statement of present levels of academic achievement and functional performance
- A statement of measurable annual goals, including academic and functional goals, and short-term objectives (if required)
- A description of how students' progress toward meeting the annual goals will be measured and when periodic report will be provided
- A statement of the special education and related services, along with supplemental aids and services that will be provided
- The projected time for the beginning of services and the anticipated frequency, location, and duration of the services
- An explanation of the extent, if any, that the student will not participate with nondisabled students in the general education class and in extracurricular and other activities
- A statement of any individual accommodations that are necessary to measure the academic achievement of students on statewide and districtwide assessments, and if the IEP determines that the student will take an alternative achievement

> assessment, an explanation of what the student cannot take in the regular assessment, and which alternate assessment is appropriate
> • A transition plan beginning not later than the first IEP in effect when a student turns 16 (earlier if required by state law)

Students' IEP teams are procedurally obligated to include all these components in students' IEPs. When specific content is missing from an IEP, the absence of these components will clearly constitute a procedural error and may result in a denial of FAPE.

Parental Participation

The most basic of all the procedural requirements of the IDEA is that a student's parents are full and equal participants with school district personnel in the development of their child's IEP. Bateman (2017) asserted that

> IDEA makes parental participation central in all decisions regarding the child's program and placement and when full and equal parent participation is abridged or denied, a denial of FAPE will most likely be found. Few, if any, of IDEA's procedural rights are more vigorously protected by courts. (Bateman, 2017, p. 91)

According to the IDEA Amendments of 2004, hearing officers may find a denial of FAPE if procedural violations "significantly impeded the parent's opportunity to participate in the decision-making process regarding the provision of FAPE to the parent's child" (IDEA Regulations, 34 CFR § 300.513[a][2], 2006).

In special education rulings by the US Supreme Court from *Rowley* (1982) to *Endrew F.* (2017), the High Court has emphasized the importance of parental participation in special education programming. As the US Court of Appeals for the Ninth Circuit noted in *Amanda J. v. Clark County School District* (2001), "procedural violations that interfere with parental participation in the IEP formulation process undermine the very essence of the IDEA" (p. 892).

When school personnel determine a student's program or placement without collaborating with a student's parents and outside of the IEP process, they have engaged in predetermination. Predetermination makes a charade out of the parent-school collaborative decision-making process regarding a student's program or placement because these decisions have already been made by school district personnel. According to the US Court of Appeals for the Ninth Circuit, "predetermination occurs when an educational agency has made its determination prior to the IEP meeting, including when it presents one placement option at the meeting and is unwilling to consider other alternatives" (*H.B. v. Las Vegas Unified School District*, 2007, p. 344). Readers should note that informal discussions of the IEP prior to a student's IEP meeting do not constitute predetermination as long as final decisions are not made until the student's parents have an opportunity to be involved. Similarly, if school districts are unable to get a student's parents involved in the creation of their child's IEP, it is important that school personnel document their efforts to secure parental participation in the IEP meeting.

Placement

After a student's IEP is developed, a team must determine the placement in which the student may receive the specially designed instruction in his or her IEP. Although IEP teams often determine students' placements, that is not actually required by the IDEA. According to the IDEA, the placement decision must be a team of persons, including the parents and other persons knowledgeable about the child, the meaning of the evaluation data, and the placement options (IDEA Regulations, 34 CFR § 300.116 [a][1], 2006). Because a student's IEP team meets all these criteria, they can serve as the student's placement team.

The team that makes the placement decision must do based on a completed IEP and in accordance with its terms (IDEA Regulations, 34 CFR § 300.115[b][2], 2006). According to the US Department of Education (1994), "the appropriate placement for a given child with a disability cannot be determined until after decisions have been made about what the child's needs are and what will be provided" (US Department of Education, Appendix C to Part 300, Question 5). Thus, placement must be determined after the IEP has been developed. To do otherwise (i.e., make the placement decision before the IEP is completed) would constitute a serious procedural error that has been referred to as shoehorning (Tatgenhorst et al., 2014).

Two major procedural requirements that govern placement decisions are the mandate to (a) place students in the least restrictive environment (LRE) and (b) use the continuum of alternative placements when doing so. In chapter 6, we examine the placement requirements of the IDEA in detail. Here we address the procedural requirements of using the continuum of alternative placements in determining LRE for students.

The LRE mandate of the IDEA requires all students with disabilities be educated with nondisabled students to the "maximum extent appropriate" (IDEA Regulations, 34 CFR § 300.114[a][2][i], 2006). If a more restrictive setting is needed to provide a FAPE to a student, the team may decide to place in a setting such as a special class or special school but only when the "nature or severity of the disability is such that education in regular classes with the use of supplementary aids and services cannot be achieved satisfactorily" (IDEA Regulations, 34 CFR § 300.114[a][2][ii], 2006). Thus, an important requirement prior to moving a student to a more restrictive setting is to make good-faith efforts to provide supplementary aids and services in an attempt to maintain a student in a less restrictive environment. In fact, this requirement is so important the US Court of Appeals for the Fifth Circuit developed a test to determine whether a school district has complied with the LRE mandate of the IDEA. In the first part of the test, a hearing officer or court must determine whether school personnel had attempted to maintain a student in the regular classroom by using supplementary aids and services (*Daniel R.R. v. State Board of Education*, 1989).

When a student's placement is being considered, and the team has determined that a student cannot be educated in the regular classroom with supplementary aids and services, the team must use the continuum of alternative placements in choosing the eventual placement. According to the IDEA regulations, "each (public school district) must ensure that a continuum of alternative placements is available to meet the needs of children with disabilities for special education and related services" (IDEA Regulations, 34 CFR § 300.115[a], 2006). The continuum includes "instruction in regular classes, special classes, special schools, home instruction, and instruction in hospitals and institutions" (IDEA Regulations, 34 CFR § 300.115[b][1], 2006). The purpose of the continuum is to ensure that students with disabilities are served in the LRE setting in which a FAPE can be provided.

The placement requirements impose several very important procedural obligations on school districts. To ensure these procedures are met when making a placement decision, a student's placement team must keep in mind the importance of the FAPE and LRE requirements of the IDEA. If the team determines a more restrictive placement along the continuum is needed to provide a student a FAPE, the team should also consider supplementary aids and services in determining the LRE along the continuum. It is also important that steps on the continuum be followed in order so that the team not skip continuum placement options when making decisions. So, for example, never go from regular class placement (step 1 on the continuum) to a special school (step 3 on the continuum) without first considering a special class (step 2 on the continuum). It is of utmost importance that these decisions be made on an individualized basis and never by category of disability or administrative convenience. Certainly, placing students in more restrictive settings to receive a FAPE was anticipated by Congress in the IDEA. Lake (2007) aptly wrote that as "a safe rule . . . a district must make a documented, diligent, and good-faith effort to educate the student in the least restrictive environment before considering, much less proposing a more restrictive one" (p. 59).

Summary of the Procedural Dimension of FAPE

The IDEA includes several procedural requirements that school districts are obligated to adhere to. According to the federal law, when school personnel commit procedural errors that (a) impede a student's right to a FAPE, (b) hinder a student's parents' opportunity to participate in the decision-making process regarding their child's FAPE, or (c) deprive a student of educational benefits, it will likely result in the denial of a student's right to a FAPE. We believe that particularly serious and likely fatal procedural errors are those that compromise (a) child find activities; (b) a full and individualized evaluation of a student; (c) IEP development, including the IEP team composition and content; (d) parental participation; and (e) placement determination. Special education must ensure that all procedural requirements of the law are followed and documented. Although the federal law enumerates these procedural requirements, it is important for readers to be familiar with any additional requirements that may be included in their state's special education law.

The Substantive Dimension

As we have seen, the IDEA imposes a detailed set of procedural requirements on school districts; however, the law is less clear on substantive requirements and does not clearly distinguish between what constitutes a procedural and a substantive violation (Berney & Gilsbach, 2017). Courts, especially the US Supreme Court, have issued rulings that have clarified the procedural and substantive distinctions of the IDEA. According to Zirkel (2017), the substantive dimension focuses on the adequacy of an IEP with respect to its likely or actual results. Essentially, a substantive violation occurs when the content of a student's IEP is not sufficient to confer a FAPE (Berney & Gilsbach, 2017; Weatherly, 2015).

The substantive dimension involves the "what" of the IEP and refers to the content of the document. The content of the IEP addresses what student needs will be addressed in the IEP, what goals and services will be included in the IEP, and what procedures and strategies will be used to measure student progress toward a student's goals. The ruling of the US Supreme Court in *Endrew F.* (2017) provided the following guidance: "To meet its substantive obligation under the IDEA, a school must offer an IEP reasonably calculated to enable a child to make progress in lights of (his or her) circumstances" (*Endrew F.* 2017, p. 1002) and that, if asked to do so by a hearing officer or judge, school authorities must be able to "offer a cogent and responsive explanation for their decisions" that shows that a student's IEP was likely to confer such progress (*Endrew F.* 2017, p. 1002). The purpose of this textbook is to address the development of students' IEPs to ensure that their programs of special education and related services enable them to make progress. How do we ensure that our IEPs are reasonably calculated to enable students to make progress appropriate in light of their circumstance? In the following sections, and in the rest of this textbook, we offer the following answers to this critical issue.

The Four IEP Content Questions

To ensure substantively correct IEP content, IEP team members must determine answers to the following four content questions:

1. **What are the student's unique academic and functional needs that must be addressed in his or her IEP?**

   This question is answered by conducting a thorough, individualized evaluation of a student and describing all his or her academic and functional needs in the present levels of academic achievement and functional performance (PLAAFP) statements at the beginning of the IEPs. The PLAAFP statements are the foundation of a student's IEP. If the PLAAFP statements are incomplete or not accurate, the rest of the IEP will most likely be invalid. A US District Court judge summarized the importance of the PLAAFP statement when he wrote:

   > If the IEP fails to assess the "child's present levels of academic achievement and functional performance" the IEP does not comply with [IDEA]. This deficiency goes to the heart of the IEP; the child's level of academic achievement and functional performance is the foundation on which the IEP must be built. Without a clear identification of [the child's] present levels, the IEP cannot set measurable goals, evaluate the child's progress and determine which educational and related services are needed. (*Kirby v. Cabell County Board of Education*, 2006, p. 694)

We believe that the notion that a student's PLAAFP statement is the foundation of the student's IEP and FAPE is correct. As Bateman (2017) asserted, a student's "IEP must stand solidly and squarely on a foundation of current, accurate evaluations of the student's level of performance in academic and functional areas" (p. 94). School personnel must ensure the PLAAFP statements include all of a student's academic and functional needs (e.g., behavior, communication) and these needs be addressed throughout his or her IEP. The PLAAFP statements are the starting points for determining a student's goals and measuring the student's academic and functional progress (*Anchorage School District*, 2008). In our opinion, if a school district is to meet the *Endrew F.* standard of enabling a student to make progress, the PLAAFP statements must serve as a baseline by which to measure student progress. In chapter 5, we provide guidance on writing PLAAFP statements.

2. **What are the annual goals that must be included in his or her IEP to address the needs identified in the PLAAFP statements?**

The IDEA requires that every student's IEPs include measurable academic and functional goals that are designed to (a) meet a student's needs that result from his or her disability, (b) enable the student to be involved in and progress in the general education curriculum, and (c) meet each of a student's other educational needs that result from his or her disability (IDEA Regulations, 34 CFR § 300.320[a][2][i][A-B], 2006). The purpose of goals, which are based on the needs identified in the PLAAFP statements, are to provide an estimate of a student's annual growth in academic and functional areas. If a school district is to meet the *Endrew F.* standard of enabling a student to make progress, it is essential that student's goals are measurable, and then that they are actually measured. As Bateman & Linden (2012) asserted, if an annual goal is not measurable it is a violation of FAPE, and if a goal is not measured it is also a violation of FAPE.

Measurable annual goals are essential to developing IEPs that enable a student to make progress, thereby conferring a FAPE. Without measurable annual goals in an IEP, a team simply cannot assess student progress. Bateman (2017) referred to the unfortunate practice of writing goals that are not measurable and then not measuring the goals as the "cycle of non-accountability" (p. 95). According to Bateman, the reason for the cycle of non-accountability is that "too few IEP team members know how to write measurable goals and too few goal writers intend that anyone ever actually measure the progress the child has made" (p. 95). We believe that when school personnel engage in the cycle of non-accountability it is not deliberate; rather, it is more likely caused by a lack of knowledge of writing goals that are measurable and then measuring them. In chapter 6 we present a three-step method for writing measurable annual goals.

3. **How will the student's progress toward these goals be monitored?**

The IDEA requires every student's IEP include a description of how a student's progress toward meeting his or her annual goals will be measured and when periodic reports on the student's progress toward meeting the annual goals will be provided, such as through issuing quarterly reports concurrent with issuing report cards (IDEA Regulations, 34 CFR § 300.320[a][3][i-ii], 2006). For school districts to show that students' IEPs are reasonably calculated to enable a student to make progress appropriate in light of their circumstances, per the *Endrew F.* standard, students' progress toward meeting their annual goals must be measured and programming decisions must be based on an analysis of this data.

The importance of writing measurable annual goals and then actually measuring students' progress cannot be overstated. In a ruling in *Rio Rancho Public Schools* (2003), an administrative appeals officer for the state of New Mexico ruled two years of a high school student's IEPs did not provide FAPE because the student's IEPs did not include present levels statements, clear goals and objectives, and a baseline by which the student's progress could be measured. Additionally, the IEP team did not issue regular reports documenting the student's progress. The appeals officer provided an apt description of the importance of monitoring student progress:

> The statements of the Student's annual goals and objectives in each IEP simply do not contain objective criteria which permit measurement of student's progress especially in light of the absence of the student's current levels of performance. A goal of "increasing" reading comprehension skills or "improving decoding skills" is not a measurable goal without a clear statement of the student's present level of performance and a specific (goal) by which the student's progress can be measured. Even if the present levels of performance were clearly stated, an open-ended statement that the student will "improve" does not meet the requirement (added by the 1997 amendments to the IDEA) for a "measurable goal." (p. 563)

The administrative appeals officer raised an interesting point about what constitutes an appropriate way to measure a student's progress. In the ruling, the officer noted that "the addition of a percentage is not helpful when the IEP fails to define a starting point, ending point . . . or a procedure for pre and post testing" (p. 563). To this hearing officer, a percentage (e.g., 80%) without a starting or ending point is not an appropriate measure.

Additionally, neither general statements about improving or increasing nor anecdotal reports of teacher observation will pass muster. A State Review Officer (SRO) in New York state ruled in *Board of Education of the Rhinebeck Central School District* (2003) that a school district's IEP did not provide FAPE largely because no legitimate data were collected on a student's progress. The SRO, who noted that subjective observational reports were used to measure a student's progress, wrote "although subjective observation provides valuable information, teacher observation is not an adequate method of monitoring student progress . . . without supporting data, teacher observation is opinion which cannot be verified" (p. 156). Clearly, special educators need to choose objective measures and collect legitimate data to analyze student progress. We address measuring students' annual goals in chapter 6.

4. **What services will be provided to the student so he or she may reach these goals?**

The 2006 regulations to the IDEA require that students' IEPs include:

A statement of the special education and related services and supplementary aids and services, based on peer-reviewed research to the extent practicable, to be provided to the child, or on behalf of the child, and a statement of the program modifications or supports for school personnel that will be provided to enable the child—

(i) To advance appropriately toward attaining the annual goals;
(ii) To be involved in and make progress in the general education curriculum . . . and to participate in extracurricular and other nonacademic activities; and
(iii) To be educated and participate with other children with disabilities and non-disabled children (IDEA Regulations, 34 CFR § 300.320[a][4], 2006).

All IEPs must include service statements, which are based on a student's needs as identified in the PLAAFP. Additionally, all of a student's annual goals require corresponding services. When a student's IEP team fails to adequately consider if such services are needed or fail to include needed services in his or her IEP, the school district will be most likely be held accountable for violating the student's right to FAPE (Tatgenhorst et al., 2014).

Recall that to be eligible under the IDEA, a student must have one or more of the disabilities that are covered under the IDEA and they must require special education and related services because of their disability. In other words, a student must need special education services, related services, supplementary aids or services, or a combination of those services to be determined eligible under the IDEA. The definitions of these different types of services are:

- Special education is "specialized designed instruction, at no cost to the parents, to meet the unique needs of a child with a disability" (IDEA Regulations, 34 CFR § 300.39[a], 2006). These services include the following: (a) instruction in classrooms, homes, hospitals, and other settings, including instruction in physical education; (b) speech and language pathology; (c) travel training; and (d) vocational education (IDEA Regulations, 34 CFR § 300.39[a][b], 2006).
- Related services are "transportation, and such developmental, corrective, and other supportive services as are required to assist a child with a disability and benefit from special education" (IDEA Regulations, 34 CFR § 300.34[a], 2006). The IDEA includes a non-exhaustive list of related services that IEP teams may provide when a student needs services to benefit from special education.
- Supplementary aids and services means "aids, services, and other supports that are education classes, other education-related settings, and in extracurricular and nonacademic settings to enable children with disabilities to be educated with nondisabled children to the maximum extent appropriate" (IDEA Regulations, 34 CFR § 300.42, 2006).
- Program modifications or supports for school personnel are provided to a student to help them to advance appropriately toward achieving the annual

goals, to be involved in and make progress in the general education curriculum, and to be educated and participate with other students with disabilities and nondisabled students.

When any of these services are required to enable a student to make progress appropriate in light of their circumstances, they must be included in the student's IEP. Additionally, certain students may need other services such as behavior interventions, assistive technology, extended school years services, and transition plans. In chapter 7, we examine these services in greater depth. In the meantime, it is important that whenever these services are needed, they must be provided or the IEP will not provide a FAPE.

The Internal Consistency of the IEP

A critical aspect of IEP development is the degree of internal consistency of the document. By internal consistency, we are referring to the gestalt of the IEP; that is, everything in the IEP must be related to the individualized needs of a student and all the components of the IEP must be interrelated. The US Department of Education summarized the importance of developing internally consistent IEPs as follows:

> There should be a direct relationship between the present levels of educational performance and the other components of the IEP. Thus, if the statement describes a problem with the child's reading level and points to a deficiency in a specific reading skill, this problem should be addressed under both (1) goals and objectives, and (2) specific special education and related services to be provided to the child. (US Department of Education, Appendix C to Part 300, Question 36)

The figure depicts the importance of connecting all parts of an IEP. All of a student's needs identified in his or her PLAAFP statements must have a corresponding service (i.e., special education services, related services, supplementary aids and services, program modifications). Most academic, instructional, and functional needs that require special education services will need a corresponding measurable annual goal. Occasionally some of a student's needs may only require a service. For example, a student with a visual impairment may need large print books in his or her classes, which would require supplementary aids and services or program modifications, but probably not an annual goal. All annual goals will need service

Figure 3.1 Internal Consistency of an IEP.

statements. Two of the authors of this textbook have served as hearing officers in their respective states in which school district's IEPs were internally inconsistent. We can attest that when IEPs are not internally consistent, they most likely will not provide FAPE.

Summary of the Substantive Dimension of FAPE

According to the US Supreme Court in *Endrew F. v. Douglas School District* (2017), to meet the substantive FAPE standards of the IDEA, students' IEPs must be reasonably calculated to enable a student to make progress in light of his or her circumstances. These substantive standards obligate IEP teams to develop the content of IEPs so as to result in student progress toward meeting their goals. To develop students' IEPs that meet the substantive FAPE requirements, IEP teams should (a) base the IEP on full, individualized and relevant assessments; (b) include PLAAFP statements that address all of a student's needs, regardless of their disability categories; (c) write meaningful, ambitious, and measurable annual goals; (d) monitor student progress by collecting and analyzing legitimate data; and (e) ensure that IEPs are internally consistent.

The Implementation Dimension

The IDEA's definition of a FAPE requires that a FAPE be "provided in conformity" with a student's IEP (IDEA Regulations, 34 CFR § 300.17[d], 2006). In a ruling of the US Courts of Appeals for the Ninth Circuit in *M.C. v. Antelope Valley Union High School District* (2017; hereinafter *Antelope Valley*), the court noted that "an IEP, like a contract . . . embodies a binding commitment and provides notice to both parties as to what services will be provided to the student during the period covered by the IEP (*Antelope Valley*, 2017, p. 1197). The notion of the IEP as a contract deserves some explanation. The IEP is not a contract in the sense that it is not a guarantee that a student will achieve all the goals written in the IEP; rather it a contract because school personnel are obligated to provide the services agreed to by parents and school personnel in the IEP. Thus, if a student's IEP is not implemented, it could be a denial of FAPE and thus violate the IDEA.

Although there has been little litigation regarding a school's failure to implement an IEP, due process hearings and court cases in this area are becoming more frequent (Zirkel, 2017). These few cases have held that failure to implement a student's IEP could be a denial of FAPE, and thus violate the IDEA. This litigation indicates that it likely will take a material or substantial failure to implement a student's IEP before the failure to implement rises to a possible FAPE violation. According to the US Court of Appeals for the Ninth Circuit in *Van Duyn* v. *Baker School District* (2007), a material failure to implement "occurs when there is more than a minor discrepancy between the services a school provides to a disabled child and the services required by the child's IEP" (p. 822). Examples of these material or substantial mistakes include (a) not implementing a student's behavior intervention plan; (b) failing to provide special education services, related services, or supplementary services that were included in a student's IEP; (c) providing fewer hours of services than were included in a student's IEP; and (d) failing to provide extended school services (King, 2009; Yell, 2019). Additionally, delaying the implementation of an IEP can also be denial of FAPE.

One of the judges in the *Van Duyn v. Baker* case issued a dissent in which he asserted that any failure to implement aspects of a student's IEP should be an automatic denial of FAPE. Moreover, in his dissent the judge noted judges should not be second-guessing parents and school district personnel's decisions by deciding which sections of an IEP are material or not. The dissent, which has been referred to as the per se approach (King, 2009; Zirkel, 2017), has not been widely adopted by courts; nonetheless, we believe it should be the approach that school districts should adopt when implementing students' IEPs. Certainly, best practice requires that school districts implement students agreed-upon IEP fully and using good-faith efforts to execute IEPs with fidelity.

Summary of the Implementation Dimension of FAPE

Students' IEP teams can follow the procedural and substantive requirements of the IDEA and still fail to prove a FAPE if they do not accurately implement important elements of the student's IEP. It is crucial, therefore, to ensure all teachers and related service providers understand and properly implement their duties consistently and in a timely manner.

Summary

The purpose of this textbook is to present a framework and process for collaboratively developing educationally meaningful and legally sound IEPs that enable eligible students to make progress. To ensure IEPs meet these standards, it is important to understand the procedural, substantive, and implementation obligations of IEP development. The procedural dimension of FAPE involves questions of "when" and "how" we accomplish procedural tasks required by the IDEA such as identifying students with disabilities, conducting evaluations, developing IEPs, and setting the timelines in which we should accomplish these tasks. The substantive dimension focuses on the adequacy of an IEP with respect to its likely or actual results. Violations of the substantive obligations occur when the content of a student's IEP is not sufficient to confer a FAPE. The implementation dimension requires that school personnel implement a student's IEP as agreed upon by his or her parents and school personnel. When IEPs meet the procedural and substantive requirements and are faithfully implemented, it is much more likely that students will make progress in light of their circumstances, thus conferring a FAPE and meeting both the spirit and intent of the IDEA and the *Endrew F.* decision.

CHAPTER 4

The IEP Process and Components

Ensuring Meaningful Parental Participation and Conducting the IEP Meeting

Our purpose in this book is to examine the IEP provisions of the IDEA and to offer guidance on using better practices when developing student's special education programs. In this chapter we explore the crucial issue of parental rights and how special educators can ensure parents become important collaborators with school district personnel in developing students' special education programming. When Congressional authors reauthorized the IDEA in 2004, they emphasized the importance of meaningful parental involvement in special education:

> Almost 30 years of research and experience has demonstrated that the education of children with disabilities can be made more effective by strengthening the role and responsibility of parents and ensuring that families of such children have meaningful opportunities to participate in the education of their children at school and at home. (IDEA 20 USC § 1400 [c][5][B], 2004)

Many hearings and special education-related cases, including every special education case from the US Supreme Court, have affirmed the critical obligation of schools to involve students in developing their child's IEP (Conroy & Yell, 2019). As the judges of the US Court of Appeals for the Ninth Circuit noted, parental participation is the "very essence of the IDEA," and when schools fail in the obligation to include parents in the IEP process, it is very likely that FAPE will be denied (*Amanda J. v. Clark County School District*, 2001, p. 892).

It is essential that school district personnel go beyond providing parents with merely an opportunity to participate to actually allowing and encouraging "meaningful" participation in the IEP process (Lake, 2007). Lake (2007) asserted that meaningful participation means that parents provide input based on a clear understanding of (a) what is being discussed at the IEP meeting, (b) what is going on at the meeting, and (c) what is or will be proposed at the meeting. To these components we add that school personnel should encourage parents to contribute to the discussion and the team should fully consider their ideas.

In this chapter we examine this critically important obligation of administrators and teachers. We first explain the IDEA's requirements regarding parental participation in IEP development. Second, we provide suggestions and strategies to ensure that parents' participation is meaningful. Third, we address how to conduct an IEP meeting that ensures meaningful parental involvement.

The IDEA and Parental Participation

Since the passage of the Education for All Handicapped Children Act in 1975, parents have been equal partners with school personnel, in planning, developing, reviewing, and revising their child's special education program. The federal law, now titled the Individuals with Disabilities Education Act (IDEA), empowers parents of eligible students with disabilities with certain rights, for themselves and for their children. In general, school districts are required to take steps to ensure one or both of the parents of a student with a disability are present in their child's IEP meeting. In the IDEA Amendments of 1997, the rights of parents were expanded to include participation in the identification, evaluation, educational placement, and provision of a FAPE for their child. We next review some of these very important rights.

Who Is a Parent under the IDEA?

This seems like a simple question with an obvious answer, but when the biological or adoptive parents of a student are not available, we need to determine who can exercise these rights for themselves and their child. Courts have ruled states have the authority to determine who can make educational decisions on behalf of a student, as long as state laws are consistent with federal law. Thus, when a student's parents cannot be located or identified, educators should look to their state's laws for guidance. A student's foster parents have full rights under the IDEA, "unless state laws, regulations, or contractual obligations with a state or local entity prohibit a foster parent from acting as a parent" (IDEA Regulations, 34 CFR § 300.30[a][2], 2006). A student's guardians or other individuals acting in place of a biological parent, like a student's grandparents, a stepparent, or other relative can also exercise parental rights under the IDEA. Surrogate parents are appointed to protect a child's rights if a student's parents cannot be identified or located, the child is a ward of the state, or the child is homeless (*Federal Register*, v. 71, p. 46,568, 2006b).

Difficult situations can arise when a student's biological parents are divorced. In such cases, officials of the Department of Education wrote that both parents have rights under the IDEA, unless a court order or state law specify otherwise (IDEA Regulations, 34 CFR § 300.519[a], 2006). If a judicial order identifies a person(s) to act as a parent on behalf of a child, then that person(s) would be provided the rights of a student's parent (IDEA Regulations, 34 CFR § 300.30[b][2], 2006). If one of the two divorced parents has a judicial order giving the parental rights to him or her, then that parent should be extended all special education parental rights. In instances when one divorced parent does not have legal or physical custody of a child, but they have an amicable agreement to joint participation in educational decision-making, it is permissible to allow participation to both (Norlin, 2011).

Divorced parents who have joint custody of a child and disagree on educational programming for their child present a very difficult problem for educators. In a 2009 letter, officials at the Office of Special Education Programs (OSEP) in the US Department of Education wrote that when a student's parents who are authorized to make decisions on behalf of their child disagree on revoking consent for providing special education services, just one of the parent's written revocation triggers a school district's duty to provide prior written notice and cease services. Additionally, if either one of the parents later requests an evaluation, school officials must treat that as an initial evaluation, not a re-evaluation (*Letter to Cox*, 2009). Confused yet? When such an unfortunate situation occurs, it is best to try and convince the parents to resolve the dispute among themselves in their child's best interest.

Parental Rights

The parental participation regulations to the IDEA can be found at 34 CFR § 300.322 and 300.501. Textbox 4.1 is a depiction of parental procedural rights under the IDEA.

Textbox 4.1: Parental Procedural Rights under the IDEA

- The right to be notified of the procedural safeguards under the IDEA. The notice must be in understandable language and explain all of these rights
- The right to be provided prior written notice whenever the school proposes or refuses to initiate or change the identification, evaluation, or placement of their child
- The right to provide informed written consent prior to the school district conducting an initial evaluation, providing special education and related services, conducting a reevaluation, and excusing an IEP team member from attending an IEP meeting in which the team member's area will be discussed
- The right to access educational records
- The right to participate in meetings regarding their child
- The right to participate in their child's IEP meeting, including placement decisions
- The right to be informed of their child's progress
- The right to an independent education evaluation (IEE) at public expense if the parent disagrees with the school district's evaluation. When an IEE is requested, school officials must quickly either file a due process hearing to show the school's evaluation is appropriate or ensure that the IEE is provided at public expense
- Right to seek an impartial mediation of disputes with the school district
- Right to present complaints through state complaint procedures or due process procedures
- Right to appeal rulings of the state agency or hearing officer
- Right to bring civil actions
- Right to seek attorney's fees

Parents have the right to be meaningfully involved in meetings regarding their child's special education. If parents and school district personnel agree, alternative means can be used to be hold meetings that allow parents the opportunity to participate by alternative means such as virtual conferencing and telephone calls (IDEA Regulations, 34 CFR § 300.328, 2006).

The IDEA includes a provision that when a student reaches the age of majority under state law, school districts should send notification to a student and his or her parents that all the rights under the IDEA transfer to the student (IDEA Regulations, 34 CFR § 300.520, 2006). The transfer of rights apply unless the student has been determined to be incompetent under state law, in which case a legally appointed guardian, usually the parent, retains the rights under the IDEA. Additionally, each state must establish procedures for appointing the parent of a student with a disability (or another person if a student's parents are not available) to represent a student's education rights throughout his or her time of eligibility under the IDEA if under state law a student who has reached the age of majority, but has not been determined incompetent, is determined to not have the ability to provide informed consent regarding the educational program (IDEA Regulations, 34 CFR § 300.520[b], 2006). In the following sections we further examine some of these parental rights.

Parents' Right to Related Services In addition to the parental rights depicted in table 4.1, the IDEA regulations include a non-exhaustive list of related services that the student's IEP team may provide to a student's parents. The related services involve counseling and training, which IDEA regulations define as (a) assisting parents in understanding the special needs of their child, (b) providing parents with information about child development, and (c) helping parents to acquire the necessary skills that will allow them to support the implementation of their child's IEP or individualized family services plan (IDEA Regulations, 34 CFR § 300.34[c] [8], 2006). The idea behind the counseling and training services is that if parents understand this information, they will be better equipped to help their child (Norlin, 2011). The counseling and training services listed in the IDEA regulations which may be provided to a student's parents include:

- Counseling and guidance of parents regarding hearing loss and audiology-related services (IDEA Regulations, 34 CFR § 300.34[c][1][v], 2006)
- Planning and managing a program of psychological counseling for children and parents (IDEA Regulations, 34 § CFR 300.34[c][10][v], 2006)
- Counseling and individual counseling with the child and family (IDEA Regulations, 34 § CFR 300.34[c][14][ii], 2006)
- Parent counseling and training (IDEA Regulations, 34 § CFR 300.34[c][8], 2006)

Additional types of training an IEP team may provide include training in the use of behavior management strategies and assistive technology that the student requires.

We believe it is best if IEP teams consider these types of training during the initial IEP meeting because it may be the first time that a student's parents will have encountered special education programming, and at this point in their child's life, working with the parent in such a way may be the most effective manner to ensure their involvement. Norlin (2011) suggested that a student's IEP ask the following questions to determine if the related service of parent counseling and training is required: (a) Is it important to provide a student's parents with specific skills needed to support implementation of their child's IEP? (b) Will parent training

TABLE 4.1   **Suggestions to Ensure Meaningful Parent Involvement**

Step	Actions
Prior to meetings	
1. Planning	• To avoid surprises during the IEP development process and at meeting, get in touch with the parents on a regular basis. • Keep parents informed of student difficulties (e.g., math, behavior) and of major decisions that need to be made about programming/placement.
2. Providing Timely Drafts of Documents	• Send a draft of the IEP that is to be discussed to the parents ahead of the meeting, according to state guidelines. • Make sure the entire team is aware that what has been developed prior to the meeting is a draft, and that changes to the program and/or placement for the child are to be expected because of team discussions.
During meetings	
3. Ensuring Parents Are Greeted upon Arrival	• Make sure there is someone to greet the parents when they arrive in the building. • Answer any basic questions they have about the process, and to make sure they get to the meeting location.
4. Establishing Rapport	• Prior to starting the meeting, talk about some common interest topics and work to make parents feel comfortable at the meeting. • Be sure parents are included in conversation, avoiding talk exclusively among staff members.
5. Making Room/ Equipment Arrangements	• Secure the needed technology (computer, screen, passwords) to display the draft IEP to allow participants to see and so that changes can be made while you are discussing them. • Provide participants notepads/pens and courtesy items such as water, tea, or coffee.
6. Planning for Alternate Modes of Attendance	• For parents who cannot attend a meeting in person, make other possible means of participation available. • Use approved alternate modes such as the phone, Skype, Zoom, or FaceTime.
7. Involving Other Meeting Attendees	• Remind parents that they can bring others (e.g., family member, advocate) to all meetings to help provide assistance and emotional support. • Make efforts to help the parents and other attendees feel comfortable with participation, for example, by using active/ reflective listening. • Be sure all meeting attendees introduce themselves, identifying roles they will play in the meeting and provision of special education services.
8. Providing Required Interpreters	• Plan ahead to determine if the parents need an interpreter for any reason (language or hearing-related). • Prearrange proper interpreter presence at the meeting.
9. Considering Meeting Room Seating Arrangements	• Be aware of room setup to promote communication and to avoid suggesting an "us-against-them" arrangement. • Allow parents their choice of seating and assure line-of-site for visuals.
10. Introducing the Agenda and Meeting Purpose	• Develop an agenda and ensure everyone has a copy prior to starting the meeting. • Clarify the purpose of the meeting (e.g., initial meeting, revision), and determine if additional agenda items are needed.

(Continued)

TABLE 4.1   Suggestions to Ensure Meaningful Parent Involvement (*Continued*)

Step	Actions
11. Individualizing and Personalizing the Meeting to the Student	• Respectfully, focus the meeting by using the student's name early and often in the meeting as a reminder that the meeting is about the student, not IEP compliance or paperwork. • Keep all the discussion and decisions focused on the specific needs of the student - not on what the district has available to provide or on the child's disability label.
12. Assuring Clear Communications and Clarifications	• Use language that is clear in describing the programs and placements under consideration. • Avoid acronyms as much as possible, but when one is used, make sure all attendees know what is being discussed. • Periodically, ask the parents if they have any questions during the meeting.
13. Planning for Notetaking and Sharing	• Assign responsibility for taking notes. • For meetings that do not have a person to do so, consider using a transcription service such as rev.com (an iPhone app) to record the meeting, and obtain a transcript of the meeting.
14. Discussing Testing Results	• For the meeting, make sure to review all recent testing data. • Be sure to review the needs, as identified in the present levels section, to assure that data to support decisions are included. • Describe test results in user-friendly terminology.
15. Discussing Placement	• Assure any placement decision is made with the intention of having the student involved in the general education classroom - or with general education peers - to the maximum extent possible. • Always base placement decisions on data that lead to instructional goals and services.
16. Explaining the Ongoing Decision-Making That Follows the Meeting	• Explain any decision with respect to the data and reasoning that support it. • Make it clear that decisions for programming and placement are not permanent, and that they will be reviewed regularly. • Explain that the IEP team will be taking data routinely to determine if the student is making progress.
17. Allowing Sufficient Time and Offering Multiple Meetings	• Allocate ample time for the meeting. • Recognize that it may take more than one meeting to develop a working, complete IEP. • Do not rush parents into agreeing to programming or placement for their child because "time is running out" for the meeting.
After meetings	
18. Planning for Follow-up Tasks and Deadlines	• At the end of the meeting, make a list of next steps/tasks, assigning responsibility for each one. • Determine due dates for tasks to be completed. • Share the listing with parents, answering any questions they may have before they leave.
19. Assuring Post-Meeting Communication	• Assign a point person who will contact the parents five days after the meeting. • Share status of follow-up tasks and answer any additional questions or concerns raised by the parents. • Offer to follow up again and assure parents that the lines of communication are open.

help to alleviate a student's problem? (c) Do a student's parents need training about their child's disability and the IEP process? (d) Is parent training necessary to implement part of the IEP?

Parents' Right to Receive Information on Their Child's Progress In chapter 6, we address the importance of including information in a student's IEP on how to measure and report a student's progress. The IDEA regulations of 2006 specifically require that IEPs include "how the (student's) progress toward meeting the annual goals . . . will be measured" (IDEA Regulations, 34 CFR § 300.320 [a][3][i], 2006) and provide an example of how "periodic reports on the progress the (student) is making toward meeting the annual goals (such as through the use of quarterly or other periodic reports, concurrent with the issuance of report cards) will be provided" (IDEA Regulations, 34 CFR § 300.320 [a][3][ii], 2006). According to officials at the US Department of Education, school districts should use the periodic reporting requirement to keep students' parents informed of their progress toward their annual IEP goals (*Federal Register*, v. 71, p. 46,664, 2006b). School districts' officials have an obligation to keep parents informed about their child's progress, but how they accomplish this is up to the state and school officials. As the judges of the US Court of Appeals for the Ninth Circuit wrote in 2017, "parental participation does not end when the parent signs the IEP. Parents must be able to use the IEP to monitor and enforce the services that their child is to receive" (*M.C. v. Antelope Valley School District*, 2017, p. 1199). Without information on a student's progress toward achieving their goals, his or her parents will not have this important information.

Parents' Rights and Their Child's Educational Records Regulations to the IDEA require that students' educational records be kept confidential (IDEA Regulations, 34 CFR § 610, 2006) and that students' parents may access these educational records (IDEA Regulations, 34 CFR § 613, 2006). The confidential and access rights of the IDEA are consistent with the rights conferred in the Family Educational Rights and Privacy Act (FERPA; 34 CFR § 99.10 *et seq*.). The IDEA and FERPA require that (a) school districts must establish written policies regarding student records and inform parents of their rights under FERPA annually, (b) parents be guaranteed access to their children's educational records, (c) parents have the right to challenge the accuracy of the records, and (d) disclosure of these records to third parties without parental consent is prohibited. A student's parents may file complaints under FERPA regarding a school's failure to comply with the law.

FERPA and IDEA cover all records, files, documents, and other materials that contain personally identifiable information directly related to a student and that are maintained by the school district or by a person acting for the district. With respect to special education, these records include students' IEPs, evaluation reports, test forms, recordings of IEP meetings, and other records with personally identifiable information. School district personnel must ensure these educational records are kept confidential and only available to school professionals with a legitimate reason to access these records (e.g., a child's special education and general education teachers, counselors, administrators). Third parties may only access students' records if given permission by parents. This access rule does not apply to persons responsible for determining eligibility for financial aid, to when a judge orders records released, and in emergency situations, to persons who act to protect the student's health and safety.

Students' parents must be permitted to inspect and review their child's educational records maintained, collected, or used by the school district. Additionally, school officials must explain and interpret records to parents if they ask school officials to do so. School officials must comply promptly with parental requests to inspect educational records. The response must be made in a reasonable amount of time. Parents may also challenge the accuracy of their child's educational records and request the records be amended. School officials may deny the parents' request, but the parents may contest this refusal in a due process hearing.

Parents' Right to Attend Meetings Regarding Their Child's Special Education In this chapter, we are exploring the crucial issue of parental rights vis-à-vis students' IEPs. It is clear students' parents must be meaningfully involved in IEP development. Beyond being a meaningful collaborator in the IEP development process, parents have the right to be involved in all meetings regarding their child's special education programming. The 2006 regulations to the IDEA guarantee parents' rights to participate in all meetings concerning "the identification, evaluation, and educational placement of the child; and the provision of FAPE to the child" (IDEA Regulations, 34 CFR § 300.501 [b][1][i-ii], 2006). To ensure parental attendance at these meetings, school district personnel must provide notice early enough to ensure that the parents will be able to be at the meeting. Because the IDEA does not provide specific timelines in some areas but relies on a standard of reasonableness, readers should determine if their state has specific timelines. Of course, school district personnel should keep thorough records of their attempts to contact a student's parents.

Readers should note that unscheduled or informal discussions among school personnel do not constitute meetings for purposes of the IDEA, if no final decisions are made regarding the student's education. Neither are preparatory activities to develop proposals or respond to parental requests considered a meeting according to the law. If, however, school personnel make unilateral final decisions during preparatory meetings, they open the school district to charges of predetermination.

Conducting the IEP Meeting

Scheduling of IEP meetings should be done early enough to ensure parents will have an opportunity to attend. The IDEA requires school districts to schedule IEP meetings at a "mutually agreeable time and place" (IDEA Regulations, 34 CFR § 300.322[a][2], 2006). Readers should note that the regulation noted that the agreement regarding the IEP meeting is made "mutually," which means school personnel also have a say in determining the meeting date. Thus, school district personnel do not need to honor every parental request (e.g., late evening meetings, meetings on the weekend). Nonetheless, school personnel must make good-faith efforts to arrange the date and time of the IEP meeting, even if has to be done via an alternative method (e.g., Zoom, GoToMeeting). Of course, meetings must be held at the agreed-upon time and place (*Dallas Independent School District*, 1998).

When parents are advised in writing about an upcoming meeting, the notification should include the purpose, time, and location of the meeting and who will attend the meeting. Parents must also be informed of other IEP participants, including those on the IEP team who have knowledge or special expertise about the student, including related services personnel and, if the student previously participated in a Part C (i.e., early childhood services) system, a Part C service coordinator or representative. Similarly, for older students of transition age, a student's parents must be notified of the (a) purpose of the meeting, including the consideration of the postsecondary goals and transition services for the student, and (b) information about other agencies that will be invited to send a representative to the meeting (IDEA Regulations, 34 CFR § 300.320[b], 2006). Additionally, when appropriate the student should be invited to the meeting, which is especially important when he or she is of transition age.

When a student's parents cannot be contacted/identified, or are unwilling to attend, school officials may need to conduct an IEP team meeting without a parent in attendance. In such cases, school personnel must carefully document their attempts to arrange a mutually agreed-on time and place. The IDEA regulations suggest keeping documentation such as—

(1) Detailed records of telephone calls made or attempted and the results of those calls;
(2) Copies of correspondence sent to the parents and any responses received; and
(3) Detailed records of visits made to the parent's home or place of employment and the results of those visits (IDEA Regulations, 34 CFR § 300.322[d][1, 2, 3], 2006).

Another circumstance requiring specific attention by school personnel occurs when a student's parents have communication needs. Additional actions, as appropriate, may be needed so that school personnel can demonstrate that they have taken whatever means are necessary to ensure that the parent understands the proceedings of the IEP Team meeting, including arranging for an interpreter for parents with deafness or whose native language is other than English (IDEA Regulations, 34 CFR § 300.322[e], 2006) when necessary. Finally, in all cases, the parent must be provided a copy of their child's IEP at no cost.

Tips for Ensuring Meaningful Parental Involvement in the IEP Process

There are many ways that school personnel can ensure meaningful parental involvement in the development of the IEP. Most of the tips and strategies that we share below focus on the IEP document and the meeting itself. Whereas these are important strategies, they are not sufficient in assuring the role of the parent in the whole process of educating a student. Communication with the parent(s) is something that should happen well before the parents are invited to an IEP meeting and the IEP is developed, and it should be viewed as a long-term communication strategy. The parents are to be a part of the process of the development of the program or IEP, and their input will be vital in developing the specific goals and the number of services the student is expected to receive.

It is important that administrators and educators involved in IEP team meetings understand the importance of the IEP meeting to a student's parents. For educators, it is another IEP meeting; for parents it is <u>the</u> IEP meeting. Parents who are going through the development of an IEP for the first time will have questions that need to be addressed. Typically, special education teachers will have had many IEP team meetings, and even though they will not yet be involved in the delivery of services, they are the IEP team members most likely to have answers to many of the parents' questions.

Additionally, prior to the IEP meeting is the time the general education and special education teachers need to work together and ensure the parents receive timely and accurate information to their questions about the process, and what special education services may look like if their child is determined to be eligible. Similarly, general educators who are new to the IEP process may have questions. Special education teachers, therefore, should reach out to the general education teachers once the evaluation commences and let them know they are available to answer questions about the process.

In addition to tips to communicating with parents, we offer some tips on what <u>not</u> to say. When parents make service or other types of requests, school personnel should never make the following types of statements: We cannot do <u>(fill in the blank)</u>; We will not do <u>(fill in the blank)</u>, We never have done <u>(fill in the blank)</u>; That will cost too much, or we only will provide <u>(fill in the blank)</u>. Any statements that begin in this way are to be avoided! Additionally, if a parental request is unreasonable or contraindicated by research, team members should respectfully discuss and consider the practice even though the team will eventually decide not to implement the practice. In such cases, it is important that team members explain their rationale in refusing to implement.

Talking Points and Assurances to Share with Parents

The information shared with parents early in—and throughout - the IEP process will be the foundations of a successful experience. There are many opportunities to explain important points, answer parents' questions, and to offer ongoing assurances. It is important to explain that the evaluation process under IDEA may take a while, possibly up to 60 days, and to let parents know they will be interviewed as part of the process related to their child's education. Parents must provide their informed written consent before the evaluation can be conducted and be told what this means. Also, teachers should let the parents know that the determination of eligibility at the end of the evaluation process does not necessarily mean their child will receive special education services, because not all students with disabilities are eligible for special education.

After the evaluation, if the student is found eligible, the parents must provide written approval before their child will receive special education services. Parents should be informed that before services can be provided their approval will be needed. Moreover, the program will begin as soon as possible after they have given their permission to begin the special education program. It is important to explain to the parents that most students eligible for special education receive most of their education in the general education classroom, and that students are removed from the general education environment if and when they require specialized services related to their disability that cannot be provided or delivered in the general education setting.

Ongoing communications about parents' rights and responsibilities are necessary. Parents should be informed that if they approve the special education program for their child, they can revoke authority for the services at any time. However, if they do revoke their approval for special education services, the student will be considered a general education student for all educational services, including provisions related to discipline. Parents must receive a copy of the procedural safeguards notice, and a school-based point person should be identified to address questions parents have about the document and the process.

Finally, the timing of ongoing requirements for IDEA services should be made clear. It is essential that the parents know that the determination about whether a child is eligible for special education and related services will be revisited every three years and that their child's IEP will be revised at least annually, or more often if needed. The latter provision assures that the programming and services in the IEP are individualized for the student—a central tenet of the IDEA. Additionally, a student's parents should be told that they can request an IEP meeting when they believe one is needed.

Parent Expectations

What can school district personnel reasonably expect of parents at an IEP meeting? Because of the different ways parents are involved with the education of their child, there is no one answer to this question. However, it is the responsibility of school personnel to help parents be comfortable with the IEP process, and to help them understand their role in ensuring the student receives a FAPE. Parents and other family members often provide the continuity of experiences for the student as the child progresses from grade to grade. Because they have experiences with their child and their child's educational experiences, they may refer to things that happened (or didn't happen) from their involvement with previous teachers and administrators. There may even be a degree of distrust with the system, the district, or teachers. Supporting the parent(s) to re-establish the trust and willingness to continue to participate in the process in order to make informed decisions about their child is a critical role for school personnel.

Parental Involvement in Developing the Present Levels, Goals, Services, and the Progress Monitoring System

Parents should be encouraged to provide information and opinions about the assessments given to their child and the services the student is (or is not) receiving. It is important to ask parents about their thoughts and ideas about how the student is functioning as part of the development of the PLAAFP. This information should be gathered as part of PLAAFP development in advance of the IEP meeting. However, when parents' input and concerns are not obtained ahead of time (e.g., due to their schedules, not receiving input forms in a timely manner, or not understanding what was requested of them), it is advisable to begin the IEP meeting by asking the parents to tell the team about their child and share their thoughts about how their child is doing and what they need. Doing this opening activity serves multiple purposes:

(1) It grounds the team to remind them they are talking about an individual child, who has academic problems, behavioral problems, or both.
(2) It leads to a discussion of the student's strengths, which can be useful in determining programming.
(3) It provides direction for the team in thinking about the concerns the parent has related to their child's program and highlights specific concerns the parent has.
(4) It provides the parent information for the PLAAFP statement that can be embedded in the PLAAFP section or added as a supplement to the information that the parent provided previously.

The opening discussion should lead to the sharing of information related to the needs of the student and about how those needs should be addressed through the student's annual goals. Specifically, parental input can help define, refine, and prioritize the annual goals that will be targeted for the upcoming year. Parents should be encouraged to discuss their educational goals for their child.

It is also important to explain how their child's progress toward achieving his or her goals will be measured, and when and how this progress will be communicated. Preferably, communication will be in person or conducted virtually. When discussing progress monitoring, the method of data collection should be explained to the parents. For example, if a student's progress in reading will be monitored by conducting weekly measures of oral reading fluency, the importance of reading fluency data should be briefly explained and a reporting schedule should be set up with the parents.

With respect to determining the services that will be provided to a student, the parent should certainly be involved in these decisions and their opinions should be carefully considered and discussed. Such discussions could certainly include discussions of educational methodology. However, readers should note "there is nothing in the (IDEA) that requires an IEP team address specific instructional methodology that will be used in a student's programming unless a student needs the program to receive a FAPE" (*Federal Register*, v. 71, p. 46,665, 2006b). In fact, the IDEA leaves decisions regarding specific educational methodologies to school personnel. Whereas school personnel on the IEP team should maintain a dialogue regarding educational methodologies with a student's parents, the choice of educational methodology is ultimately the school personnel's decision (Tatgenhorst et al., 2014).

Specific Steps for Ensuring Meaningful Parental Involvement

Throughout the IEP meeting, it is imperative that all school personnel who are part of the IEP team work diligently to create and maintain a professional and courteous environment. As part of the IEP team, parents' engagement and contributions are central to a positive outcome of such meetings, and so it is important to think strategically about how to best assure their sense of value and influence. To begin, always tell the student's parents that all school personnel in attendance are there to discuss and plan for *their child's* educational programming. At the beginning of the IEP meeting, school personnel on the team should introduce themselves to the parents. During the meeting, it is essential that everyone who works for the school district pays attention to the meeting and to the comments from the parents. This professionalism means that attendees are focused on developing an appropriate program and placement for the student; they are not "multitasking" with email, grading, or other tasks. Of course, person-first language and personal references to the student should be used throughout the meeting. Table 4.1 includes suggested steps and actions to support parent engagement before, during, and after IEP meetings.

Meeting Leadership and Agendas

Every IEP meeting should be led by a designated team member who will assume responsibilities for facilitating the discussion and moving the team toward decisions. This team member may be, but does not need to be, the LEA representative. An important component of an IEP meeting should be the development of the meeting agenda. The agenda should be shared with all team members in advance so that they may be prepared to contribute to relevant agenda items. A sample IEP meeting agenda is presented in textbox 4.2.

Textbox 4.2: Sample IEP Team Meeting Agenda

IEP Team Meeting
Date | Time 1/15/2021 9:00 AM| Location David School, Room 100
Type of Meeting: Initial IEP
Meeting Leader: Mr. Mitchell
Notetaker: Mr. James

Notes:

Agenda Items:
(a) Welcome and purpose of the meeting
(b) Introduction of the team members
(c) Basic rules for the meeting
    (a) Listen to others
    (b) Only one person talks at a time
    (c) Respect the views of others
    (d) Be open to other ideas
    (e) Ask questions for clarification
    (f) Preserve confidentiality
(d) Presentation of the meeting agenda
(e) Parents' statement about how their child is doing in school and concerns
(f) Five special considerations
(g) Develop present levels of academic achievement and functional performance statements
    (a) Student's strengths
    (b) Student's needs

(h)   Craft measurable annual goals
(i)   Measuring student progress
    (a)   Frequency and method for reporting student progress
(j)   Special education services
    (a)   Related services
    (b)   Supplementary services
    (c)   Program modifications
    (d)   Frequency, duration, and location of services
    (e)   Placement (focusing on the LRE)

Other Items:

Follow-up Tasks/Persons Responsible

Follow-up Communication/Persons Responsible/Date

Notes

The meeting leader should adopt a step-by-step process, to ensure all the needs of the student are addressed when creating the student's program of special education. As a part of identifying the needs for the PLAAFP statement, team members work to identify why the student has specific needs. They can do this by gathering information from the general education teacher(s) regarding why they believe the student may be struggling and why the student might not be as engaged as others. If the student is currently receiving special education services, these same questions should be asked of the special education teacher. Finally, ensure the parents are afforded an opportunity to provide insights they may have about why they believe their child is having problems. The leader of the meeting should encourage and facilitate parents' contributions. You cannot always decide why the student is having problems, but it is a good place to start and then work to address the needs as they were identified.

We offer the following suggestions to assist the meeting leader in this critical task and role:

1. Do not just focus on the areas where the student is having problems; work to understand and describe areas where the student is having successes. When teams are able to identify areas in which a student is succeeding in addition to identifying the educational problems he or she is experiencing, it is more likely that the team will develop a plan that capitalizes on the student's strengths.
2. If a student is having behavior problems that impede his or her learning or the learning of others, be certain that these problems are documented and considered. This ensures the team addresses how the behavior may affect a student's access, engagement, and progress in grade-level general education instruction and environments as well as in understanding why this behavior is occurring.
3. Ensure the team understands that the development of the IEP for a student can and often should go beyond academics. Therefore, the team should address any functional issues the student is having in the school-related programming.
4. Ensure the team addresses every need that is identified for the student.
5. Ensure the team addresses the student as an individual and not as a member of a specific disability category. Just because the student may have a label as a

student with a learning disability or some other disability, this does not mean the student is or should receive all the same services as other students who have the same disability label.

6. When developing goals, ensure the IEP team understands how baseline, level of attainment, and procedures for monitoring progress are all connected.
7. Ensure there is someone on the team who will check with staff to ensure all progress-monitoring measures are regularly used and that they track the progress toward goals for the student.
8. Emphasize how many special education services can be provided in the general education environment. Always lead the team in thinking about how we can do a better job of including the student in the general education classroom for as much time as possible.
9. Ensure the parents know that if they have questions or concerns about their child's programming, they can call a representative of the district and expect a timely answer to their questions or concerns. Additionally, the parents can ask for a revision to the IEP at any time they believe one is necessary.

The Individualized Education Program Team

It is very important to emphasize that the final development of a student's IEP is a team process. An individual may be requested to develop a draft of the IEP prior to the team meeting; however, the final version must represent the information of all IEP participants. One person cannot dictate the program or the components of the program. The IEP is a consensus document. All team members have a say in the development of the IEP, but this does not mean everything a member of the team suggests has to be in the final program described in the IEP. Any requested services must be fully considered by the team to determine if services are needed for the student to receive a FAPE.

Mandatory School-Based Members

The mandatory members of the IEP team are delineated in 34 CFR §300.321 of the IDEA regulations. Specifically, the IEP team for each child with a disability includes—

(1) The parents of the child
(2) Not less than one regular education teacher of the child (if the child is, or may be, participating in the regular education environment)
(3) Not less than one special education teacher of the child, or where appropriate, not less than one special education provider of the child
(4) A representative of the public agency who—
    (i) Is qualified to provide, or supervise the provision of, specially designed instruction to meet the unique needs of children with disabilities
    (ii) Is knowledgeable about the general education curriculum; and
    (iii) Is knowledgeable about the availability of resources of the public agency.
(5) An individual who can interpret the instructional implications of evaluation results

(6) At the discretion of the parent or the agency, other individuals who have knowledge or special expertise regarding the child, including related services personnel as appropriate

(7) Whenever appropriate, the child with a disability

For students of transition age, there may be other participants on the IEP meetings. Below we describe the roles of required participants and suggest actions the person in each role can take to prepare for an IEP team meeting. Readers should note state laws and regulations on IEP team membership and procedures may exceed those of the IDEA, so it is important to stay up to date on your state's requirements.

Parents Parents play a vital role in the development of the IEP. Special education rulings from the US Supreme Court from the first special education case, *Board of Education v. Rowley* (1982), to the most recent, *Endrew F. v. Douglas County School District* (2017), have emphasized the critical need for parental involvement. Parents know their child's likes and dislikes and have a history with the student that few others have. Addressing and working with the parents can be one of the most important parts of the IEP team. (Recall the tips for meaningful parental involvement in table 4.1 of this chapter.) Parents can bring that expertise about their child to the meeting and will have the opportunity to share their insights, concerns, and suggestions.

A student's parents are equal partners on their child's IEP team and their suggestions must receive the full consideration during the IEP process. Nonetheless, a parent's suggestions do not have to be accepted. Neither do a student's parents have an absolute veto over the IEP. The goal of an IEP meeting is to reach consensus; the law does not require that members vote at a meeting (*Federal Register*, v. 64, p. 12473, Appendix A, 1999). School districts are responsible for the provision of FAPE and the IEP team makes the final decision. If parents do not agree with the IEP, the school district personnel must provide the parents of their prior written notice of the district proposal or refusal. The parents always have the option to request mediation or a due process hearing. When agreement cannot be reached, the consensus of the IEP team is to determine appropriate services and provide parents with prior written notice of the services and an explanation of the parents to seek resolution of any disagreement through a due process hearing (*Letter to Richards*, 2010).

Public Agency/Local Education Agency (LEA) Representative When it is used in an IEP meeting, the term "LEA" often refers to the administrator who is a representative of the school district. The LEA representative must be (a) qualified to provide or supervise the provision of special education, (b) knowledgeable about the general education curriculum, and (c) knowledgeable about school district resources. The comments to the 2006 IDEA regulations noted that "it is important however, that the (school district) representatives have the authority to commit (school district) resources and be able to ensure that whatever services are described in the IEP will actually be provided" (*Federal Register*, v. 71, p. 46,670, 2006). Furthermore, according to officials at the US Department of Education, they did not include this specific language in the regulations because the school district "will be bound by the IEP that is developed at an IEP meeting" (*Federal Register*,

v. 71, p. 46,670, 2006b). Some states specifically require the LEA representative to have the authority to commit funds and resources for the special education and related services required by the student.

School district officials may determine who the LEA representative will be as long as they meet the aforementioned qualifications (*Federal Register*, v. 71, p. 46670, 2006). The person who can serve this role varies from state to state, and even sometimes within a state. In some districts it is only a special education supervisor or director, whereas in others it can be a principal who may act in this role. We believe that a school principal, an associate principal, or a district-level special education administrator would be best positioned to be the LEA representative. We caution against the use of school counselors or school psychologists, who will likely not meet the criteria mentioned above, and special education teachers may not be knowledgeable about school district resources. Norlin et al. (2010) warned that in parental challenges to student IEPs, if a hearing officer or judge determines that the person who serves in this role is not qualified or knowledgeable as required by the IDEA, it is likely that this error will be considered a substantive denial of FAPE.

Additional roles of the LEA representative include:

(1) Ensuring the implementation of the IEP.
(2) Convening the IEP team when there are needs, changes, or timeline requirements.
(3) Ensuring the IEP is implemented even during disputes.
(4) Documenting IEP implementation.
(5) Ensuring fair procedures related to student discipline.

Special Education Teacher The IDEA requires that "not less than one special education teacher of the child" (IDEA Regulations, 34 CFR § 300.321 [a][3], 2006) be included on a student's IEP team. The special education teacher is often a main contributor to the IEP team meeting. They often provide important information and experience related to the eventual special education program and are able to answer questions related to the services the student will be receiving. Special educators usually can address (a) how to modify the general education curriculum to help the student, (b) the supplementary aids and services necessary for the general education classroom, and (c) strategies to modify testing to meet student needs. The special education teacher on the IEP team should be the teacher who will be primarily responsible for implementing the student's IEP. It should be noted, however, that it is a common misconception that the special education teacher should be the sole or primary person responsible for developing a student's IEP. This is incorrect because the entire team is responsible for developing, reviewing, and revising a student's IEP. In any case, the decision as to who will serve on the IEP team is left to local and state officials (*Federal Register*, v. 71, p. 46,670, 2006b).

General Education Teacher The IDEA requires that a student's IEP team include "not less than one regular education teacher of the child" (if the child is, or may be, participating in the regular education environment" (IDEA Regulations, 34 CFR § 300.321 [a][2], 2006). In 2017, Barbara Bateman suggested that failing to have a general education teacher[1] on the IEP team makes a school district vulnerable to charges of predetermination of placement. This is because if a general education teacher is not included on the team, the clause "is, or may be" means that school personnel are essentially saying that a student is not and will never be in general education. Placement cannot be determined until a student's IEP is finalized, so a general education teacher should be on the team (Bateman, 2017). In situations in which a student does not have a current general education teacher, the US Department of Education has recognized that a teacher who is or may be responsible for implementing part of the IEP should be on the team so he or she may participate in discussions about how best to teach the student (IDEA Regulations, 34 CFR § 300, Appendix A, Question 26, 1999).

The general education teacher of a child with a disability, as a member of the IEP team, must, to the extent appropriate, participate in the development, review, and revision of the child's IEP, including assisting in the determination of—

(1) Appropriate positive behavioral interventions and strategies for the child; and
(2) Supplementary aids and services, program modifications or supports for school personnel that will be provided for the child. General educators can offer information about the expectations for the student with respect to (a) curricular priorities within the academic content standards of the state, and (b) behavioral capabilities needed for successful inclusion and participation in the regular class setting.

In the discussion accompanying the 2006 IDEA regulations, the regular education "should be a teacher who is, or may be, be responsible for carrying out a portion of the IEP" (*Federal Register*, v. 71, p. 46,675, 2006). According to the US Court of Appeals for the Sixth Circuit, "The input provided by a regular education teacher is vitally important in considering the extent to which a disabled student may be integrated into the regular education and how the student's individual needs might be met within that classroom" (*Deal v. Hamilton County Board of Education*, 2004, p. 864).

A Person to Interpret Instruction Implications of the Evaluation The IDEA regulations require that an individual who can interpret the instructional implications of evaluation results be part of the IEP team. Often, this role is filled by a school psychologist, but it can also be filled by other members of the team (e.g., special education teacher) as long as he or she is qualified. Evaluation data are used in determining how the student is currently doing in school and identifying the student's areas of need. Whoever fills this particular role on an IEP team must have the "skills or knowledge to assist the IEP team in determining the special education services, related services, and other supports that are necessary in order for the child to receive FAPE" (*Federal Register*, v. 71, p. 46,670, 2006b). In addition to sharing findings from psychological tests and observations, the person in this role helps summarize and provide information related to the PLAAFP statement in the IEP. They also monitor student progress to ensure students are making progress toward their IEP goals.

---

[1] Although the IDEA and implementing regulations use the term "regular education," we will use the term "general education."

Others with Knowledge about the Child or Special Expertise

The IEP team may include "other individuals with knowledge or special expertise about the student, including related services personnel as appropriate" (IDEA Regulations, 34 CFR § 300.321 [6], 2006). The determination of the knowledge of special expertise of an invited member of the IEP team has is made by the party, either the parent or school personnel, who invited that person to be a member (IDEA Regulations, 34 CFR § 300.321 [c], 2006). Neither the IDEA nor the regulations limit the number of persons either party may invite to the IEP team.

Related service providers could include occupational or physical therapists, adaptive physical education providers, psychologists, or speech-language pathologists. Either the parent or school district personnel can invite these individuals to participate on the team. Examples of individuals parents may invite include: an advocate, an independent evaluator, a professional with special expertise about the child and his or her disability, or others who have been working with the student in some capacity (e.g., tutor, advisor). Parents may also bring a family friend for support during the meeting but only if the person can contribute to the IEP meeting with their knowledge or special expertise (Norlin, 2011). School personnel should ensure the parents know they can bring persons to the meeting to assist them in understanding programming necessary to develop the IEP for the child.

The Student The student may also be a member of the IEP team. A student may be a participating member of the team, and according to the IDEA, "whenever appropriate, the child with a disability" should also be invited (IDEA Regulations, 34 CFR § 300.321 [7], 2006). Clearly, when the team is discussing transition planning, the student is an expected participant in the meeting. In such situations, the IEP team should invite and strongly encourage the student to participate. If a transition-aged student does not participate in the meeting, additional steps must be taken to ensure that the student's preferences and interests are taken into account in developing a transition program (see chapters 5 and 7 for further information on transition planning and services).

Transition Services Agency Representative(s) When a student is of transition age as determined by a state (or age 16 if there is no state requirement, as required by the IDEA), representatives from transition service agencies are important participants in an IEP meeting. In the discussion of transition services, the school district must invite a representative of any other agency that is likely to be responsible for providing or paying for transition services (IDEA Regulations, 34 CFR § 300.321 [c], 2006). A school district must obtain the parent's consent before the agency's representative may participate in an IEP meeting (see *Letter to Gray*, 2008). The information provided by this representative can help the team plan any transition services the student needs. This person also may commit resources of the agency to help provide needed transition services.

When Students Reach the Age of Majority When a student reaches the age of majority, which is determined by individual states (usually the age of 18), the law may require all of the rights under the IDEA be transferred to the student instead of the parents. The IDEA permits, but does not require, that states may transfer the IDEA Part B rights to students with disabilities when they reach the age of majority (IDEA Regulations, 34 CFR § 300.520 [a], 2006). If a school district does not transfer these rights to the student, if required to do so by state law, it is a violation of the procedural obligations of the IDEA. Therefore, there may be some students who are 18, 19, or 20 years old who are attending the IEP meeting without a parent. Just as when working with parents to keep them informed about their child's progress, we need to make sure the adult student is fully informed of his or her progress.

Consideration of Special Factors in IEP Development

All IEP teams must consider six special factors in the development and revision of each student's IEP (see IDEA Regulations, 34 CFR § 300.324[a][2][i-v], 2006). The special factors specified by the IDEA regulations are:

 (i) In the case of a child whose behavior impedes the child's learning or that of others, consider the use of positive behavioral interventions and supports, and other strategies, to address that behavior;

 (ii) In the case of a child with limited English proficiency, consider the language needs of the child as those needs relate to the child's IEP;

(iii) In the case of a child who is blind or visually impaired, provide for instruction in Braille and the use of Braille, unless the IEP team determines, after an evaluation of the child's reading and writing skills, needs, and appropriate reading and writing media (including an evaluation of the child's future needs for instruction in Braille or the use of Braille), that instruction in Braille or the use of Braille is not appropriate for the child;

(iv) Consider the communication needs of the child, and in the case of a child who is deaf or hard of hearing, consider the child's language and communication needs, opportunities for direct communications with peers and professional personnel in the child's language and communication mode, academic level, and full range of needs, including opportunities for direct instruction in the child's language and communication mode; and

 (v) Consider whether the child needs assistive technology devices and services (IDEA Regulations, 34 CFR § 300.324[a][2], 2006).

The IEP team must determine if any of these factors are relevant for the child and, if so, address the factor in the child's IEP. Depending on your state, most likely these components are in the early part of the IEP and are also an important part of the development of the IEP. Too often, the answers to these questions are pro-forma checkboxes on an IEP form. We encourage all IEP teams to take them seriously and thoroughly discuss these considerations in the development, review, and revision of each student's IEP. During the initial IEP meeting, as well as IEP review or revising, the team must examine these five special factors (Lake, 2007).

With respect to the behavior decision, if the team determines that behavior is indeed a concern, regardless of a student's category of disability, these behaviors must be addressed in the student's IEP. When the team decides the behavior is a serious problem, then the team should consider "appropriate positive behavioral interventions and supports and other strategies" to address that behavior (IDEA Regulations, 34 CFR § 300.324 [3][i], 2006). Neither the IDEA nor the regulations specify what problem behaviors are covered under the law;

nonetheless, Drasgow and colleagues (2014) inferred from previous litigation that these behaviors included (a) disruptive behaviors that distracted a teacher from teaching and a student and his or her peers from learning, (b) noncompliance, (c) abuse of property, (d) verbal abuse, and (e) aggression toward students or staff. It is important that IEP team members understand that the behaviors that must be considered are any that affect a student's learning or the learning of other students. It is not limited only to dangerous or illegal behaviors (Lake, 2007; Yell, 2019).

The requirement in the IDEA about including positive behavior supports was originally in the law with the amendment of 1997. Thomas Hehir, then the director of the US Department of Education's Office of Special Education Programs, wrote that "the key provision in IDEA '97 is using positive behavioral interventions and supports" for students who exhibit significant problem behaviors (*Letter to Anonymous*, 2008). Thomas Hehir's policy letter seemed to clearly support the use of positive behavior support with all students with disabilities who exhibited problem behavior. Thus, if a student exhibits problem behaviors that the team determines are serious but has no plan to address these concerns in a meaningful manner, the IEP is inconsistent with the requirements of IDEA to address all of a student's needs and may be a denial of FAPE.

For students with blindness or visual impairment, the question IEP team members should ask is: "Is the student blind or visually impaired?" If the team answers "yes," there needs to be a description of the instruction in Braille and the use of Braille. This is necessary unless after an evaluation the team determines that instruction in Braille or the use of Braille is not appropriate for the student. It is important for the evaluation to analyze any future needs the student may have related to Braille instruction. Students' needs related to their visual impairments may significantly change over time. It is important for the team to make all determinations after the completion of an evaluation determining issues related to sight. This evaluation should include the student's reading, writing and computing skills, needs and appropriate literacy media including the student's future needs. The results of this assessment should be included in the present levels section of the IEP.

Specifically, the evaluation could potentially include:

- Information documenting the student's medical condition and visual prognosis
- A functional vision assessment, assessing the student's use of vision in all areas of education (not just academic)
- Description of how the student uses sensory channels to acquire information
- The student's ability to read, write and compute (for both short and sustained durations)

IEP teams should consider this information for all students suspected of having a visual impairment. This may include students with autism as well as students with multiple disabilities. Additionally, there may be a need for the consideration of assistive technology for these students to determine if that is needed to help access the curriculum and the contents of the classroom.

When a student has communication problems, the question IEP team members should ask is: "Does the student have communication needs?" If the team answers "yes," there must be a plan to address the student's communication needs. Communication is more than just providing information to the teacher; it also includes language and communication with peers. To make the determination about whether there are needs, it is important that for all students suspected of having hearing loss, an evaluation is completed that addresses the student's preferred mode of communication, the academic functioning level of the student, the need for any assistive technology devices or services, and whether an interpreter is needed, and if so, for how long and in which settings. For students for whom manual communication is their primary method, the IEP team could consider programs and placements where the other students, teacher, and personnel use similar forms of communication.

Typically, the determination related to communication needs is made with the assistance of a speech-language pathologist, with strong consideration given to the possible modes of communication the student uses with other persons. Additionally, the team should consider how effective the student is in communication. Finally, like other areas, the family may be helpful in determining if there are concerns related to the student's communication skills and needs.

With respect to determining if a student may have with assistive technology needs, the primary question is: "Does the student need assistive technology devices and/or services?" Increasingly, students are needing various forms of assistive technology to allow them to access the curriculum and to allow them to participate with their peers. IEP teams need to think very broadly about a student's need for assistive technology and not just limit the determination to academic content.

Although there are many different definitions of assistive technology, according to the regulations to the IDEA:

> Assistive technology means any item, piece of equipment, or product system, whether acquired commercially off the shelf, modified, or customized that is used to increase, maintain, or improve the functional capabilities of a child with a disability. The term does not include a medical device surgically implanted, or the replacement of such device. (IDEA Regulations, 34 CFR § 300.5, 2006)

Assistive technology service is different from assistive technology. Assistive technology services are any services that assist a student with a disability in the selection, acquisition, or use of an assistive technology device. This could come in the form of evaluators who help determine services, and the evaluator could come from various fields: occupational therapy, physical therapy, speech, or an autism specialist.

As a part of the determination about whether a student needs assistive technology, there are questions the IEP team must consider (see Exhibit X). It is important to point out that the determination about the supports is a team decision, that it should be highlighted in the needs sections of the IEP, and that the school district is responsible for ensuring the student receives the services that are delineated.

IEP teams also must ask the question, "Does a student have limited English proficiency?" The primary issue for team members to answer is how the language needs of students who are English language learners related to the programming offered as a part of the IEP.

Summary

A long line of special education-related cases, including rulings from the US Supreme Court, have confirmed the critical obligation of school personnel to ensure that parents are partners in the special education process, from evaluation to IEP development and review. These rights include meaningful participation in meetings regarding the special education of their child. School district personnel must make good-faith efforts to work with a student's parents and meet the requirements of the IDEA. According to the US Court of Appeals for the Ninth Circuit, if a student's parents' rights, which are the "very essence of the IDEA" (*Amanda J. v. Clark County School District*, 2001, p. 892), are abridged or short-circuited in any way, it is very likely that the student will be denied a FAPE.

CHAPTER 5

The IEP Process and Components

Conducting Assessments and Crafting Present Levels of Academic Achievement and Functional Performance Statements (with Dawn Rowe)

According to a principal author of the Education of All Handicapped Act (now the IDEA), Senator Robert T. Stafford from Vermont, the IEP was "the central part of this act as wrote it and intended it to be carried out" (Stafford, 1978, p. 79). The IEP has always been the cornerstone of the IDEA. The IEP is the blueprint of a student's FAPE and is the center of many, if not most, IDEA-related disputes (Bateman, 2017). It is absolutely critical, therefore, that administrators and teachers understand how to craft educationally appropriate and legally sound IEPs. Our purpose in this chapter is to provide information on procedures and strategies that school-based teams and parents in collaboration can use to develop relevant and meaningful IEPs.

In chapter 3, we noted that four questions must be answered in the IEP to provide a FAPE to eligible students with disabilities. The four questions are as follows:

1. What are students' unique academic and functional needs that must be addressed in their IEPs?
2. What are the annual goals that must be included in students' IEPs to address their needs identified in the PLAAFP Statements?
3. How will students' progress toward their annual goals be monitored?
4. What services will be provided to students so they may reach their goals?

The IDEA (IDEA 20 USC § 1414[d][1][i][2006]) and regulations to the IDEA (IDEA Regulations, 34 CFR § 300.320) specify the contents to be included in each student's IEP. In this chapter we review the following components, which are crucial in the development of students' IEPs: conducting the assessment and developing the present levels of academic achievement and the functional performance (PLAAFP) statement. The assessment and PLAAFP statements answer our first question (i.e., What are the student's unique academic and functional needs that must be addressed?) and underlie a student's IEP, the basis of his or her free appropriate public education (FAPE). When there are problems with the assessment and the PLAAFP statement, e.g., the assessment fails to consider a student's unique educational needs or the PLAAFP statements do not establish a baseline by which to craft the annual goals and monitor progress, the entire IEP will most likely will be defective (Bateman, 2017; Norlin et al., 2010; Yell, 2019).

In this chapter, we provide strategies for ensuring that students' assessments and PLAAFP statements are relevant, meaningful, and lead to an IEP that enables a student to make progress in light of his or her circumstances. We first address the assessment process.

Assessment

The process of developing IEPs for students with disabilities begins with a full and individualized assessment. The purpose of assessment, or evaluation[1] as it is called in the IDEA, is to collect student information to make decisions about the student (Salvia et al., 2017). Special education involves the following four assessments: (a) assessment for eligibility, (b) assessment for instructional planning, (c) assessment for progress monitoring, and (d) assessment for accountability. Before reviewing these categories, we discuss the IDEA's requirements regarding the collection of assessment data and the special education process.

Assessment Requirements in the IDEA

The IDEA includes a number of legal requirements that school officials must meet when assessing students for eligibility and to assist the IEP team in determining the content of a student's IEP. Before discussing these requirements, it is important to point out that if a student is being screened by a teacher or a specialist for appropriate instructional strategies for curriculum implementation, that is not considered as special education evaluation to determine eligibility, so parental permission is not needed (IDEA Regulations, 34 CFR 300.302). For example, if a school district uses a response to intervention (RTI) process, a schoolwide positive behavior interventions and supports system (PBIS), or a multi-tiered system of support (MTSS) and requires that all students be screened for the system for inclusion in the system the district uses, informed parental consent is not required. Similarly, if additional screening assessments or progress monitoring procedures are required for determination of appropriate placement in tiers, and not as a special education evaluation, that is permissible as long as such screening may be a possibility for all students.

Additionally, there is a difference in requirements between the initial assessment and additional assessment data collected after a student is already in special education. Before the initial assessment can be conducted of a student, his or her parents must provide the school district with informed written consent allowing them to conduct the assessment. The IDEA's requirements regarding an initial assessment are listed in table 5.1.

If further assessments are conducted after a student is in special education, his or her parents must be provided with a prior written notice.

---

[1] In the IDEA and regulations, the terms "assessment" and "evaluation" are used interchangeably. In this chapter and throughout the book, we will exclusively use the term "assessment" when referring to an initial assessment and "evaluation" when referring to the annual and 3-year reevaluations.

TABLE 5.1   Initial Assessment, Selected Requirements (emphasis ours)

- School districts must conduct a <u>full and individualized</u> assessment/evaluation before the initial provision of special education and related services to a student (IDEA Regulations, 34 CFR § 300.301[a], 2006).
- Either a student's parents or school district personnel may initiate a request for the initial evaluation (IDEA Regulations, 34 CFR § 300.301[b], 2006).
- The initial evaluation must be conducted within 60 days of receiving parental consent for the evaluation or within the time frame established by a state (IDEA Regulations, 34 CFR § 300.301[c][1][i & ii], 2006).
- The initial evaluation must consist of procedures to determine (a) if the student has an <u>IDEA-eligible disability</u> and (b) the <u>educational needs</u> of the student (IDEA Regulations, 34 CFR § 300.301[c][2][i & ii], 2006).
- The time frame does not apply if (a) the parent repeatedly fails or refuses to produce their child for the evaluation or (b) the student enrolls in another school district after the time frame has begun and before the student is determined eligible by the initial school district. The new school district must make sufficient progress to ensure the prompt completion of the student to be evaluated (IDEA Regulations, 34 CFR § 300.301[d][1][2]), 2006).
- *Screening* for instructional purposes by a teacher or a specialist <u>is not evaluation</u> under the IDEA (IDEA Regulations, 34 CFR § 300.302, 2006). For example, screening for determining appropriate instructional strategies or for a school's RTI or MTSS system is not considered an evaluation for determining special education eligibility.
- A school district must provide notice to a parent that describes any assessment/evaluation procedures that school district personnel will use in the assessment (IDEA Regulations, 34 CFR § 300.304[a], 2006).
- The requirements for conducting the assessment/evaluation must be met (IDEA Regulations, 34 CFR § 300.304[b], 2006).
  a) School district personnel must use a variety of assessment tools and strategies to gather <u>relevant functional, developmental, and academic information</u>, including information *provided by a student's parents*, that assists in determining if the student has an IDEA disability and the content of his or her IEP (IDEA Regulations, 34 CFR § 300.304[b][I & ii], 2006).
  b) School districts may not use any single measure or assessment to determine if a student has a disability and requires special education and related services (IDEA Regulations, 34 CFR § 300.304[b][2], 2006).
  c) School district personnel must use <u>technically sound instruments</u> that may be used to assess the relevant contributions of cognitive, behavioral, physical, and developmental factors (IDEA Regulations, 34 CFR § 300.301[3r c], 2006).
- Requirements about assessments/evaluation materials must be met (IDEA Regulations, 34 CFR § 300.304[c], 2006).
  a) Selected and administered so the materials are not discriminatory on a racial or cultural basis (IDEA Regulations, 34 CFR § 300.304[c][i], 2006).
  b) Are administered in the student's native language or other mode of communication unless it is clearly not feasible to do so (IDEA Regulations, 34 CFR § 300.304[c][ii], 2006).
  c) The assessment materials are used for the purposes for which the assessments or measures are valid and reliable (IDEA Regulations, 34 CFR § 300.304[c][iii], 2006).
  d) The assessment materials are administered by trained and knowledgeable personnel (IDEA Regulations, 34 CFR § 300.304[c][iv], 2006).
  e) The assessment materials are administered in accordance with any instructions by the test producer (IDEA Regulations, 34 CFR § 300.304[c][v], 2006).
  f) The student is assessed in all areas related to the suspected disability including, if appropriate, health, vision, hearing, and social and emotional status, general intelligence, academic performance, communicative status, and motor abilities (IDEA Regulations, 34 CFR § 300.304[c][iv], 2006).
  g) The assessment/evaluation is sufficiently comprehensive to address all of the student's special education and related service needs, whether or not commonly linked to the student's classification category (IDEA Regulations, § 300.304[c][6], 2006).
  h) Assessment tools and strategies must provide relevant information that directly assists in determining the educational needs of the student (IDEA Regulations, § 300.304[c][7], 2006).
- After the assessment/evaluation is completed, a group of qualified professionals and a student's parents meet to determine the student's eligibility for special education and the educational needs of the student (IDEA Regulations, 34 CFR § 300.306[a][1], 2006).

Assessment in the Special Education Process

The special education process usually begins with a referral to a school's multi-disciplinary team[2], which is a group of knowledgeable professionals that review referrals and determine if the student may have an IDEA-eligible disability and need special education services, in which case the student is referred for eligibility assessment. Referrals may be made by teachers and other school-based personnel or a student's parent (IDEA Regulations 34 CFR § 300.301[b], 2006).

If a student's parents do not provide consent for the initial evaluation to determine eligibility or if they fail to respond after school personnel have made reasonable efforts[3] to obtain consent, school officials may seek an initial evaluation by using the due process hearing mechanism of the IDEA. Nonetheless, they are not required to pursue these mechanisms and do not violate their obligations under the IDEA if they decline to seek an initial assessment (IDEA Regulations 34 CFR § 300.300[a][3][i-ii], 2006). Additionally, when a student is found eligible for initial special education and related services and school officials have made reasonable attempts to secure parents' permission for the initial provision of special education, if parents refuse to provide consent for services or fail to respond to efforts to secure their permission, school officials <u>may not</u> use the mediation or due process procedures of the IEP to obtain agreement or a ruling that they may provide services to the student (IDEA Regulations 34 CFR § 300.300[b][3], 2006). In such situations, school officials will not be in violation of their obligations under the IDEA to make a FAPE available to a student (IDEA Regulations 34 CFR § 300.300[b][4][i], 2006).

After consent is received, school personnel have 60 days to complete an assessment of the student[4]. The initial assessment has two purposes: (a) to determine if a student is eligible for special education services and (b) to help develop the content of the student's IEP. A student is determined eligible under the IDEA if he or she has an IDEA-eligible disability and if because of that disability, he or she needs special education. We next review the four purposes of assessment in special education: (a) assessment for eligibility, (b) assessment for instructional planning, (c) assessment for progress monitoring, and (d) assessment for accountability.

Assessment for Eligibility The first use of assessment in the special process occurs when determining a student's eligibility for special education services. To be eligible for special education services under the IDEA, students must have one or more of the following disabilities: autism, deaf-blindness, deafness, emotional disturbance, hearing impairment, intellectual disability, multiple disabilities, orthopedic impairment, other health impairment, specific learning disability, speech or language impairment, traumatic brain injury, and visual impairment, including blindness (IDEA Regulations, 34 CFR § 300.8, 2006). For younger children from age three to nine, the category of developmental disabilities may be used in lieu of the IDEA's 13 categories of disabilities if a

---

[2] States and school district may have different names for the team that receives and analyzes referrals (e.g., child study team, intervention teams, teacher assistance teams).

[3] School officials must document their efforts to obtain parental permission by keeping records of phone calls, home visits, or maintaining copies of all correspondence.

[4] Readers should check to see if their state requires that the assessment be completed in fewer days.

child experiences developmental delays in one or more of the following areas: physical cognitive, communicative, adaptive, or social or emotional development (IDEA Regulations, 34 CFR § 300.8, [b][1], 2006). Readers should determine how their states define developmental disabilities and the age range that is allowed by the state.

It is especially important to note that it is not enough to have one or more of these disabilities to be eligible for services under the IDEA; a student's disability must also require that he or she needs special education and related services (IDEA Regulations, 34 CFR § 300.8, [a][1], 2006). Moreover, the regulations to the IDEA add to the definition of many disability area that a student's disability must adversely affect his or her educational performance. Although the IDEA requires that a student's disability must require special education and also negatively affect a student's educational performance to be eligible under the IDEA, the educational performance clause has nonetheless been a source of controversy because there is no definition of the term in the IDEA. This has led to inconsistent interpretations of what constitutes educational performance in the courts and often depends on state law where case was heard. We believe, however, that a close reading of the IDEA indicates that educational performance includes academics and functional areas (e.g., behavior, communication). Why else would the Congressional authors of the IDEA require that school districts "gather relevant functional and developmental information," in addition to academic data about the child, including information provided by the parents, that may assist in determining whether the child is a child with a disability . . . (and) the content of the child's IEP (IDEA Regulations, 34 CFR § 300.304 [b][1][i-ii], 2006). Would Congress require the collection of such information if a student's educational performance only referred to academic achievement? We think not!

According to the IDEA, students cannot be determined eligible for special education if the team finds that the determining factors leading to the conclusion that a student may have a disability and need special education services were due to (a) lack of appropriate instruction in reading, including instruction in the essential components of reading instruction[5], (b) lack of appropriate instruction in math, or (c) limited English proficiency (IDEA Regulations, 34 CFR § 300.306 [b][1][i-ii-iii], 2006). This section of the law seems to be taken from the notion driving the No Child Left Behind Act of 2001 that too often general education reading and math programs do not use scientific research-based instructional procedures, which results in students becoming curriculum casualties. In other words, some students may not have a disability, rather, they are casualties of poor curricular reading and math choices and instruction in general education. Unfortunately, neither the IDEA nor the regulations to the law provide guidance on how the decision regarding the lack of instruction in reading and math is to be made.

Assessment Tests and Procedures for Determining Eligibility Of the many types of procedures that may be included in the eligibility phase, the IDEA includes norm-referenced tests; criterion-referenced test; existing evaluation data;

---

[5] These are the essential components of reading instruction as identified by the National Reading Panel in 1999: phonemic awareness, phonics, fluency, vocabulary, and comprehension.

information provided by a student's parents; current classroom-based, local, or state assessments; and classroom-based observations by teachers and local service providers. The purpose of these types of procedures are to collect functional, behavioral, adaptive, physical, social, and cultural information and information on any other needs the student may have (IDEA Regulations, 34 CFR § 300.306 [c][1] [i], 2006). It is important that readers be acquainted with any specific requirements in their state for eligibility determination.

Tests given to students to classify them and determine their eligibility usually include commercial standardized norm-referenced tests. The different types of norm-referenced tests frequently used in determining eligibility under the IDEA include the following:

- Achievement tests, which assess a student's skill development in reading, math, written language, such as the Kaufman Test of Educational Achievement, Stanford Achievement Tests, Woodcock Johnson Tests of Achievement
- Behavioral checklists, which examine a student's behavior visà-vis societal expectations, such as the Achenbach Child Behavior Checklist, Autism Diagnostic Observation Schedule (ADOS), Behavior Assessment Scale for Children (BASC)
- Intelligence tests, which assess a student's reasoning and problem-solving abilities, such as the Differential Ability Scales (DAS) and Wechsler Intelligence Scales for Children (WISC)
- Adaptive behavior scales, which assess if a student performs daily living skills at an age-appropriate level, such as the Adaptive Behavior Assessment System (ABAS), Scales of Independent Behavior-Revised (SIB-R), and Vineland Adaptive Behavior

These tests are frequently used in making special education eligibility decisions. A primary reason for using commercially developed norm-referenced tests for eligibility is that many of the most frequently used norm-referenced tests are carefully developed by experts in test construction and have very good psychometric qualities such as reliability and validity. Reliability is how consistently a test measures a particular characteristic, and validity is whether a test truthfully measures what it was constructed to measure (Tindal & Marston, 1990). Moreover, commercially developed standardized tests usually have accurate norming or standardization samples, which refers to the group of test takers upon which the test was based. When deciding on a student's eligibility for special education services, we want the standardization sample to be representative of the population for whom the test was intended.

Commercially developed norm-referenced tests that have adequate psychometric properties are used to compare the performance of the student taking the test to the specified norm group. These tests give the team making the eligibility decision information on a student's relative standing with other students of the same age or age. This is useful to determining eligibility because the results of the test provide information on a student's cognitive performance, achievement, or behavior and how discrepant it is from that of his or her peers (Tindal & Marston, 1990). In fact, the scores from a norm-referenced tests (e.g., age scores, grade scores, standard scores) are all variations of percentile ranks that are very practical for making comparisons. These scores are useful when determining eligibility for services, but they are virtually useless when planning the content of a student's instruction of the special education services and totally useless for monitoring a student's growth toward achieving his or her goals.

Assessment for Instructional Planning

The assessments conducted of students with disabilities, in addition to assisting in determining eligibility, must also help IEP teams to develop special education programs. In other words, the assessments must be such that they assist an IEP team to "determine the educational needs of the child" (IDEA Regulations, 34 CFR § 300.301 [2][ii][c], 2006) and to help to develop "the content of the child's IEP, including information related to enabling the child to be involved in and progress in the general education curriculum" (IDEA Regulations, 34 CFR § 300.304 [b][1] [ii], 2006). For this reason, a student's IEP team must include "an individual who can interpret the instructional implications of the (assessment) results" (IDEA Regulations, 34 CFR § 300.321 [a][5], 2006). Whereas examination of specific items in norm-referenced tests may give IEP teams a general idea of where a student's skill deficits are, they do not pinpoint deficits or assist teams or a student in determining what to teach.

Assessments that focus on a student's specific skills and knowledge are more useful in determining the services and programming a student may need. Such tests are diagnostic because they help pinpoint a student's areas of strengths and areas of weakness. Criterion-referenced tests are often used to assess a student's level of mastery in particular areas because these tests compare student performance to clearly specified criterion or content in these areas (e.g., reading, math). The scores usually provide a level of performance in terms of a predetermined standard of mastery so that a teacher can determine where to begin instruction. Additionally, the scorer may also conduct an error analysis of the test items to ascertain where the student's skills break down and plan instruction from that point.

In functional areas, such as adaptive living skills, procedures such as task analysis breaks a larger, more complex task into its component step or tasks. These smaller tasks are then assessed to determine where the student's skills break down. A student is then taught the component skills in sequence beginning with the skills that have not been mastered and followed with skills taught in sequence, building on one another until the larger task is mastered. If a student exhibits serious problem behavior, a functional behavior assessment could be conducted to assist the IEP team in planning positive behavioral programming.

In situations in which students present behavior problems, an extremely important assessment procedure to plan programming is a functional behavioral assessment (FBA). The use of an FBA is intended to assist IEP teams to determine the function of a student's behavior so the team may plan and deliver appropriate behavioral programming that addressees these functions, teaches socially acceptable replacement behavior, and structures the environment in such a way as to render the inappropriate irrelevant, ineffective, and inefficient

(O'Neill et al., 1996). Although the IDEA only mandates the use of an FBA in situations in which a team changes a student's placement for disciplinary reasons or has conducted a manifestation determination (see discipline procedures in the IDEA Regulations at 34 CFR §§ 300.521 through 300.529, 2006), we believe an FBA should be part of the assessment procedure for determining the goals and services provided in a student's IEP when the student present serious behavior problems.

The second type of assessments conducted for special education, therefore, are used for planning the content of a student's IEP. Assessments used for determining instruction are not useful for eligibility determination but are extremely important to determine the goals and services to include in a student's IEP.

Assessment for Progress Monitoring

The third use of assessment in the IDEA requires that a student's progress toward his or her annual goals be measured and reported on a regular basis. The purpose of assessment for progress monitoring, which is sometimes referred to as formative assessment or individually referenced assessment, is to measure students on some aspect of academic or functional skills repeatedly and then to compare newer values with previous values. If these individually referenced assessments are collected systematically and frequently, we can make decisions about a student's progress. If our analysis of the data show a student is not doing well enough to make his or her annual goals by the end of the year, we can then make instructional changes and continue to collect progress data to determine if the instructional change was successful.

There are four primary characteristics of effective formative assessment. First, formative assessment is a direct measure of the area of interest. For example, if the area of concern is reading, the formative assessment may involve measure of oral reading fluency, or if the area of concern is basic math, the formative assessment may include a test of random math problems. Second, formative assessment must be repeatable. To create a useful data base for progress monitoring, assessments must be given frequently (e.g., one a week). Norm-referenced tests, such as the Woodcock Reading Mastery Test, can only be given once or twice a year, whereas, individually referenced assessment, such as a curriculum-based measures (CBM) can be administered daily or several times per week (Deno, 1992). Third, individually referenced tests often use a performance graph to essentially provide a picture of changes in a student's performance over time. For example, the CBM graph depicted in figure 5.1 clearly shows a student's past performance, present performance, and probable future growth. Graphs are an excellent communication tool and are easily explained and understood. Deno (1992) wrote that using graphs enhanced communication because "parents are so pleased to have clear and direct information on how their children are doing in school" (p. 9). Fourth, individually referenced tests are goal referenced. That means that you take the baseline information on a particular skill from the assessment, project an annual goal from the baseline information, and enter data from the repeated assessments during the course of the year to help determine if a student is to track to meet his or her goal.

Student: _____ Grade/Age: _____ Teacher: _____

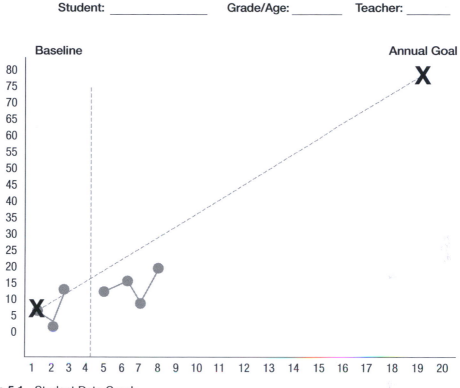

Figure 5.1 Student Data Graph.

Assessment for Accountability

The purpose of the Every Student Succeeds Act of 2015 was to ensure that students in every public school achieve important learning goals. To increase student achievement, the law required that school districts assume responsibility for all students. The primary way in which this was accomplished was by requiring states to measure student progress on statewide achievement tests. The purpose of these statewide assessments was twofold: (a) To provide information about individual student achievement and (b) to gauge the success of schools and school systems by holding educators accountable for student attainment of educational outcomes.

Similarly, under the IDEA, accountability has changed from a more compliance-oriented process to one that stressed, and continues to stress, the importance of improving students' academic and social/behavioral outcomes. Thus, both the ESSA and IDEA stress accountability for results. In general, assessments for accountability purposes emphasize academic outcomes, measured through students' participation in state testing programs. With respect to participation in state assessments, all students with disabilities must participate in state assessment system, and IEP teams make the decision of *how* not *if* the student will take part in a state test. IEP team decisions on the appropriate assessment option for each student with disabilities are made on an annual basis.

States must give assessments for accountability purposes in the academic areas of reading/language arts and mathematics for students in grades three through eight and once in high school (Every Student Succeeds Act, 20 USC §1111[c][4]

[B], 2015). Student's IEP teams have two options when deciding how a student will participate in accountability systems. First, the student may take the same general assessment based on academic achievement standards (GA-AAS) as their peers without disabilities. Approximately, 99% of students are expected to take part in the GA-AAS with or without accessibility features and accommodations. If the IEP team decides that a student needs accommodations, the IDEA requires that the team include a statement of any individual appropriate accommodations that are necessary to measure the academic achievement and functional performance of the student (IDEA, 34 CFR § 300.320[a][6][i], 2006).

Second, an IEP team may decide that students will participate in an alternate assessment based on alternate academic achievement standards (AA-AAAS). It is expected that 1% of students may participate in AA-AAS. (We discuss the provisions of accessibility and accommodation supports in chapter 7). The 1% limit is meant to avoid inappropriate inclusion of students with disabilities in an assessment based on different achievement expectations. If the IEP team decides that a student will participate in an alternate assessment, the IDEA requires that the team include a statement of why the student cannot participate in the regular assessment and why the alternate assessment selected is appropriate for the student (IDEA, 34 CFR § 300.320[a][6][ii][A-B], 2006).

There are three primary questions a student's IEP team must answer to determine how a student will participate in a state's alternate assessment: (1) Does the student have a significant cognitive disability? (2) Is the student's instruction linked to grade-level content and reflective of the state's academic content standards? and (3) Does the student require extensive direct, individualized instruction and substantial supports to achieve measurable gains in the grade- and age-appropriate curriculum. The IEP team's decisions are <u>not to be based on</u> expectations of low performance on the general assessment, certain special education eligibility labels or the receipt of certain services, and achievement that is significantly below grade-level expectations.

To determine if the student has a significant cognitive disability, the IEP team should review student records indicating a disability or multiple disabilities that have a significant impact upon intellectual functioning and adaptive behavior. Students may have been identified under various categorical labels—most often intellectual disabilities, autism, and multiple disabilities. Determinations are made about the degree to which a student's instruction is linked to grade-level content from the state's academic content standards. IEP teams must consider if the instruction is reflective of those standards, how instruction addresses the knowledge and skills that are appropriate, and if the instruction is challenging for the student. The level and extent of supports needed can be judged by examining (a) the extent to which extensive, repeated, and individualized instruction is provided and (b) the student's use of individualized methods of accessing information in alternative ways to "acquire, maintain, generalize, demonstrate and transfer skills across multiple settings" (see Illinois State Board of Education, 2019).

To see your state's guidelines for decisions about the appropriate assessment option for an individual student, see the information gathered by the National Center on Educational Outcomes at: https://nceo.info/state_policies/policy/participationswd. Ultimately, the IEP team will decide how students' participation in assessments for accountability will help students meet the intent of IDEA that they "achieve to the highest levels they can by making progress relative to challenging academic content standards in light of the individual circumstances" (Shriner & Thurlow, 2019, p. 136).

Additional Issues in Assessment

Identification of Students with Learning Disabilities

In the Individuals with Disabilities Education Improvement Act of 2004, special procedures for identifying students with learning disabilities were added to the IDEA (see IDEA Regulations, 34 CFR § 300.307, 2006). States "(1) must not require the use of a severe discrepancy between intellectual ability and achievement for determining whether a child has a specific learning disability; (2) must permit the use of a process based on the child's response to scientific, research-based intervention; and (3) may permit the use of other alternative research-based procedures for determining whether a child has a specific learning disability" (IDEA Regulations, 34 CFR § 300.307 [a][1-2-3], 2006). The requirement that school personnel should follow when identifying a student as having a learning disability can be found in the IDEA Regulations, 34 CFR § 300.307 to § 300.311, 2006.

The IDEA also requires that to ensure the poor achievement of a student is not due to the lack of appropriate instruction in reading or math, the team must consider "data that demonstrates that prior to, or as a part of, the referral process, the child was provided appropriate instruction in regular education settings, delivered by qualified personnel" and that "data documentation of repeated assessments of achievement at reasonable intervals, reflecting formal assessment of student progress during instruction, which was provided to the child's parents" (IDEA Regulations, 34 CFR § 300.309 [b][1-2], 2006). Additionally, the school "must ensure that the child is observed in the child's learning environment (including the regular classroom setting) to document the child's academic performance and behavior in the areas of difficulty" (IDEA Regulations, 34 CFR §§ 300.310 et seq., 2006).

When identifying a student with learning disabilities under the IDEA, states and school districts have used a discrepancy formula that used achievement and intelligence tests and compared them to determine if there was a mismatch between a student's intellectual ability and his or her achievement. If there was a large enough discrepancy between intelligence and achievement, the student was often determined to have a learning disability. Prior to the reauthorization of the IDEA in 2004, the President's Commission on Excellence in Special Education issued its final report, *A New Era: Revitalizing Special Education for Children and Their Families* (2002). The Commission recommended on the basis of "expert recommendations made repeatedly in testimony and the scientific literature expert that . . . IQ achievement discrepancies (and therefore IQ tests)" be eliminated as a method used to determine the presence of a learning disability (p. 25). In fact, one the commissioners on the panel memorably encouraged "this Commission to drive a stake through the heart of . . . the discrepancy formula" as a means to identify students with learning disability (p. 25)! Congress prohibited states from requiring that school districts use a discrepancy formula in determining if a student has a learning disability and was eligible for special education services under the IDEA; nonetheless, school district officials could decide to use a discrepancy formula in their districts.

Response to Intervention Congressional authors of the IDEA clearly preferred a method of identification of students with learning disabilities recommended by the Commission: response to intervention (RTI). The Commission also noted that the current method of identification (i.e., the discrepancy formula) relied on a "wait-to-fail" model that should be abandoned and replaced by models that are based on "response to intervention and progress monitoring" (p. 25). In the IDEA, Congress adopted the Commission's RTI method and allowed a school district to "use a process that determines if the child responds to scientific, research-based intervention, as part of the evaluation procedures" (IDEA, 20 USC 14145 [b][6] [B], 2004). According to the Commission

> Children should not be identified for special education without documenting what methods have been used to facilitate the child's learning and adaptation to the general education classroom. The child's response to scientifically based interventions attempted in the context of general education should be evaluated with performance measures.

Interesting enough, the President's Commission recommended that making special education eligibility decisions by using the response to intervention "concept be extended to other high incidence disabilities" (p. 26). This would include emotional disturbance and intellectual disabilities. Congress did not include the response to intervention language in other disability categories, although states would be free to do so as long as it resulted in the same students be identified as would be under the federal categories. Response to intervention clearly has become more than just a method to identify students with learning disabilities and is now a school wide strategy for use with all students in a school.

Officials in the Office of Special Education Programs (OSEP) in the US Department of Education became concerned with the possible inappropriate use of response to intervention. In 2011 Melody Musgrove, the director of the OSEP, wrote a memorandum to State Directors of Special Education titled *A Response to Intervention (RTI) Process Cannot Be Used to Delay-Deny an Evaluation for Eligibility under the Individuals with Disabilities Education Act (IDEA)*. In the letter, Dr. Musgrove asserted that there had been reports that some school districts were using RTI strategies to delay or deny timely evaluation for special education services. She reiterated the obligation of school districts personnel to evaluate students with disabilities cannot be impeded by a school's RTI process. When a parent requests a special education evaluation, school officials must either begin the evaluation process or deny the parent's request, in which case school officials must provide written notice to the student's parents explaining the reasons that the evaluation was denied and giving them a copy of their procedural safeguards. Of course, the parent can challenge the decision in a due process hearing.

Transition Assessment

Ensuring that all students transition from high school into postsecondary settings prepared for college, careers, and life starts with the collection of sound data for decision-making (Bangser, 2008; Brand & Valent, 2013). Data collected through the transition assessment process helps IEP teams understand student strengths, interests, needs, and preferences and provides information to students, families, and educators to ensure a student's high school coursework and activities align with the student's postsecondary goals (Neubert & Leconte, 2013; Rowe et al., 2015).

Transition assessment provides a foundation of information that sets the stage for the transition components of the IEP when a student reaches age 16 (or earlier if required by your state). It is recommended assessment data be collected by an interdisciplinary team using formal and informal assessments on an ongoing basis to identify students' strengths, interests, needs, and preferences (Neubert, 2003; Neubert & Leconte, 2013; Rowe et al., 2015). Beginning the assessment process early allows time for students to develop an understanding of who they are and what they want to do after high school including postsecondary education, employment, and community living activities. In middle school, transition assessment helps student to understand their interests and talents, while exploring and experiencing the importance of general workplace readiness skills (e.g., attendance, teamwork, dependability, problem-solving). In high school, transition assessment sets the stage for students to further refine their interests and preferences and explore potential employment, postsecondary education, and independent living environments, while identifying appropriate courses to take and employment experiences that will help them develop the necessary skill set to attain their goals.

Transition assessment data also assists students in understanding their individual needs, preferences, and interests, so they can advocate for themselves with employers, instructors at postsecondary education institutions, and personnel in community or adult service agencies. As the student approaches school completion, transition assessment data also helps adult service providers in planning and providing appropriate support services beyond high school.

Transition assessment is a process of gathering information to inform transition planning and instruction. The process moves from determining what to assess and selecting and conducting appropriate assessments to using the data (Rowe et al., 2015). A sound transition assessment process requires careful planning and includes measures that assess student (a) interests and preferences, (b) knowledge, (c) skills and aptitudes, and (d) actual ability to demonstrate skills. When considering transition, it is also important to examine the current and future environments in which students will use the skills.

Planning for Transition Assessment Knowing what to assess requires an understanding of the expectations in current and future environments. In other words, what skills will be required for a student to understand and be required to demonstrate to be successful in middle/high school (e.g., current environment) and postsecondary education, employment, and independent living (e.g., future environments as defined by IDEA, 2004). The term "transition assessment" covers a wide range of skills from academic to social/emotional, to vocational, and community living skills. Understanding expectations of the different environments in which students would need to exhibit these skills may require observation and systematic data collection; however, there are some existing tools that teams can leverage to get a baseline understanding of the general knowledge and skills needed to be successful in these environments. For example, the Common Core State Standards initiative defined the expectations for reading, writing, speaking and listening, language, mathematics, and other college and career readiness skills needed for entry into credit-bearing courses at two- and four-year colleges or entry into the workforce (Common Core State Standards Initiative, 2012). There are also additional workforce standards IEP teams can draw from to understand the knowledge and skill expectations in particular career fields (see Advance CTE, https://careertech.org/career-clusters). The area of independent living might be a bit more challenging. There are no set of general knowledge and skills for this particular area to draw from. Depending on a student's post-school goals, this future area may require systematic observation to determine the required competencies.

Selecting Appropriate Assessments In general, results of one transition assessment will not provide a comprehensive understanding of specific content, as it relates to how the information will be applied to postsecondary settings. As Rowe et al. (2015) indicate, an extensive selection of assessments exist and new assessments continue to be developed, sometimes making selecting appropriate assessment tools overwhelming.

Determining the appropriate battery of assessments to use with one student or groups of students requires knowledge to enable critical examination of assessments. Critical examination provides information to determine the appropriateness of the assessment for any given context (e.g., accessibility, purpose, validity, reliability). There are two types of transition assessments, formal assessments and informal assessments. Formal assessments are used for learning about a wide variety of skill levels in various areas (e.g., vocational, academic, social). They include published measures that have been tested for reliability and validity that compare student scores to those of others (Mazzotti et al., 2009; Rowe et al., 2012). A review of student records will typically uncover some formal transition assessment data, which can be a starting place (e.g., three-year re-evaluation data, adaptive behavior scales). Some examples of formal assessments include academic achievement tests (e.g., Woodcock Johnson), adaptive behavior scales (e.g., Vineland), aptitude tests (e.g., Armed Services Vocational Aptitude Battery), and some interest inventories (e.g., Self-Directed Search). An advantage of formal assessments is the inclusion of a norm or comparison group. This allows the IEP team to compare the student's performance to that of a peer group (Rowe et al., 2012).

Informal assessments, on the other hand, are more subjective than formal assessments and require triangulation of data or collecting data from multiple sources to increase the validity of the information gathered (Rowe et al., 2012). Informal transition assessments can involve systematically observing students in various academic, work, and social situations to determine what skills they currently have to be successful in that environment as well as skills that need development. Informal assessment can also involve talking to students, families, and other stakeholders about a student's likes and dislikes, as well as setting up experiences for students to allow them an opportunity to experience something that may be of interest and having them rate the experience. Informal assessments are often teacher-made and result in anecdotal information as opposed to a number score (Mazzotti et al., 2009). Informal assessments could include:

- Observation: watching or listening to an individual's behavior and systematically recording relevant information,
- Interviews/Questionnaires: structured or unstructured conversations through question-and-answer format,
- Environmental Analysis: carefully examining the environment in which an activity normally occurs, or

- Curriculum-Based Assessments: task analysis, portfolio assessments, work sample analysis, criterion-referenced tests (Test et al., 2006; Neubert & Leconte, 2013).

The assessment you select all depends on the skills you want to learn more about. For example, what does the IEP team need to know to support the student in meeting the expectations in the next environment (e.g., next class, next grade level, graduation, postsecondary education, employment)? If a student has post-school goals related to living independently and the IEP team has no knowledge of the student's skills or aptitude for financial literacy, then they will need to select multiple assessments that will provide information to inform the team regarding these areas. Living independently requires some level of responsibility for finances or knowledge of where to get assistance and/or support. If employment is a goal, and the team is aware of the student's employment skills but is unaware of skills regarding mobility and transportation, then the team would select assessments related to this skill area as this would be an expectation for employment. Transition assessments should provide results that inform decisions regarding instruction, transition services, community experiences, and future planning students need to achieve their postsecondary goals. When determining which assessments to use with students, it is important to be critical consumers (i.e., someone who uses a wide range of criteria to evaluate products before purchasing or using).

Present Levels of Academic Achievement and Functional Performance The Office of Special Education and Rehabilitative Services (OSERS) in the US Department of Education issued a question and answer (Q&A) document on the US Supreme Court's unanimous ruling in *Endrew F. v. Douglas County School District* (US Department of Education, 2017). According to officials at OSERS, the purpose of issuing this document was to inform parents, educators, and other stakeholders of this seminal ruling with a synopsis of this important case and describe how the decision in the *Endrew F.* case should inform school district's efforts to improve academic and functional outcomes for students with disabilities. In the Q&A, OSERS specifically analyzed the standard that the Supreme Court set for determining if a school has provided sufficient educational benefits to confer a FAPE. The standard announced by the High Court was as follows: "a school must offer an IEP reasonably calculated to enable a child to make progress appropriate in light of the child's circumstances" (*Endrew F,* 2017, p. 288).

Question 11 of the Q&A was "What does progress appropriate in light of the child's circumstances mean?" (p. 6.). In part of their answer, officials at OSERS targeted the phrase in light of the child's circumstances and wrote that "this reflects the focus on the individualized needs of the particular child that is at the core of the IDEA" (p. 6). We believe that for school-based personnel and parents to collaboratively fashion IEPs that focus on a student's individualized needs, they will need to develop educationally appropriate and legally compliant PLAAFP statements on which to base a student's programming. The key to meeting the *Endrew F.* standard, therefore, hinges on the effectiveness of an IEP team in (a) gathering and interpreting relevant and current assessment data, (b) developing clear and meaningful PLAAFP statements that identify all of a student's needs, and (c) basing the rest of the IEP on the needs identified in PLAAFP statements.

This view is also consistent with the answer to question 12 in the Q&A document: "How can an IEP team ensure that every child has the chance to meet challenging objectives?" (p. 6). In the response, officials in the department emphasized that an "accurate statement of the child's present level of academic achievement and functional performance" (p. 6) is required because such a statement sets the foundation for ambitious goals and services based on the student's unique circumstances (US Department of Education, 2017).

Compliance and Better Practices PLAAFP Statements

There are differences between merely "compliant" PLAAFP statements and a present level statement representing "better practices." Special educators should ensure that their PLAAFP statements are both compliant and reflect better practices.

There are a number of characteristics that should be present in compliant and better practices PLAAFP statements. First, a compliant PLAAFP includes a statement of the child's levels of academic achievement and functional performance and how the student's disability affects the student's involvement and progress in the general education curriculum. A PLAAFP statement that is compliant and written in accordance with better practices includes a foundational statement of the child's performance that supports decision-making based on current and reliable evaluation data. Second, evaluation data in a compliant and better practices PLAAFP statement should include results of the student's performance on a variety of assessments (e.g., state assessment, district assessment, individually administered measures) that is written in a parent-friendly manner with the details about those results. Third, a compliant and better practices PLAAFP statement will provide a quantitative baseline about current functioning and include some discussion of assessment results in relation to the student's peers and/or specific skills and behaviors that influenced them. Fourth, a compliant and better practices PLAAFP statement should be the foundation of the rest of an IEP. Keep in mind that every need identified in the present levels must be addressed by a goal, a service, or both a goal and service. With these four elements, a well-written PLAAFP statement establishes a solid foundation for deciding how best to address the student's needs, including through the development of annual goals and service statement in prioritized areas of the specially-designed instruction for the upcoming year. The PLAAFP, however, does not delineate the routine teaching plans or daily instructional approach(es) that teachers may use. Table 5.2 is a depiction of the required components of a better practices PLAAFP statement.

TABLE 5.2   Components of Better Practices PLAAFP Statement

Identifies Student Need	Effect on General Education	Serves as Baseline	Connected to a Goal, Service, or Both

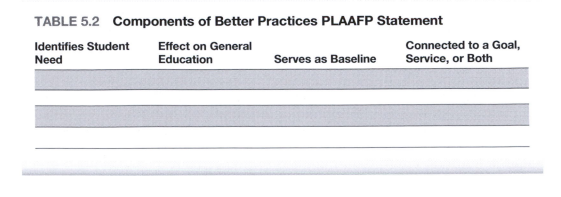

What Do Better Practices PLAAFP Statements Mean for IEP Teams?

The PLAAFP statements should address all of a student's unique individual needs for academic/educational achievement and functional performance. Additionally, any social development, physical development, and needs related to managing or modifying a student's environment (e.g., the need for peer or adult support in classes for redirection to task, organization of materials, and behavioral/self-monitoring levels) may also be appropriate. Baseline data on needs in specific skills related to identified eligibility areas and that can be used to write annual goals must be found in the PLAAFP, including:

- Data from multiple sources of academic and functional assessments, and other data that are "relevant and current" (*Endrew F.*, 2017, p. 11)
- Parent/guardian input about their child's functioning and needs
- Current information about the student's status in relation to general curricular (e.g., standards) expectations describing specific needs relative to the content and skills within the state standards
- Data related to student needs in other areas (e.g., behavior, self-regulation/care skills, foundational academics)

A good PLAAFP statement should include current data from tests, measures, and observations from each need listed in the statement. It is very important that the data in the statement should be described in a way that is readily understandable to a student's parents. A good rule of thumb is that a PLAAFP statement should have enough information to allow anyone reading it to be able to (a) identify a student's needs, (b) understand a student's current baseline of performance from which annual goals can be developed, (c) plan a student's individualized instruction in the services provided in his or her IEP, and (d) gauge student progress in relation to the student's needs vis-à-vis the academic content standards and to their individual circumstances. A well-written PLAAFP statement provides the data—and the explanations of those data in clear, understandable terms—with respect to the skills needed to ensure student progress and success. When the PLAAFP statement includes such information, a student's IEP team may use the statement as evidence to assist them to plan how the student will be supported throughout the rest of the IEP. Table 5.3 is an example of some key elements and phrases to look for in the summary statements for each domain covered in the PLAAFP. These summary statements can help make it clear there is a documented deficit interfering with the student's acquisition of priority skills and helps point the IEP team to the instructional focus for the subsequent annual goals. These elements are consistent with the findings and implications of *Endrew F.*, and the table lists only a single example. For each element, other options may be sensible. Table 5.4 presents questions to assess PLAAFP statements.

When we talk with educators about best practices PLAAFP statements, we ask them, "If you removed the student's name from the PLAAFP and its summary, could someone who knows the student identify him/her based on what is written?" If so, then it is possible to go to the next step of writing observable, measurable goals. If not, the level and specificity of information and explanation might not be

TABLE 5.3 Structure of PLAAFP Summary Statements

Key Phrase	Explanation	Example
"Based on . . ."	A summary of the assessment data and observational information upon which the student's need or identified deficit area is based	Based on the district progress monitoring measures of reading comprehension, review of the student's state assessment results, and feedback from content area teachers, the student . . .
"The student has difficulty with . . ."	Academic, behavioral, or functional skills the student is not demonstrating or that need significant improvement	the student has difficulty with recognizing the organization and sequencing of facts and concepts in a text . . .
"Which hinders the student's ability to . . ."	How access to the general curriculum/content standards is affected by the student's area of difficulty	which hinders the student's ability to comprehend multiple forms of text in content area materials and assignments.
"And makes _____ an instructional priority."	Skills that will be addressed with specially-designed instruction through special education services	This makes teaching strategies for identifying the organization and categorization of text-based information an instructional priority.

Adapted from: CCSSO, 2012

TABLE 5.4 Test Questions for PLAAFP Statement

1. Does the PLAAFP provide a descriptive snapshot of the student including *both* strengths and areas of need?
2. Is parent/guardian input present and clearly considered?
3. Do statements about the student have data to support them?
    3a. Are multiple sources/types of data used?
4. Are the data understandable to the parents/guardians/student/another teacher?
    4a. Do the data provide information about skills that are strengths or weaknesses for the student?
    4b. Does the PLAAFP make it clear what content/skill(s) are an instructional priority for the student?
    4c. Are the content/skills listed specific enough that you could identify areas for standards-referenced instruction based on the PLAAFP?
5. Are PLAAFP summary statements present for each skill area included?
6. Could you write observable and measurable individualized goals based on the PLAAFP?
7. If you remove the student's name, could someone who knows the student well identify the student based on reading this PLAAFP statement?

Source: IEP Quality Project, University of Illinois, J. G. Shriner, Principal Investigator.

sufficient to provide a descriptive snapshot of the student, making it difficult to build on student strengths and address areas of need.

Keep in mind that PLAAFP statements establish, in a general sense, the baseline of student performance at a single point in time—the descriptive snapshot just mentioned. Also, baseline data have meaning if they are related to both the student's current skills and the target skills in the goals to be developed. It is not advisable to make forced connections between baseline data and those skills. The data source used to measure student skills for the PLAAFP should be consistent with the measurement strategy intended to be used in the criterion statements of annual goals. In a best practice scenario, whatever data sources are used to determine the student's current level of performance (academic or functional) should link to what will be used for progress monitoring.

For example, if a curriculum-based measurement of reading is used to determine Words Correct per Minute (WCPM) for a PLAAFP statement, a similar measure that can yield WCPM is needed for criterion statements within annual goals. Use of "teacher-made tests" or "percent correct" for progress monitoring would not give the same type of information to measure improvement in WCPM.

It is necessary, therefore, to determine if the measure used to monitor and evaluate progress going forward is consistent with that used for baseline. If a measure is going to be used only for part of the IEP year (or not at all), then it is important to establish a new baseline with a new, applicable measure. Consider the following scenario.

1. The baseline data for written language found in the PLAAFP from a sending school (Pleasantville Elementary) are based on the "Bateman Test of Writing Progress."
2. This test is not used in the receiving school (Pleasantville Middle). Rather, they use the "Yell Sample of Writing."
3. Both tests sample the same skills (e.g., ability to write word/sentences/paragraphs using correct forms) and yield reliable data from which valid inferences about student performance and progress can be made.
4. The receiving school (Pleasantville Middle) must establish a new baseline for the student's writing skill using the "Yell Sample of Writing."
5. Because the tests both have adequate technical characteristics, the skills needed by the student that are included in the annual goal for writing should remain the same, but the criterion statement will change to reflect the use of the new test.

Another scenario we have observed in our work with teachers is that of a changing focus of writing instruction needed as students move from grade-to-grade in a school. Rather than emphasizing writing production (number of words), as is typical in early elementary grades, the instructional focus of upper-elementary often is on writing of connected text that includes elements of construction, completeness, and clarity. In this case, both the student's skill needs and the measurement strategy to determine progress needed to be re-examined. The IEP team in this case chose to establish a new baseline of student performance, using a writing rubric sensitive enough to detect student growth and to refine the skill focus of the annual goals to make progress in the general curriculum.

Practices That IEP Teams Should Avoid When Writing PLAAFP Statements

The PLAAFP statement is the foundation of the IEP. We have addressed these important areas that must be present in better practices PLAAFP statements (e.g., including information that allows the PLAAFP statement to be used as a baseline). We next review practices that IEP teams should avoid when crafting a student's PLAAFP statements.

Do Not Use a Disability Label in Place of a Statement of Need Statements such as "Jeremy has a learning disability in reading" provide no foundation for further development of Jeremy's IEP because it does not contain baseline information by which Jeremy's goals can be developed nor his progress be measured. Remember, all goals and services that follow in a student's IEP must be based on his or her needs without regard to the student's category of disability.

Do Not Use Old Information in the PLAAFP Statements PLAAFP statements must be based on current information. If an IEP team is aware of a student's need but only has old information (i.e., one year or older) on which to base the PLAAFP statement, the team should secure additional assessments in that area. Remember that students' PLAAFP statements describe the disability-related problems so that the rest of the IEP can be developed; if the information on which an IEP is old, it is likely that the IEP may not confer FAPE. As OSEP officials noted in the 1999 regulations to the IDEA, a student's present levels statement must be based on information that is current (*Federal Register*, v. 64, p. 12,428, 1999a).

Do Not Write PLAAFP Statements That Are Too Vague or General When PLAAFP statements are too vague or general (e.g., "Jeremy has problems with reading"), the statement will not provide sufficient information to develop the student's IEP. Because vague or general statements will not provide data-based baseline information, there will be no basis for the IEP team to monitor a student's progress.

Do Not Include Unnecessary Information in PLAAFP Statements Only include information that is pertinent to developing the special education and related services in students' IEPs. The PLAAFP is the starting point for specifying the services that will address a student's particular need and will become the baseline for measuring a student's progress. Cluttering up an IEP with PLAAFP statements that are not relevant and will not be addressed in the rest of the IEP will lead to internally inconsistent IEPs (see chapter 3 on internally inconsistent IEPs).

Do Not Substitute Scores from Assessments for Explanations of Those Scores The information included in the PLAAFP statements must be understandable to parents so they can assist in developing goals and services for their child. IEP teams need to craft brief and detailed PLAAFP statements, and when information on test scores is included, it should be accompanied with an explanation of the score. The PLAAFP statement, as well as the rest of the IEP, should be as "understandable and meaningful for parents as possible" (*Federal Register*, v. 64 p. 48, 12592, 1999a).

Textbox 5.1 Present Levels of Academic Achievement and Functional Performance Test Questions

We find it helpful to examine PLAAFP using a set of test questions to gauge the degree to which the statement includes the elements of a better practice PLAAFP. Such test questions cover specific characteristics we would hope to see (e.g., current and relevant assessment data; explanations of the skills reflected in students' test scores, indications of instructional needs/priorities). When considered in totality, the test questions will help establish if the information considered in the PLAAFP is sufficient enough to (a) provide a descriptive snapshot of the student such that someone familiar with that student could recognize to whom the statement refers, (b) establish a meaningful starting point (baseline) for the subsequent years' worth of instruction in areas of high-priority need, and (c) provide the foundation for the annual goals that will follow. In the following section we present three examples of PLAAFP statements to test again a table of essential PLAAFP elements. Table 5.5 depicts the questions of the PLAAFP tests. Assess the student's example PLAAFP statement using the questions in table 5.5

The answers to the PLAAFP examples can be found in tables 5.6, 5.7, and 5.8. Our comments on the example PLAAFP statements follow each table.

PLAAFP Example 1

Rosie is entering fourth grade and has improved in mathematics since last year. She can add and subtract and identify most money. She has limited budgeting experience. She can estimate two-digit numbers but not more than that.

Rosie has trouble controlling her behavior. She gets easily upset when interacting with peers and does not take direction from authority. Once off task it is really hard to reengage her.

Comments: **Strengths of Rosie's PLAAFP**—We know only that Rosie is perceived as doing better in math than she had done previously. **Needs of Rosie's PLAAFP**—Statements of math skills are offered without substantiation. Other statements are broad descriptors that could apply to many students. Data are absent and no parent input is mentioned.

TABLE 5.5 PLAAFP Test Questions

PLAAFP TEST QUESTIONS:	YES	NO
1. Does the PLAAFP provide a descriptive snapshot of the student including *both* strengths and areas of need?		
2. Is parent/guardian input present and clearly considered?		
3. Do statements about the student have data to support them?		
3a. Are multiple sources/types of data used?		
4. Are the data understandable to the parents/guardians/student/another teacher?		
4a. Do the data provide information about skills that are strengths or weaknesses for the student?		
4b. Does the PLAAFP make it clear what content/skill(s) are an instructional priority for the student?		
4c. Are the content/skills listed specific enough that you could you identify areas for standards-referenced instruction based on the PLAAFP?		
5. Are PLAAFP Summary Statements present for each skill area that connect the data to priorities for instruction and general curriculum access included?		
6. Could you write observable and measurable individualized goals based on the PLAAFP?		
7. If you remove the student's name, could someone who knows the student identify the student based on reading this PLAAFP statement?		

Adapted from: Shriner, J. G., & Carty, S. (2018). *Utilizing IEPQ as professional development with staff.* Presentation at Illinois State Board of Education, Directors' Conference. Springfield, IL: IEP Quality Project, University of Illinois. https://www.isbe.net/Documents/Session-20-IEP-Utilizing-IEP-Q-PD.pdf; https://iepq.education.illinois.edu

TABLE 5.6 PLAAFP Test Questions Example for Rosie

PLAAFP TEST QUESTIONS:	YES	NO
1. Does the PLAAFP provide a descriptive snapshot of the student including *both* strengths and areas of need?		X
2. Is parent/guardian input present and clearly considered?		X
3. Do statements about the student have data to support them?		X
3a. Are multiple sources/types of data used?		X
4. Are the data understandable to the parents/guardians/student/another teacher?		X
4a. Do the data provide information about skills that are strengths or weaknesses for the student?		X
4b. Does the PLAAFP make it clear what content/skill(s) are an instructional priority for the student?		X
4c. Are the content/skills listed specific enough that you could identify areas for standards-referenced instruction based on the PLAAFP?		X
5. Are PLAAFP summary statements present for each skill area that connect the data to priorities for instruction and general curriculum access included?		X
6. Could you write observable and measurable individualized goals based on the PLAAFP?		X
7. If you remove the student's name, could someone who knows the student identify the student based on reading this PLAAFP statement?		X

PLAAFP Example 2

James is an 11-year old student eligible for services as a student with learning disabilities.

Strengths: Math skills are a strength for James. He is liked by his peers.

Parental concerns: James' parents say he enjoys doing his video games with friends and that he is happiest when he is part of a "team game" where puzzles are solved. He avoids most reading except for his comic books. He does not like to do homework involving reading of any type. They worry that once he gets to middle school, the work will be too hard, and he will stop wanting to go to school.

Academic: James' reading fluency is deficient according to *aimsWeb Plus* data. On the *fluency* test he is currently reading 95 words per minute with a goal of 123 words per minute. His comprehension is on target to meet for the year. He is obtaining a score at the 17th percentile in *comprehension* and his benchmarking was "emerging." Due to his low fluency level, fluency and comprehension are still a concern. On the most recent state assessment, he fell "below standards" in the areas of Reading for Information and Reading Literature. On the district's reading benchmarking assessments, he scored at the 11th percentile. In math, James got a score of 11 on his math *concepts and applications*, which is above level. His *math computation* score is 26 points, which is above level. He "approached expectations" in the area of Problem Solving and was "meets expectations" in Number Sense and Numeracy on the last state assessment.

Functional: James gets along well with peers and adults at school. At times, honesty can be a problem for him. He will lie occasionally to get out of what he does not want to do. When he is caught, he has cried and shut down. Homework is a problem for him. He is capable of a lot more than what he does. He has motivation problems. His speech, language, vocational, independent functioning, and social are all age appropriate.

Comments: **Strengths of James' PLAAFP**—The PLAAFP includes parents' concerns, and some data on student performance in academics are included. **Needs of James' PLAAFP**—The information presented is largely a listing of scores and performance descriptors, but very little explanation of what these mean is offered. Skill(s) that are associated with the scores are not defined. Summaries of the priorities for access to the general curriculum and goals are not offered. No data accompany the statements about the student's functional performance. Statements are mostly general and do not provide a personalized description of the student.

TABLE 5.7 PLAAFP Test Questions for James

PLAAFP TEST QUESTIONS:	YES	NO
1. Does the PLAAFP provide a descriptive snapshot of the student including *both* strengths and areas of need?		X
2. Is parent/guardian input present and clearly considered?	X	
3. Do statements about the student have data to support them?	X	
3a. Are multiple sources/types of data used?	X	
4. Are the data understandable to the parents/guardians/student/another teacher?		X
4a. Do the data provide information about skills that are strengths or weaknesses for the student?		X
4b. Does the PLAAFP make it clear what content/skill(s) are an instructional priority for the student?		X
4c. Are the content/skills listed specific enough that you could identify areas for standards-referenced instruction based on the PLAAFP?		X
5. Are PLAAFP summary statements present for each skill area that connect the data to priorities for instruction and general curriculum access included?		X
6. Could you write observable and measurable individualized goals based on the PLAAFP?		X
7. If you remove the student's name, could someone who knows the student identify the student based on reading this PLAAFP statement?		X

PLAAFP Example 3

Tyler is an eight-year-old, second-grade young man who has been participating in regular education with special education in a class for autism for about 18% of his day and speech/language support services since the end of his Kindergarten school year. Academically, a review of previous standardized testing, current benchmark assessment data, and most recent grade report indicate Tyler is demonstrating Average to Above Average performance across the reading, writing, and math domains. Standardized and benchmark testing places his performance in these areas between the 50th-75th percentiles and standards-based report card grades in the academic areas are consistently 3s (meets expectations) and 4s (exceeds expectations). Grade reports, anecdotal teacher reports, and direct observations of the student do indicate primary needs with regard to speaking and listening, work/study habits, and social skills. Although these need areas are consistent with his current goal areas, a review of IEP progress monitoring data does suggest growth in these areas. During small group speech/language sessions, Tyler has met his conversational turn-taking skills by attending to peer's turn and waiting for his own turn in 90% of observed opportunities. Tyler continues to need to work on generalizing this skill to less structured settings. He also struggles to understand a range of nonverbal social communication behaviors including personal space, tone of voice, facial expressions, eye contact, and orienting body toward speaker. These areas of need are validated by ratings on the Pragmatic Language Skills Inventory completed by both Tyler's regular education and autism support teachers. Baseline data collected via structured observation of the student during indoor recess over the course of three separate days indicated Tyler established eye contact and oriented body toward the speaker only 15% of the time when peers initiated conversation with him (same-aged peers were observed to establish eye contact and orient body toward the speaker and average of 83% of opportunities). Additionally, within the classroom setting, Tyler engaged in conversational turn-taking skills by attending to peer's turn and waiting for his own turn in only 25% of observed opportunities (compared to same-aged peers who were observed to attend and wait turn in 92% of opportunities). Finally, parent and teacher ratings on the ASRS also highlight continuing needs with regard to the executive functioning areas of attention and self-regulation (Clinically Significant range). When this goal was first written into Tyler's IEP, baseline data indicated that he was on-task an average of 37% of the time during academic instruction (compared to peers who were on-task an average of 89% of the time). Most recent progress monitoring of on-task behavior using partial interval recording observations during academic instruction in the regular classroom yielded findings of 60%, 62%, and 54% on-task behavior across three separate 20-minute observation periods (compared to peers who were on-task an average of 92% of the time). Although this is good progress from initial goal development, a goal continues to be warranted in this area. As part of this annual review, the IEP team has ruled out the presence of any socio-cultural considerations. Tyler's parents brought several examples of his work done in classes that showed excellent work, but on which there were multiple comments about his ability to cooperate and patriciate with peers. Medically it is noted student is prescribed Methylphenidate by pediatrician, but no cognitive or academic skill concerns are noted. No emotional, motor skills, or daily living skills needs are reported. Tyler is not of transition age at this time.

Comments: **Strengths of Tyler's PLAAFP**—The PLAAFP is a very good one. Data from multiple sources describe both strengths and needs and are presented to demonstrate the priorities for the student and are described adequately and clearly. Parental input/concerns about the student's current levels of performance in classroom/social situations are offered. **Needs of Tyler's PLAAFP** - The Autism Spectrum Rating Scales (ASRS) is mentioned, but not explained with respect to the information about needs areas (executive functioning, attention, and self-regulation). The PLAAFP focuses on functional skills, but no summary statement about how these skills affect access to the general curriculum (and the relevant skills from within the standards) is offered.

TABLE 5.8   PLAAFP Test Questions for Tyler

PLAAFP TEST QUESTIONS:	YES	NO
1. Does the PLAAFP provide a descriptive snapshot of the student including *both* strengths and areas of need?	X	
2. Is parent/guardian input present and clearly considered?	X	
3. Do statements about the student have data to support them?	X	
3a. Are multiple sources/types of data used?	X	
4. Are the data understandable to the parents/guardians/student/another teacher?	X	
4a. Do the data provide information about skills that are strengths or weaknesses for the student?	X	
4b. Does the PLAAFP make it clear what content/skill(s) are an instructional priority for the student?	X	
4c. Are the content/skills listed specific enough that you could identify areas for standards-referenced instruction based on the PLAAFP?		X
5. Are PLAAFP summary statements present for each skill area that connect the data to priorities for instruction and general curriculum access included?		X
6. Could you write observable and measurable individualized goals based on the PLAAFP?	X	
7. If you remove the student's name, could someone who knows the student identify the student based on reading this PLAAFP statement?	X	

Summary of Better Practices PLAAFP Statements

The PLAAFP statements provide the basis on which the rest of the IEP rests. The PLAAFP statements in an IEP serve three primary functions: (a) describing the needs of a student, (b) providing a basis for developing a student's goals and services, and (c) establishing a baseline which the IEP team can use in monitoring student performance and measuring student progress. When PLAAFP statements are incomplete or inaccurate, it is likely the rest of the IEP will be invalid, possibly leading to a violation of the FAPE requirement of the IDEA. Table 5.9 reviews the practices to follow and to avoid in constructing PLAAFP statements that we have addressed in this chapter.

TABLE 5.9   Practices to Follow and Practices to Avoid

Practices to Follow	Practices to Avoid
Include data from which a goal can be determined and progress can be monitored	Do not use a disability label as a PLAAFP statement
Write in clear and understandable language	Do not use outdated information in the statement
Include information from the student's parents	Do not use vague or overly general language
Include comparison data with the student's nondisabled peers	Do not clutter up with extraneous information
Ensure all needs in the PLAAFP statement are addressed by a goal, a service, or both	Do not just list scores in the statement; if you do, provide an explanation

CHAPTER 6

The IEP Process and Components

Developing Measurable Annual Goals and Monitoring Student Progress

Thus far, we have discussed one of the four following questions we have used to structure chapters 5, 6, and 7 of this book:

1. What are students' unique academic and functional needs that must be addressed in their IEPs?
2. What are the annual goals that must be included in students' IEPs to address the needs identified in the PLAAFP statements?
3. How will students' progress toward these annual goals be monitored?
4. What services will be provided to students so they may reach these goals?

The first question concerns the assessments and the PLAAFP statements, which we addressed in chapter 5. The second and third questions are answered in this chapter on the measurable annual goals and the methods and procedures special educators used to measure students' progress toward achieving their annual goals. In chapter 7, we examine the services we provide to students in special education.

When the Education for All Handicapped Children (EAHCA; now titled the IDEA) was passed in 1975, it required that eligible students' IEPs include "a statement of annual goals and short-term instructional objectives" (IDEA, 20 USC § 1401 [20], 1990). Since the law's inception, therefore, annual goals have been required in all students' IEPs.

Huefner (2000) asserted that IEP goals are often written by IEP teams in a broad and abstract (e.g., improve reading) manner. Apparently recognizing this problem when Congress reauthorized the IDEA in 1997, the annual goals were changed to "a statement of measurable annual goals, including benchmarks or short-term objectives" (IDEA, 20 USC § 1414[d], 1997). After 1997, therefore, IEP teams were required to include measurable annual goals and they would have a choice between also including benchmarks, which were major milestones toward achievement of a goal, or short-term objectives, which were measurable intermediate steps to measure a student's progress.

In the reauthorization of 2004, Congress eliminated the benchmark requirements. Congress also eliminated the short-term objectives requirement except for students taking alternate assessments[1]. Since the original passage of the EAHCA, in 1975 goals have been mandated; however, it was not until 1997 that the IDEA required that annual IEP goals had to be measurable.

Unfortunately, writing measurable annual goals has often been a difficult task for many IEP teams. When a student's goals are not measurable, the IEP team cannot monitor his or her progress, which makes IEP goals meaningless. The result can be frustration for parents, administrators, and teachers and may lead to hearings and litigation. The purpose of this chapter is to (a) review measurable annual IEP goals, (b) present a clear and simple process to develop measurable annual IEP goals, and (c) examine the importance of measuring a student's progress toward achieving his or her goals in terms of academic and functional performance.

The importance of writing meaningful and measurable annual goals was colorfully stated by a US district court judge in *Escambia County Board of Education v. Benton* (2005). The case involved a 12-year-old student diagnosed with autism spectrum disorder, Jarred Benton. The Bentons contented that the school district had failed to provide him with a FAPE in violation of the IDEA. One of the issues in the case was that the IEP team failed to write measurable annual goals. The court, finding for Jarred Benton, held that:

> Without meaningful measurable objectives and goals, Benton's educators and parent were engaged in a futile endeavor to pin the tail on a moving donkey while blindfolded in a dark room. In other words a meaningful, measurable goal gives Benton a target to work towards and his educators and parents a way to evaluate his progress . . . a program cannot possibly confer an educational benefit to Benton if his teachers and parents do not know where they are trying to take Benton and how they will know when he has arrived (p. 1264).

A Method for Ensuring That Annual IEP Goals Are Measurable

The process we suggest for developing measurable annual IEP goals is based on the work of American psychologist Robert F. Mager, who developed a system, which he called criterion-referenced instruction, in his role as a trainer in the US Air Force in the late 1950s. He later refined his method for use by educators in his textbook *Preparing Instructional Objectives* (Mager, 1962). His method was widely used in education to develop objectives during the 1960s and 1970s, which led to the widespread adoption of a rigorous, objectives-based approach to the design of courses and teaching materials.

We believe that Mager's method of preparing instructional objectives is an excellent method for ensuring that a student's annual IEP goals are measurable. We have added a couple of components to Mager's system so it corresponds to the requirements for IEP annual goals. According to Mager (1997), the purpose of goals, or instructional objectives as he called them, is to describe the intended

---

[1] Many states and school districts still require that students' IEPs have short-term objectives.

outcomes, rather than the processes that will achieve the outcomes. As Mager wrote, "They describe the ends rather than the means" (p. 19). When applied to IEPs, the goals are the outcomes we want our students to achieve, not the methods, procedures, and strategies we will use to achieve the goals. We address the services, methods, procedures, and strategies to achieve the goals in chapter 7.

Readers should note officials in school districts and states may suggest or require their own methods of writing measurable annual IEP goals. In such cases, IEP teams should adhere to these procedures. Thus, we are suggesting **A** method, not **THE** method. Nonetheless, we believe a goal writing method will need to include Mager's three components to be measurable: (a) target behavior, (b) conditions, and (c) criteria for acceptable performance. In this section we present the Mager method to craft measurable annual IEP goals. To Mager's method, we propose adding a reference to the timeline, which aligns with the IDEA requirement that goals be written for one year.

Identify the Target Behavior or Performance The target behavior or performance refers to what we want the student to be able to do in order to demonstrate the mastery of a goal. The target behavior in the annual IEP goal must be related to a need identified in the PLAAFP statement and should be described in such a way that the parent, child, and any staff member can look at the IEP goal and understand what skill the child should be demonstrating or what goal the child should be achieving. Observable behaviors allow more than one teacher or observer to agree upon the extent to which the behavior has occurred. They are descriptive and student-focused. Measurable behaviors can be counted or quantified in a reliable manner.

Goals that fail to be observable or measurable usually involve the use of value words (demonstrates "respect," shows "anger," is "cooperative," is "nice," etc.) and phrases that refer to an internal process ("will understand," "will improve," "will learn," "will realize," "will master," "will appreciate," and so on). These words and phrases are subjective and likely will be judged and measured differently by separate observers. It is often helpful to use the phrase, "by doing what" to further define the expected behavior the student must show. What action will the student do that can be observed by multiple people? For example, if a goal to "improve" math skills is planned ("improving" by itself is not measurable), explicit statements of what the student will do in demonstrating the behavior can make the goal acceptably and objectively observable. For example, *John will improve his math reasoning skills* **as demonstrated by** *answering three fourth-grade level word problems involving fractions and percents with 100% accuracy in three out of four trials.*

Observable and measurable behavior statements can be described and observed without judgment or bias. For example, "*John will be respectful to school staff*" is **not** observable or measurable because different staff members may have different views on what constitutes respectful behavior. Instead, the goal should be written to specify the desired behaviors that John learn and exhibit, such as "*John will interact appropriately by speaking to school a voice level that is consistent with that being used by the staff member with whom he is conversing for the entire school day for three consecutive days.*" Writing the goal in this way also provides information about the specific behaviors John will be taught. Other ideas for making functional or social goals more explicit include phrases such as, "will complete steps in a (given) task," and "verbally initiate a conversation" (Hedin & DeSpain, 2018). Examples of observable target behaviors include words read aloud, identifying letters of the alphabet, words spelled correctly, number of math facts correct. Poor target behaviors that are open to many interpretations include understanding, appreciating, enjoying, and knowing.

Identify the Conditions The conditions in a goal statement identify the circumstances under which the terminal performance of goal will be demonstrated by the student at the end of the instructional period (in the case of annual goals, one year of instruction). Conditions include a description of the **materials to be used to measure the goal** and, if the terminal performance is not one the student is expected to do independently, the **level of assistance or accommodation** to be provided. Conditions should be detailed enough to be sure the desired performance would be recognized by another competent person and detailed enough so that others understand the intent of the goal writer (Mager, 1997).

As such, condition statements may start with phrases such as: "Given . . .," "From the (text, material, etc.) . . .," "When provided with . . .," and "While in a group of two or more other peers . . .." Further, condition statements may include things such as the curriculum and grade level of materials that will be used *in general terms* (some states, such as Illinois, recommend against the naming of specific, commercial, or published programs—see: https://www.isbe.net/Pages/Spe cial-Education-Individualized-Education-Program.aspx). We recommend against writing what will be denied to a student, unless the annual measurable goal is designed to reduce the use of supports/accommodations. Writing what a student may not have ("without the use of a calculator") may be important in these circumstances but may also be clarified in the accommodations section of the IEP.

Identify the Criteria for Acceptable Performance or Mastery The criterion statement for a goal identifies the expected levels of performance the student is to show on the observable behavior and skills within a goal—in other words, expected level of performance or mastery. The importance of specific, measurable levels of performance within criterion statements was highlighted in a recent due process hearing from Massachusetts. In this instance, a student had a reading comprehension goal of "will read fictional, expository, and informational texts at his independent and instructional reading level with satisfactory comprehension and appropriate fluency" (*In Re: Martin v. North Middlesex Regional School District*, 2020, p. 10). The goal was followed by objectives, but these did not indicate targets for student performance. The hearing officer in this case determined the reading goal on the IEP was too vague. Terminology such as "satisfactory" comprehension and "appropriate" fluency did not describe measurable, specific targets that would allow the IEP team to measure the student's progress. Similarly, an administrative appeals officer in *Rio Rancho Public Schools* (2003) found two years of IEPs did not provide FAPE because they contained goals that were not measurable. In the ruling, the appeals officer wrote that a "goal of 'increasing' reading comprehension skills or 'improving decoding skills' is not a measurable goal without a clear statement of the student's present level of performance and a specific (goal) by which the student's progress can be measured" (p. 563).

Criteria may be written in many forms, including (a) accuracy targets, (b) fluency rates, (c) time to respond, (d) threshold or number of appropriate responses, (e) quality ratings/rubrics, and (f) duration/latency of responding. Often, statements combine more than one criterion (e.g., within 10 seconds of being asked a question in three consecutive trials) to indicate the expected consistency, maintenance, or generalization of the target behavior. This latter consideration is important because a statement written to indicate that if a student meets a criterion once the goal has been met is appropriate only in very limited circumstances. However, often the goal behavior would require multiple demonstrations to ensure the student has truly met the goal or objective. In this case, the addition of statements such as "in three out of four consecutive trials," "in four out of five observed opportunities," or "on average over the course of two weeks" should be included in the full criterion statement.

It is also important that criterion statements for goals and objectives be reflective of the measures used in establishing the baseline of student performance and related logically and meaningfully to the behavior being measured. In our work on the IEP Quality Project, we see many criteria stated in terms of percentages, even though percent correct is not always applicable to the goal behavior because the target behavior can neither be expressed as a rational percentage, nor is the percentage related to a valid baseline measure of the behavior. For example, the behavior of "paragraph writing," by itself, could not be measured at 85-90% accuracy. But it is possible to monitor progress on the behavior of "paragraph writing" using a rubric that quantifies critical features and elements. For example, if writing a persuasive paragraph is the target behavior, then points could be assigned to the elements of topic identification, position identification, statement of reason(s), evidence statement, transition phrases, and conclusion. In addition, points could be assigned to the conventions of writing, including grammar, punctuation, and spelling. Thus, caution to avoid the overuse of "percent correct" is warranted when both a logical starting point (baseline) and defensible ending point (criterion) cannot be articulated clearly (see *Rio Rancho* ruling described in chapter 3).

Similarly, as the use of commercial progress monitoring programs has increased over time (e.g., AimswebPLUS, FastBridge), we have observed a concomitant rise in the strategy of listing the normative-referenced criteria referencing percentile rankings of these programs as the sole criteria found in IEP goals (Shriner et al., 2017). For example, we see IEPs from districts where every annual goal in reading and math is written in the form, "*Jimmy will score at the XXth percentile on the* _____." Whereas the benefit of this approach is the assurance that data are being collected about a student's progress, there can also be some issues with writing IEP goals using percentiles as the only criterion measure. Overreliance on a percentile only approach can lead to the question if IEPs are *individualized*. While not all students may have the same percentile target, this goal could still be written for every child, regardless of special education status or specific instructional need. In this approach, "scoring at XXth percentile" is not a behavior and the measurability of the criterion comes at the *expense of* observability and specificity of the desired target behavior(s). It is also best practice to provide the target rate of words read per minute. Doing so helps ensure another

TABLE 6.1   Depiction of the Requirements of a Better Practices Measurable Annual Goal

Target Behavior (What will be measured)	Conditions or Given (How the goal will be measured)	Criterion for Acceptable Performance (To show mastery of goal)

teacher or school personnel who receives the student's IEP will have a meaningful reference point for the instruction intended on that IEP goal. A reasonable way to do this is to write, "*Jimmy will score at the XXth percentile by orally reading 70 words correctly per minute on the fourth-grade materials over three consecutive attempts.*" Although the conventions for testing using curriculum-based measures of reading fluency are known (e.g., the student reads aloud), specifying this goal in a parent-friendly manner (e.g., 70 words correctly per minute) leaves little question about the behavior to be measured. Similarly, a reading goal of "The student will score at the Level M (3.2 to 3.6) of the reading program" identifies only the desired performance level. The goal does not identify the intent/focus of the specially designed instruction to be provided and could be rewritten as "given a grade level text, read independently, and five inferential questions, the student will answer the questions and cite textual evidence for her answer, orally or in writing, with 80-100% accuracy in three consecutive trials to meet Level M criteria of the district-chosen reading program."

In mathematics, a goal written as "*The student will increase math score to the 35th percentile according to the _____ norms by the end of the sixth grade,*" while measurable, describes no observable behaviors (e.g., write correct answers, solve problems using a template) and does not tell us the instructional focus for the year beyond the content area domain of mathematics. Furthermore, no logical connections to prioritized content from within the academic standards for mathematics are evident in this goal. A well-written goal that includes the required information may, in fact, be longer, but it will be clear and usable. The "measurement-only" goal above could be rewritten as "*With a focus on numeration, place value, and estimation, the student will solve written problems on sixth-grade probes obtaining an average of 15 points (35th percentile) across three probes.*"

Additional Elements of Goals

Because school districts or states may require IEP teams include additional information in their annual IEP goals, it is important that readers understand their school district's or state's requirements. Two examples of additional

IEP requirements are from Colorado and South Carolina. Because IEP goals are written for one academic year, the state of Colorado requires that goals include a time frame or data by which the goals are projected to be met (e.g., "In 36 weeks," "By May 19, 2022"). The purpose of requiring a date in the goal is to reinforce the time-sensitive nature of the goals. Officials in the South Carolina Office of Special Education Services prefer that annual goals include data from the present levels of performance along with the criteria for acceptable performance. So, for example, if a student had an oral reading fluency rate of 84 correct words per minute listed on his or her PLAAFP statement and the IEP team included an annual goal of 124 correct words per minute, the goal would be written as follows: *In 36 weeks, when given a fourth-grade oral reading passage and one minute to read aloud, (student's name) will increase the number of correct words per minute read from 84 to 124.*

Goals Should Be Ambitious but Reasonable In *Endrew F.* v. *Douglas County School District* (2017), the US Supreme Court ruled a school must offer an IEP reasonably calculated to enable a child to make progress appropriate in light of the child's circumstances. The Supreme Court further found that an educational benefit standard not focused on student progress "would do little to remedy the pervasive and tragic academic stagnation that prompted Congress to act" (p. 999) and "after all, the essential function of an IEP is to set out a plan for pursuing academic and functional advancement" (p. 999). Annual goals are the IEP team members' best estimate of what a student will learn or be expected to do in the next school year to address the effects of his or her disability.

Question 12 in the US Department of Education's (2017) Questions & Answers (Q&A) document on the meaning of *Endrew F.* was "How can an IEP team ensure that every child has the chance to meet challenging objectives?" (p. 6). In answering the questions, officials noted that "The IEP must include annual goals that aim to improve educational results and functional performance for each child with a disability. This inherently includes a meaningful opportunity for the child to meet challenging objectives" (p. 6). A student's annual goals, therefore, should be ambitious but reasonable. Recall that the US Supreme Court in *Endrew F. v. Douglas County School District* (2017) put school district officials on notice that the courts "may fairly expect those authorities to be able to offer a cogent and responsive explanation for their decisions that shows the IEP is reasonably calculated to enable the child to make progress appropriate in light of his circumstances" (p. 993). It would be exceedingly difficult, if not impossible, to provide such an explanation if a student's IEP contains goals so unambitious that if achieved, the student would not make reasonable progress. An incident like this occurred in *Carter v. Florence County Four* (1991), in which a school district was found to have failed to provide FAPE to a student because her goals were so unambitious that even if they had been met, the goals would have caused the plaintiff, Shannon Carter, to "continue to fall behind her classmates at an alarming rate" and therefore "ensured the program's inadequacy from its inception" (p. 158). We believe it is important that when IEP teams craft a student's annual IEP goals, they error on the side of ambition. It is likely that a hearing officer or judge will find unambitious goals to be a denial of FAPE.

Goals and Involvement and Participation in the General Education Curriculum In a standards-based approach, annual goals are, in a sense, an IEP team's answer to the following question: "What skills does the student require to master the content of the curriculum?" *rather than* the question: "What curriculum content does the student need to master?" It is important that logical connections to academic content standards are evident. A forced or trivial connection of an annual goal to academic content standards is neither appropriate nor useful in promoting meaningful access to the general curriculum (Karvonen, 2009). As the officials in the US Department of Education wrote with respect to providing general curricular access that also ensures a FAPE is made available to students with disabilities under the IDEA:

> The alignment of [the IEP and standards] must guide, but not replace, the individualized decision-making required in the IEP process [and that] the IDEA's focus on the individual needs of each child with a disability is an essential consideration when IEP Teams are writing annual goals. (US Department of Education, 2015, p. 3)

Reader should note that students' IEPs should only include annual goals for areas of the general curriculum for which a student requires special education and related services in order to be involved in and make progress in the general education curriculum. Bateman & Linden (2012) asserted that IEP teams should not clutter up student's IEP with goals that are not specifically related to the student's needs as identified in his or her PLAAFP statements.

Well-written, appropriate goals, including those for which standards-referenced, specially designed instruction is needed, help teachers prioritize students' needs and preserve the link to the standards and focus on offsetting or reducing the learning or behavioral problems resulting from the student's characteristics through the teaching of valid replacement behaviors. For example, a student performing very poorly on written tests in a particular academic content area and who is highly distractible may have a goal to address written expression skills, not the specific content area that requires written expression. He or she also may have a goal focused on improving self- monitoring/regulation skills. These goals are complementary and the student's IEP encompasses larger planning issues for the year.

Identifying High-Quality Measurable Annual IEP Goals

So, how do you know if an annual goal is of high quality? To help answer this overarching question, we offer a set of annual goal "test questions" that is shown in table 6.2.

The questions and explanations in the table were assembled by the staff at the IEP Quality Project and stem from our work with educators in several states (e.g., Shriner et al., 2013, 2017) and through an examination of due process hearings and state-complaint proceedings in which the substantive elements of the IEP related to annual goals were at issue.

We offer a possible tool to allow IEP teams to review annual goals to ensure they meet legal policy and best practice guidelines for annual goals. In addition, these questions are rooted in practices to assure that the goals are specific, standards-based, and prepared in light of the student's individual circumstances.

TABLE 6.2 Test Questions for Well-Written Annual Measurable Goals

Question	Explanation
Can I tell this goal was written for **this** student?	Individualization of goals is essential. "Stock" goals should be avoided. Use caution if referencing a goal bank.
Do I know the skills to which this student is working toward mastery based on this goal?	The instructional intent/focus of the goal should be clear. After reading a goal, another teacher or a parent should know what skills are addressed.
Are these skills specific to the student (e.g., *using context clues while reading*) and not just general skills areas (e.g., *reading comprehension*)?	Skill specificity is important to ensure implementation is as intended. Using terms understood by all who work with the student promotes shared understanding.
Are the skills based on data listed/explained in the PLAAFP, and is no further assessment needed to support the need for this goal?	Data in the PLAAFP should be sufficient to show that a need/deficit is important and should be addressed. "Why" a goal is included should be clear.
Could I begin instruction based on this goal?	Although the specific instructional *approach* is not specified, a goal should be actionable by a teacher familiar with the instructional *domain*.
Could I evaluate student progress based on this goal?	The goal criterion statement should be based upon a reliable and valid measurement strategy that allows for progress (or lack thereof) to be monitored.
Does the evaluation logically match the target skill?	The measurement of behavior(s) should be meaningful and replicable (e.g., "Student includes parts of a paragraph based on a rubric" rather than "Student writes a paragraph with 90% accuracy").

Adapted from:
Shriner, J. G., & Carty, S. (2018). *Utilizing IEPQ as professional development with staff.* Presentation at Illinois State Board of Education, Directors' Conference. Springfield, IL: IEP Quality Project, University of Illinois. https://www.isbe.net/Documents/Session-20-IEP-Utilizing-IEP-Q-PD.pdf; https://iepq.education.illinois.edu

Whereas these questions and our brief explanatory notes are not all-inclusive and may not capture all nuances of a student's IEP, they are a good starting point for teams to use as a gauge of goal quality. Some team members may prefer to use these to review goals they have drafted on their own as a self-assessment. We have found other teams sometimes "swap" goals with colleagues they trust for review and discussion. When examining any particular annual goal, it is possible there may be disagreement on some of the answers that leads to productive discussion, discovery of goal elements (conditions, behavior, criteria) that may need clarification, and, perhaps, change in subsequent practice. Table 6.3 presents the questions for examining goals in a checklist format.

Examples of using these goal test questions are shown below. The goal assessment questionnaire tables (6.4, 6.5, 6.6, 6.7, and 6.8) with answers follow each goal and our comments on each goal follow the table.

TABLE 6.3 Goal Assessment Form

GOALS CHECKLIST QUESTIONS:	YES	NO
Can I tell the goal was written for this student? (Is it individualized?)		
Do I know what skills this student is working to master based on this goal?		
Are the skills specific to the student and not just general skills areas?		
Could I begin instruction on specific skills based on this goal?		
Could I evaluate student progress based on this goal?		
Does the evaluation match the student skill(s)?		

Adapted from:
Shriner, J. G., & Carty, S. (2018). *Utilizing IEPQ as professional development with staff.* Presentation at Illinois State Board of Education, Directors' Conference. Springfield, IL: IEP Quality Project, University of Illinois. https://www.isbe.net/Documents/Session-20-IEP-Utilizing-IEP-Q-PD.pdf; https://iepq.education.illinois.edu

---

Textbox 6.1 Goal Test Questions and Sample Goals

1. Carlos will improve his reading skills (by meeting the following objectives):

TABLE 6.4 Goal Test Questions and Sample Goals Example 1

GOALS CHECKLIST QUESTIONS:	YES	NO
Can I tell the goal was written for this student? (Is it individualized?)		X
Do I know what skills this student is working to master based on this goal?		X
Are the skills specific to the student and not just general skills areas?		X
Could I begin instruction on specific skills based on this goal?		X
Could I evaluate student progress based on this goal?		X
Does the evaluation match the student skill(s)?		X

Comments: This goal cannot stand on its own. It has no conditions, skills/behaviors, or criteria for mastery. Could be for any student; we want all students to improve their reading skills. Not individualized or indicative of special education services.

2. Bea will demonstrate appropriate classroom behavior for five consecutive days.

TABLE 6.5 Goal Test Questions and Sample Goals Example 2

GOALS CHECKLIST QUESTIONS:	YES	NO
Can I tell the goal was written for this student? (Is it individualized?)		X
Do I know what skills this student is working to master based on this goal?		X
Are the skills specific to the student and not just general skills areas?		X
Could I begin instruction on specific skills based on this goal?		X
Could I evaluate student progress based on this goal?		X
Does the evaluation match the student skill(s)?		X

Comments: No conditions, no defined observable, measurable behavior (what is appropriate?), no defined way to measure progress because the behavior and conditions are not defined. Does not get at the replacement skills being taught, which should be the focus of behavior goals.

3. Mickie will write a persuasive paragraph of five or more sentences that contains a clear introduction and conclusion sentence at 80% correct.

TABLE 6.6   Goal Test Questions and Sample Goals Example 3

GOALS CHECKLIST QUESTIONS:	YES	NO
Can I tell the goal was written for this student? (Is it individualized?)	X	
Do I know what skills this student is working to master based on this goal?	X	
Are the skills specific to the student and not just general skills areas?	X	
Could I begin instruction on specific skills based on this goal?	X	
Could I evaluate student progress based on this goal?		X
Does the evaluation match the student skill(s)?		X

Comments: There is some indication of what skills the student is working on and instruction could begin but is lacking clear conditions. Criteria are not matched to skills being measured. How do you measure 80% correct of a writing sample? Could change this to a rubric (e.g., Self-Regulated Strategy Development Rubric for Persuasive Essays), or to having all three components in a certain number of trials. Adding conditions may also help with meeting criteria for mastery.

4. Maurice will increase his reading fluency skills to the 25th percentile based on Commercial Progress Monitoring program norms by the end of sixth grade.

TABLE 6.7   Goal Test Questions and Sample Goals Example 4

GOALS CHECKLIST QUESTIONS:	YES	NO
Can I tell the goal was written for this student? (Is it individualized?)		X
Do I know what skills this student is working to master based on this goal?		X
Are the skills specific to the student and not just general skills areas?		X
Could I begin instruction on specific skills based on this goal?		X
Could I evaluate student progress based on this goal?	X	
Does the evaluation match the student skill(s)?		X

Comments: Scoring at a certain percentile is not a behavior. What is being taught? What is the instructional focus to improve overall fluency? Goal can apply to any student in the school, not individualized. Norms vary. Can't be used by another LEA that doesn't use this assessment as words correct per minute (wcpm) is not specified; norms alone can't be equated.

5. Given a sixth-grade oral reading passage and with a focus on using contextual analysis, Connor will read 135 wcpm (45th percentile) based on the district's Commercial Progress Monitoring program on three consecutive probes.

TABLE 6.8 **Goal Test Questions and Sample Goals Example 5**

GOALS CHECKLIST QUESTIONS:	YES	NO
Can I tell the goal was written for this student? (Is it individualized?)	X	
Do I know what skills this student is working to master based on this goal?	X	
Are the skills specific to the student and not just general skills areas?	X	
Could I begin instruction on specific skills based on this goal?	X	
Could I evaluate student progress based on this goal?	X	
Does the evaluation match the student skill(s)?	X	

Comments: Goal is specific to student. Conditions, observable behavior, and criteria are included. Instructional focus is identified. Criterion is matched to behavior. Specifying wcpm allows goal to be used by another LEA using a different assessment and norms.

Practices That IEP Teams Should Avoid in Crafting Annual Goals

We have addressed the important components that must be present in better practices annual goals. We also encourage IEP teams to avoid the following practices when crafting a student's annual goals.

Avoid Unambitious Annual Goals According to the US Supreme Court in *Endrew F.*, every student should have the chance to meet "challenging" objectives, that a student's IEP "must aim to enable the (student) to make progress," and "the essential function of an IEP is to set out a plan for pursuing academic and functional advancement" (*Endrew F.*, 2017, p. 992). To meet this standard, annual goals should be ambitious, although they should also be reasonable. The IEP is not a guarantee that a student will achieve his or her goals; however, it is likely that with the new FAPE standard if goals are determined to be so unambitious that even if they are achieved they will not lead to meaningful progress, they will be more likely to violate FAPE than will overly ambitious IEP goals.

Do Not Clutter a Student's IEP with Goals Unrelated to His or Her Needs Do not write goals in areas that are not related to a student's needs as identified in his or her PLAAFP statements. Especially avoid including goals for content standards from the general education curriculum (e.g., social studies) that are not related to a student's needs. A student may need accommodations or modifications included in the services section of his or her IEP to be involved in and progress in the general education curriculum, but that does not mean they need goals. Measurable annual goals are developed to meet the unique individual needs of a student.

Avoid Vague or Overly General Goals Vague goals such as "increasing reading performance" or "improving mathematical skills" are woefully short of the standards necessary for a goal to be measurable (Bateman, 2017; Tatgenhorst, et al., 2014). Similarly, the use of percentages without a starting or ending point will not pass muster.

Developing Short-Term Objectives

In states and school districts that require short-term objectives (STOs) for all students in special education, measurable annual goals become the starting point for developing STOs.[2] STOs should include the following information: (a) when a student will master the objective (timeline), (b) what the student will do to show that he or she has achieved the STO (behavior and conditions), and (c) how well they will perform to show mastery (criteria for acceptable performance). With those components in place, additional considerations for further refining annual, measurable goals through short-term objectives (STOs) is an important part of IEP development. Doing so is, in one sense, the point at which the IEP and instructional implementation plans meet, and there are two main—and complementary – questions about how to break down the goal into meaningful STOs. First, what element of the measurable annual goal (i.e., conditions, behaviors, or criteria) may be modified most logically to produce good short-term objectives? Second, what is the instructional approach likely to be used in order to meet the measurable annual goal? Considerations of these questions will guide the decisions about how the goal is addressed.

Many authors have offered strategies for addressing how to break down goals (e.g., Bateman & Linden, 2012; Lignugaris/Kraft et al., 2001; Pierangelo & Giuliani, 2007). A *sequential approach* can be used to address changing skill levels or environments. Expanding the difficulty level of skills across objectives is common when the content area material is amenable to logical sequencing. For example, using a General Outcomes Measures (GOM) approach, the entire curricular expectations of a school year in mathematics, for example, might include operations with single- and multidigit numbers as well as operations with fractions with like denominators, percentages, and numbers involving decimals. A goal written with the GOM used as a progress measuring tool would state the end-of-year target for instruction. Objectives then could be prepared in a "cumulative" skill approach and address specific operations and numerical formats of increasing complexity to support the overarching IEP goal. Depending on what the IEP decides will work most appropriately is based on the individual characteristics of the student. For example, the objectives may begin with smaller addends, increase to larger addends without regrouping, and then address problems requiring regrouping.

It is also possible that any of the three components of the annual goal, behaviors, conditions, and criteria may be modified to produce good short-term objectives. Again, knowledge of the student's learning characteristics and likely instructional approaches is key in determining a sensible approach for any given child. For example, to address a reading goal focused on evidence-based vocabulary instruction, the modification of *conditions* to reflect less complex vocabulary for the initial objective and gradually increasing the vocabulary levels in later objectives might make sense. Alternately, if the instructional approach is "balanced" to address reading and writing the vocabulary words, a focus on each of the *behaviors* (reading/writing), one at a time, might be reasonable. Finally, the

---

[2] In the reauthorization of 2004, Congress removed the STO requirement from IEPs, except for students with disabilities who take alternate assessments. Whereas some states have removed the STOs from their state requirements (e.g., South Carolina), other states have kept the STO requirement (e.g., Illinois).

criterion required for mastery might be altered if a constant level of material (e.g., fourth-grade vocabulary) is used and the desired behaviors are expected throughout the year. In this case, perhaps modifications to the accuracy targets of objectives (beginning with 60% and ending with 90% by year's end) might best reflect the student's improvement on the fourth-grade words.

Using Goals to Monitor Student Progress

After writing annual goals, a student's IEP must include information on "how the (student's) progress toward meeting the annual goals . . . will be measured" (IDEA Regulations, 34 CFR § 300.320 [a][3][i], 2006). Additionally, they must include information on how "periodic reports on the progress the (student) is making toward meeting the annual goals (such as through the use of quarterly or other periodic reports, concurrent with the issuance of report cards) will be provided" (IDEA Regulations, 34 CFR § 300.320 [a][3][ii], 2006). According to the US Department of Education, students' IEP team should use the periodic reporting requirement to keep students' parents informed of their progress toward their annual IEP goals (US Department of Education, 2017). Moreover, Chief Justice of the US Supreme Court John Roberts noted in his majority opinion in *Endrew F. v. Douglas County School District* that "(t)he IEP must aim to enable the child to make progress. After all, the essential function of an IEP is to set out a plan for pursuing academic and functional advancement" (*Endrew*, 2017, p. 992). The most certain way for IEP teams to show that a student's IEP is likely to or actually does show student progress is to collect data on student progress and use this data in making instructional decisions.

The importance of collecting data to monitor student progress was addressed in a presentation at the Tri-State Law Conference in Omaha, Nebraska, in 2015 by Kathleen S. Mehfoud. Mrs. Mehfoud, a recently retired attorney for Reed Smith LLP in Richmond, VA, represented school districts in special education lawsuits. When she represented school districts in FAPE cases, Mrs. Mehfoud reported that "*When I have a school district with a FAPE case the first thing I do is go to the teacher and say: 'Give me information on your student's progress.' If the teacher doesn't have data, I consider advising the school district to settle.*" Readers should note that Mrs. Mehfoud made this statement two years before the Supreme Court's ruling in *Endrew F. v. Douglas City School District* (2017). Certainly, data collection will be more important following the *Endrew F.* decision. By showing data on a student's progress on his/her goals, school district personnel have proof by which they can establish that the student's progress is appropriate under the student's circumstances. The documentation also helps to prove the IEP was implemented.

The purpose of monitoring a student's progress is to make the specially designed instruction in the IEP as effective as possible through systematic examination of the student's growth toward achieving their goals. Adopting a progress monitoring system and then collecting and analyzing the data collected are critical tasks facing a student's IEP team. Important decisions regarding progress markers that must be made by a student's IEP team are (a) how to monitor a student's progress toward the annual IEP goals, (b) how frequently to monitor progress, (c) when and how to analyze the progress monitoring data, and (d) when and how to report the student's progress to his or her parents. We next examine these critical decisions.

How to Monitor a Student's Progress toward the Annual IEP Goals

The aim of monitoring a student's progress toward his or her annual goal is to enable educators, students, and their parents to determine if the student is on a path to achieve the goal and, if not, to revise the IEP. This is referred to as formative evaluation because we are collecting data during instruction so we may make instructional changes during the course of instruction. In comments to the 2006 regulations to the IDEA, officials in the US Department of Education wrote the following about the importance of collecting data during instruction.

> We believe that one of the most important aspects of good teaching is the ability to determine when a child is learning and then to tailor instruction to meet the child's individual needs. Effective teachers use data to make informed decisions about the effectiveness of a particular instructional strategy or program. A critical hallmark of appropriate instruction is that data documenting a child's progress are systematically collected and analyzed and that parents are kept informed of the child's progress. Assessments of a child's progress are not bureaucratic, but an essential component of good instruction. (*Federal Register*, v. 71, p., 46,656, 2006c)

According to Deno (1992), the purpose of using data in a formative manner is to enable teachers to improve student performance by creating a database which allows teachers to evaluate the effectiveness of a student's instruction. If IEP teams collect and analyze data and then use it to improve specially designed instruction, they are more likely to meet the *Endrew F.* standard of enabling a student to make progress appropriate in light of his or her circumstances.

The resources section of this textbook includes a number of excellent resources to assist special education in identifying and using data-based progress monitoring systems. We suggest that readers become familiar with the OSEP-funded National Center on Intensive Intervention (intensiveintervention.org), which maintains and updates charts assessing various academic and behavioral progress monitoring tools.

Characteristics of Progress Monitoring

Deno (1992) identified the most important characteristics of a progress monitoring system. First, the measures must be reliable and valid so the results are meaningful. Second, they must be easy to administer so teachers and others use them consistently. Third, the measures must be designed to enable teachers to use them repeatedly and frequently so they can be used as often as the team determines necessary. Fourth, the data collection system must be time efficient and cost effective to ensure they will be used by otherwise very busy teachers. We would add to these four characteristics that teachers should be able to graph the data collected. A student's teacher should be able to graph the baseline data from the PLAAFP statement, take the criteria for acceptable performance from the measurable annual goal, connect the baseline and goal with a goal line, and then graph the progress monitoring data. Figure 6.1 is a depiction of the graphing process.

Clearly, in the intervention 1 phase, data indicated that the student was not on track to meet his or her goal. Data from the intervention 2 phase, however, indicated progress and the student was likely to meet his or her goal. Table 6.9 depicts the characteristics of a better practices data collection system.

Student: _____   Grade/Age: _____   Teacher: _____

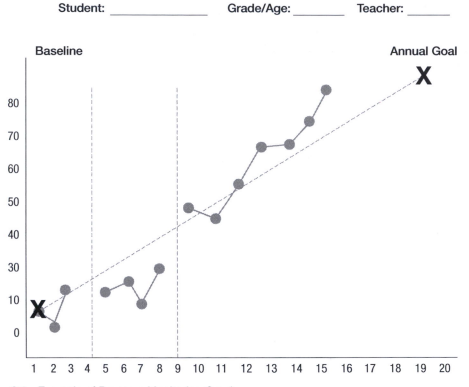

Figure 6.1   Example of Progress Monitoring Graph.

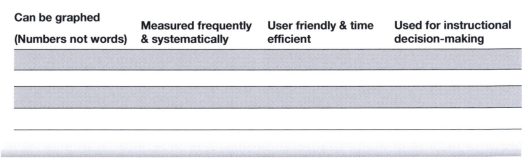

TABLE 6.9   Characteristics of Better Practices Data Collection

Can be graphed (Numbers not words)	Measured frequently & systematically	User friendly & time efficient	Used for instructional decision-making

When and How to Analyze the Progress Data

Students' IEP teams will need to make decisions regarding the nature of the data they collect. We emphasize that the progress monitoring data IEP teams collect should meet the four criteria that Deno (1992) suggested along with the use of a graph to display the data. Unless a graph is used "it is almost impossible to clearly see changes in the trend of student performance" (Deno, 1992, p. 9). Moreover, a graph seems to be intuitively understandable and thus enhances communication with parents and other professionals. A graphic demonstration of a student's progress monitoring data will assist special education administrators if they are asked by a hearing officer or judge to give a cogent and responsive explanation of why an IEP would likely result or actually resulted in student progress.

TABLE 6.10   Example of Progress Monitoring Form

Name of person collecting and reporting data: _____

Names of persons on IEP who will analyze the data: _____ _____

_____ _____

Name of LEA representative: _____

Goal #1:

Data to be collected: _____

Frequency of data collection: _____

Dates to report data collection and analysis to IEP team members and parents: _____,

_____, _____, _____,

Goal #2:

Data to be collected: _____

Frequency of data collection: _____

Dates to report data collection and analysis to IEP team members and parents: _____,

_____, _____, _____,

Signatures

LEA representative: _____

Person responsible for data collection and reporting: _____

IEP team member: _____, _____, _____,

_____, _____

Parents: _____, _____

*Add additional pages for goals as needed

When and How to Report the Student's Progress to His or Her Parents

The regulations to the IDEA require that students' IEPs include a description of "When periodic reports on the progress the child is making toward meeting the annual goals (such as through the use of quarterly or other periodic reports, concurrent with the issuance of report card) will be provided" (IDEA Regulations, 34 CFR § 300.320[a][3][ii], 2006). Although the law clearly requires that students' progress be monitored and reported, and suggests a means for reporting (e.g., periodic reports concurrent with the issuance of report cards), it leaves the manner in which IEP teams accomplish this to school districts and state officials. Thus, it is important that teachers are aware of policy in their school district or state. The greater the amount of data collected, the more accurate it will be for decision-making (Deno, 1992), so we suggest that IEP teams require students' special education teachers to collect, analyze, and report progress monitoring data at least monthly. It is critical that the progress monitoring data collection system be included in a student's IEP and that the agreed-upon system be implemented, analyzed, and reported as agreed upon in the IEP. Table 6.10 is an example of a progress reporting form that may be useful to IEP teams.

Practices IEP Teams Should Avoid in Measuring Student Progress

We believe that monitoring students' progress toward their annual IEP goals is absolutely necessary if IEPs are to meet the *Endrew F.* standard. We also suggest IEP teams avoid the following errors when determining a measurement strategy.

Don't Substitute Subjective Judgment for Objective Data in Measuring Student Progress Measuring student progress using subjective judgment as opposed to objective data collection procedures will most likely lead to ineffective decision-making. A hearing officer in *Board of Education of the Rhinebeck Central School District* (2003) asserted the use of subjective teacher observation was not an adequate method of monitoring student progress. Additionally, a judge in a US District Court in New Jersey found a student's IEP had no objective way to measure student progress and denied the student FAPE because the IEP (a) impeded the student's parents ability to participate, (b) resulted in goals that could not be measured, and (c) did not allow the IEP team to identify needed changes to the student's program.

Don't Write Vague or General Measures of Student Growth We have noted the importance of staying away from vague and general statements (e.g., "increasing" or "improving" student performance) in writing annual goals. If IEPs do not include baseline data from the PLAAFP statement and instead use terms such as "increasing" or "improving," the goals will be too vague to be measured. Hearing officers and judges have found using terms such as measuring goals by using "unit tests" (*Chris D. v. Montgomery County Board of Education*, 1990), "teacher observation" (*Board of Education of the Rhinebeck Central School District*, 2003), or percentages with no beginning or ending point (*Rio Rancho*, 2003) to be inadequate methods to measure student progress.

Don't Use Commercially Developed Achievement Tests to Monitor Growth There are a few problems with using standardized achievement tests for progress monitoring. First, such tests cannot be given frequently enough to be useful to measure student growth. Second, commercially developed achievement tests are intended to measure a student's standing relative to a norm sample of same-aged students and are not designed to directly measure short-term student growth.

Summary of Better Practice IEP Annual Goals and Measurement

The measurable annual goals included in a student's IEP "are instrumental to the strategic planning process used to develop and implement the IEP" (IDEA Regulations, Appendix A, 64, 48, 1999). The annual goals lead the way for the IEP team to develop the specially designed instruction (e.g., special education services) that will be effective in enabling a student to reach his or her goals. We suggest annual IEP goals include the components first suggested by Robert Mager in 1962: (a) an observable target behavior to be performed by a student, (b) a condition or method by which to measure the goal, and (c) a criterion for acceptable performance. States or school districts may also require additional information in an annual goal (e.g., timeline for achieving a goal, baseline data from a student's PLAAFP statement). Goals should also be ambitious enough that achieving them will result in a student making meaningful progress.

Moreover, the IEP must include information as to how the goals will be measured on a systematic and regular basis to determine if a student is making progress toward achieving these goals. These progress markers will enable administrators, teachers, students, and parents to monitor a student's progress during the year and will enable the team to change or modify his or her IEP when needed. Table 6.11 summarizes the procedures to follow and procedures to avoid in writing measurable goals and then measuring student progress toward these goals.

TABLE 6.11 Practices to Follow and Practices to Avoid in Writing Measurable Annual Goals and Monitoring Student Progress

Practices to Follow	Practices to Avoid
Address needs identified in the PLAAFP statement.	Do not clutter the IEP with detailed goals in areas not related to a student's needs.
Write in clear and understandable language.	Do not substitute a state's academic content standards for individual goals.
Write goals that are ambitious.	
The goal can be graphed.	Do not use vague or overly general language in goals or measurement descriptions in IEPs.
Methods to measure progress are specific and describe how far and by when.	Do not clutter up goals with extraneous information.
A reporting schedule should be addressed in the IEP meeting and included in the IEP.	Do not substitute subjective judgment for measuring student progress toward his/her goals rather than objective data.
The goal passes the stranger test.	
Remember, data are numbers, not words.	Do not use commercially developed test for monitoring student progress.
Develop and implement a schedule for collecting and analyzing progress monitoring data.	
Ensure the measuring and reporting schedule is implemented and reported as agreed upon.	

CHAPTER 7

The IEP Process and Components

Developing Special Education Services, Related Services, and Supplementary Aids and Services (with Paula Chan)

We have structured our discussion in the second section of this text around the following four questions that guide the development of students' IEPs:

1. What are students' unique academic and functional needs that must be addressed in their IEPs?
2. What are the annual goals that must be included in students' IEP to address the needs identified in the PLAAFP statements?
3. How will students' progress toward these annual goals be monitored?
4. What services will be provided to students so they may reach these goals?

The first question is answered in assessments and the PLAAFP statements, which we address in chapter 5. The second and third questions are answered in the measurable annual goals and the methods and procedures special educators used to measure students' progress toward achieving their annual goals (see chapter 6). The fourth question, regarding the identification of the services an IEP team includes in a student's specialized instruction, is the topic we address in this chapter.

When students need services or accommodations to receive a FAPE, those services must be included in their IEP. The IDEA requires that all students' IEPs must include:

> a statement of the special education and related services and supplementary aids and services, based on peer-reviewed research to the extent practicable . . . and a statement of program modifications or supports for school personnel that will be provided for the (student) to (1) progress toward the annual goals, (2) be involved in and make progress in the general curriculum and participate in extracurricular and other nonacademic activities, and (3) be educated and participate with children with and without disabilities (IDEA, USC § 1414 [d][1][A][i][IV], 2004).

In comments to the IDEA regulations, officials in the US Department wrote, "The (school district) must ensure all services set forth in the child's IEP are provided consistent with the child's needs . . . and are provided in a manner that appropriately meets the child's needs (*Federal Register*, Vol. 64, No. 48, Appendix A, Comments to the IDEA Regulations, 12478, 1999).

In this chapter, we address the different types of specially designed instruction, including special education services, related services, supplementary aids and services, program modifications, and supports for school personnel. Moreover, we examine services that may need to be provided to a subset of students with disabilities such as transition services, extended school year (ESY) services, and behavior intervention plans. Additionally, the IDEA requires all these services be based on peer-reviewed research (PRR) to the extent possible. We begin with an examination of this requirement of the IDEA.

Specially Designed Instruction and Peer-Reviewed Research

Motivated by national reports such as *A Nation At Risk* (1983) that showed public school students in the United States were falling behind their counterparts in other countries in the areas of reading, mathematics, and science, Congress began passing laws to combat this problem. Moreover, student assessments, especially the National Assessment of Student Progress (NASP, 2012), revealed the low achievement levels of American students were not improving despite large infusions of federal funding to improve education (Yell, 2019). The purpose of the laws, which included the Reading Excellence Act of 1998, the No Child Left Behind Act (NCLB) of 2001, and the Educational Sciences Reform Act of 2002, was to remedy these problems by requiring educators to use research-based practices.

The thinking that drove these laws was that if public school teachers used procedures, strategies, and programs that had been shown to be effective by the best available scientific evidence, student achievement would improve (Yell et al., 2017). The Coalition for Evidence-Based Policy (2002) summed up these requirements to use educational research in our schools as follows:

> The field of K-12 education contains a vast array of educational interventions—such as reading and math curricula, school-wide reform programs, after-school programs, and new educational technologies—that claim to be able to improve educational outcomes and, in many cases, to be supported by evidence. This evidence often consists of poorly designed and/or advocacy-driven studies. State and local education officials and educators must sort through a myriad of such claims to decide which interventions merit consideration for their schools and classrooms. Many of these practitioners have seen interventions, introduced with great fanfare as being able to produce dramatic gains, come and go over the years, yielding little in the way of positive and lasting change . . . (the laws) call on educational practitioners to use "scientifically-based research" to guide their decisions about which interventions to implement. We believe this approach can produce major advances in the effectiveness of American education.

Perhaps the major impetus to reform educational practices through federal law was NCLB, passed in 2001. Under NCLB, states and school districts were required to use scientifically-based research (SBR) to improve student achievement. The law defined SBR as "research that applies rigorous, systematic, and objective procedures to obtain relevant knowledge" (Elementary and Secondary Education Act [ESEA], 20 USC § 1208(6)). Secretary of Education Rod Paige asserted that NCLB demanded the use of methods that really work: "No fads, no feel-good fluff, but instruction that is based upon sound scientific research" (Paige, 2002, p. 1). O'Neill (2004) confirmed this view when he asserted that Congress's purpose in including SBR in NCLB was to warn schools, school districts, and states that no longer should educators rely on untested practices without proof of effectiveness because such practices led to widespread ineffectiveness and academic failure.

In December 2004, IDEA 2004, the Individuals with Disabilities Education Improvement Act, was signed into law. The reauthorized IDEA included the PRR requirement, which required that a student's IEP must contain: "A statement of the special education and related services and supplementary aids and services, based on peer-reviewed research to the extent practicable---that will be provided to the child" (IDEA, 20 USC § 1414[d][1][A][i][IV]).

Although the IDEA now contained the PRR requirement, the US Department of Education declined to define the term "peer-reviewed research." The Department did note, however, that the term was adopted from the following criteria that school districts could use to identify SBR from the ESEA: "Research that has been accepted by a peer-reviewed journal or approved by a panel of independent experts through a comparably rigorous, objective, and scientific review" (NCLB, 20 USC § 1208[6][B], 2006). In the final regulations to the IDEA, issued on August 14, 2006, the US Department of Education defined PRR in the commentary as generally referring "to research that is reviewed by qualified and independent reviewers to ensure that the quality of the information meets the standards of the field before the research is published" (*Federal Register*, Vol. 71, Comments to the IDEA Regulations, p. 46664, 2006).

In comments to the 2006 regulations, officials in the US Department of Education clarified the PRR requirement. According to the department:

> Services and supports should be based on peer-reviewed research to the extent that it is possible, given the availability of peer-reviewed research . . . . States, school districts, and school personnel must, therefore, select and use methods that research has shown to be effective, to the extent that methods based on peer-reviewed research are available. This does not mean that the service with the greatest body of research is the service necessarily required for a child to receive FAPE. Likewise, there is nothing in the act to suggest that the failure of a public agency to provide services based on peer-reviewed research would automatically result in a denial of FAPE. The final decision about the special education and related services, and supplementary aids and services that are to be provided to a child must be made by the child's IEP team based on the child's individual needs . . . if no such research exists, the service may still be provided, if the IEP team determines that such services are appropriate. (*Federal Register*, Vol. 71, No 156, Comments to the IDEA Regulations, pp. 46663-46665, 2006)

Yell & Rozalski (2013) suggested special education teachers adhere to the following recommendations:

- Understand and remain current with the research in their areas and use academic and behavioral interventions that have support in the research literature.

- Be prepared to discuss PRR in IEP meetings and to be able to explain the research behind the special education services that will be implemented.
- Acknowledge and discuss research that parents propose at IEP meetings. If research does not support a particular procedure advocated by a student's parents, be prepared to discuss not only the parent's suggestions and opinions but also the lack of support in the PRR.
- Implement interventions with fidelity. This means teachers should implement interventions in accordance with how they were designed to be implemented.
- Attend professional development activities on new and emerging research. Special education is a highly researched field and teachers and IEP team members should keep up with research in their respective fields.

Table 7.1 includes websites on peer-reviewed procedures in special education.

TABLE 7.1   Websites with Peer-Reviewed Interventions

Name and URL	Description
Best Evidence Encyclopedia www.bestevidence.org	The Best Evidence Encyclopedia is the website of the Center for Data-Driven Reform in Education (CDDRE) of the School of Education at Johns Hopkins University. The Center, which is funded by the Institute of Education Sciences in the US Department of Education, is intended to give educators and researchers information about the evidence base of various educational programs.
Center on Positive Behavioral Interventions and Supports (PBIS) www.pbis.org	The Center on Positive Behavioral Interventions and Supports is devoted to giving schools information and technical assistance for identifying, adapting, and sustaining effective school-wide disciplinary practices. The website is sponsored by OSEP in the US Department of Education.
IRIS Center iris.peabody.vanderbilt .edu	The IRIS Center for training enhancement is a free online resource that translates research on the education of students with disabilities into practice. The website is sponsored by OSEP in the US Department of Education.
National Center on Intensive Intervention (NCII) http://Intensiveinterv ention.org	NCII builds the capacity of state and local education agencies, universities, practitioners, and other stakeholders to support implementation of intensive intervention in literacy, mathematics, and behavior for students with severe and persistent learning and/ or behavioral needs, often in the context of their multi-tiered system of support (MTSS) or special education services. NCII's approach to intensive intervention is data-based individualization (DBI), a research-based process that integrates the systematic use of assessment data, validated interventions, and intensification strategies.
National Technical Assistance Center on Transition (NTACT) https://transitionta.org/	NTACT is dedicated to ensuring full implementation of the IDEA and helping youth with disabilities achieve desired post-school outcomes. The website is sponsored by OSEP in the US Department of Education.
What Works Clearinghouse (WWC) ies.ed.gov/ncee/wwc	The WWC reviews the existing research on different programs, products, practices, and policies in education. The goal is to provide educators with the information they need to make evidence-based decisions. The Clearinghouse focuses on the results from high-quality research to answer the question "What works in education?" The website is sponsored by the Institute of Education Sciences in the US Department of Education.

Specially Designed Instruction: Special Education Services

Students can only be determined eligible under the IDEA if they need special education services because of their disability or disabilities. The services to which eligible students with disabilities may be entitled include special education, related services, supplementary aids and services, accommodations and support for personnel, and program modifications.

The type of special education service a student receives is entirely dependent on need(s) described in the statement of the student's present levels of academic achievement and functional performance (PLAAFP) in the IEP. It is important to remember the needs of the student drive the services, not the student's disability label, and not what happens to be available in the special education classroom in a school. Additionally, the terms that are used to describe services may be different from state to state. However, the basics as described below are the same, no matter what term is used to describe them. Two important aspects drive a student's type of service:

- The service must be individualized to meet students' unique educational needs. The needs of students, identified in their PLAAFP statements, drive the level and type of services they are to receive.
- The full range or continuum of services must be made available to meet the needs of students.

District personnel cannot say that they do not have "that service" or that "level of service"; rather, students must be provided with the programming they need to enable them to make progress in light of their circumstances (i.e., the *Endrew F.* standard for providing a FAPE). If a district does not have a certain service, they must either contract with a provider, share services with another district, or otherwise arrange for the student to receive the service in their district. Regardless of how it is done, the district has the ultimate responsibility of ensuring that the needed service is provided.

The IDEA defines special education services as "specially designed instruction, at no cost to the parents, to meet the unique needs of a child with a disability" (IDEA Regulations, 34 CFR 300.37[a][1], 2006). Special education services may include instruction conducted in a classroom, home, hospitals and institutions, and other settings. It may also include instruction in physical education, speech and language pathology, travel training, and vocational education (IDEA Regulations, 34 CFR 300.39[a-b], 2006).

When IEP teams determine the special education services to be provided to a student with disabilities, the team must (a) base the services on the needs identified in the student's PLAAFP statements, (b) adapt the content, methodology, or delivery of instruction to be appropriate for the student in question, and (c) ensure access to the general education curriculum (IDEA Regulations, 34 CFR 300.39[b][3], 2006). So, for example, if a student's PLAAFP statement shows that the student has a need in reading, the IEP team will need to address this need by including special education services in reading. The team must determine how and where these services will be provided. Depending on the extent of a student's reading needs, the team may decide that the student needs a different curriculum than general education students receive or they may decide to supplement the current general education curriculum with additional instruction. Of course, the IEP team would need to include a goal in reading and measure the student's progress toward the goal. Of course, to meet the *Endrew F.* standard, the student's special education services must enable them to make progress appropriate in light of their circumstances; so if the student were not making sufficient progress, the team would then look at changing the services in some way.

Beginning Date, Duration, Frequency, and Location

Regulations to the IDEA require that all services included in students' IEPs (i.e., special education services, related services, supplementary aids and services, program modifications, and supports for school personnel) include the date services begin and the anticipated frequency, location, and duration of those services and modifications (IDEA Regulations, 34 CFR 300.320[a][7], 2006). The services provided in an IEP must be specified; therefore, it is not sufficient to merely list the services. According to a comment in the 2006 regulations, students' IEPs must include specific information on the services provided "so that the level of the (school's) commitment of resources will be clear to parents and other IEP team members" and that this information must be provided "in a manner that can be understood by all involved in the development and implementation of the IEP" (*Federal Register*, Vol. 71, No. 46, p. 46,667, 2006b). Table 7.2 is a depiction of important elements in the services section of the IEP.

Service Delivery Models

The following section delineates the specific models of services that students may receive. Again, the label for the service in your state may be different. These services may be provided in a number of settings along the continuum of alternative placements. As always, the individual needs of the student dictate the level and intensity of the services a student is to receive. All options are to be made available to the students when needed to provide the student with an appropriate education.

Indirect Services. Indirect services are not provided directly to an eligible child and are designed for students who need very minimal support. Indirect services

TABLE 7.2   **Characteristics of Better Practice IEP Services**

Addresses a Need from the PLAAFP Statement	Based on PRR	Described Specifically (Frequency, Location, Duration)	Implemented as Agreed-Upon at the IEP Meeting

are consultative supports provided to the general education teacher in the form of suggestions, steps, and guidance from the special education teacher and/or related-service provider(s) on appropriate strategies for instruction, behavior management, data collection, observation, and feedback. A special education teacher or related-service professional provides these services to others who are working directly with a child. Indirect services may include:

- Regular consultation with a general education teacher or other school staff on situations resulting from a child's disability
- Monitoring a child's progress in a specific area
- Monitoring equipment or assistive technology used by a child
- Assistance in modifying the curriculum or the environment for an eligible child
- Direct observation of a child

Push-in Services. Push-in services are often provided to students with disabilities who require minimal intervention. This option often is considered as an opportunity for students to interact more with their nondisabled peers. Typically, a specialist (a speech-language pathologist, an occupational therapist, or even a special education teacher) works very closely with the general education teacher to provide services for the student. The services provided could be either a related service, assisting with the provision of differentiated instruction, or specific instructional support. The students who are eligible for special education and related services typically do not leave the classroom throughout the day, because the services are provided in the classroom and service providers come to the student. Some of the students within the classroom may receive some pull-out services in addition to their assisted learning in the classroom.

Pull-out Services. Some students may have needs that are greater than can be addressed adequately in the general education classroom. Even though a student's needs are relatively significant, districts must try to provide services for that student in as least of a restrictive location as possible. However, some students may have more intense needs, and when pull-out services are planned in order to meet those needs, the specialists who work with the student need to have close contact and communication with the general education teacher(s). Delivering students' special education through pull-out classes is sometimes referred to as resource room services (Bateman & Linden, 2012).

Self-Contained Classrooms. There are some students who have needs greater than can be met in a general education classroom or in a pull-out program. They may require a lower student-to-teacher ratio and more individual time to assist them with developing needed knowledge and skills. The pace and structure of the general education classroom may prevent them from receiving an appropriate education. These classrooms often are based in general education buildings, and there may be interaction with nondisabled peers during the course of the day. This interaction with nondisabled peers may happen during transportation to and from school, in before and after-school activities, during nonacademic programming, over lunch, or during whole-school activities or assemblies. Although school districts and states may have different regulations, often self-contained classrooms involve a student attending this classroom for over 50% of their school day. Generally, in self-contained classrooms, a special education teacher is responsible for most or all of the academic instruction.

Specially Designed Instruction: Related Services

In addition to special education services, a student may require related services. Related services are those services "required to assist a child with a disability to benefit from special education" (IDEA Regulations, 34 CFR § 300.24[a], 2006). To be eligible for related services, students must first qualify for special education under one of the qualifying disability categories. Related services cannot be provided as stand-alone services, with the exception of speech-language services. (Speech-language services can be the only services required for a student who qualifies for special education in the categories of Speech or Language Impaired but can also be as related services for students who are eligible in other categories). An IEP cannot contain <u>only</u> related services. In addition, only services necessary to help a student with a disability benefit from special education can be provided.

Determining Eligibility for Related Services

Eligibility for related services is determined on an individual basis as part of the IEP process. The student's needs identified in the PLAAFP statements clarify any specific need that should be addressed through a related service. After an IEP team identifies an eligible student in need of a related services, the IEP requires a statement of the "anticipated frequency, location, and duration" of all special education services, included the related services, to be provided (IDEA Regulations, 34 CFR § 300.320 [a][7], 2006). In table 7.3 we provide a list of possible related services.

TABLE 7.3   Nonexhaustive List of Related Services

Included Related Services	Excluded Related Services
Audiology services	Medical devices (surgically implanted)
Counseling	Maintenance of device
Interpreting services	Optimization of the function device
Occupational therapy	Replacement of device
Orientation and mobility services	Services performed by a medical doctor (except diagnostic to determine needs)
Parent counseling and training	
Physical therapy	
Psychological services	
Recreation, including therapeutic	
Rehabilitation counseling	
School nurse services	
Social work services	
Transportation	

This is not an exhaustive list but gives examples to illustrate the range of related services. The specific related services necessary for the eligible student will depend on the unique circumstances of the student. Readers should note that the only areas in which a school district does not need provide related services are services (a) which can only be provided by a licensed physician, except for diagnostic or evaluation services, or (b) which include medically implanted devices such as cochlear implants or are required for the optimization of such devices (however, children with surgically implanted devices may receive other related services as necessary). The *Endrew F.* standard exemplifies this expectation in that the services must be reasonably calculated to enable a student to make progress appropriate in light of the student's circumstances.

Processes for Determining Related Services

After careful review of a student's evaluation information and PLAAFP statements, the IEP team determines the specific related service(s) the student is to receive (if any) and includes those services in the student's IEP. If a related service is deemed necessary, the appropriate related-service professional should be involved in developing the IEP. That individual may be invited by the school or parent to join the IEP team as a person "with knowledge or special expertise about the child" (IDEA Regulations, 34 CFR § 300.322[a][6], 2006). Unless a related service is a special education service needed in order to receive a FAPE (e.g., speech and language services), the Office of Special Education Programs (OSEP) in the US Department of Education took the position that the IDEA does not require that a student's IEP must include separate goals or STOs for related services (Letter to Hayden, 1994). Officials at OSEP reasoned that because related services are needed to enable a student to benefit from their special education programming, goals that evaluate the effectiveness of special education automatically evaluated a supporting related service. They give the example of a related service of transportation being provided solely to enable the student to get to school. So, if a student had an IEP goal in reading and writing and was in a resource room for reading, transportation to the school with the resource room would be essential to benefit from his or her special education. If the special education program was successful, the student would reach the goal. Transportation would clearly be a critical related service in the student's IEP; however, it would not require a separate goal.

A student's IEP must also specify the following factors with respect to each related service:

- *When* the service will begin.
- *How often* it will be provided and for what amount of time.
- *Where* it will be provided [IDEA Regulations, 34 CFR § 300.320[a][7], 2006).

All students should be treated individually. Keep in mind that a student with a disability may not require any related service, whereas other students may require a combination of services. The list of related services builds upon other developmental, corrective, or supportive services that may be required to help a student with a disability benefit from special education.

After the type and number of related services are noted in the student's IEP, the school district must ensure all of the related services specified are, in fact, provided. Changes in the amount or type of services listed in the IEP cannot be made without another IEP meeting.

General Strategies for IEP Teams

When working on the IEP team, it is important to pay attention to the work being done by the related-service provider, because they often are only with the student for a limited amount of time each week, and the skills taught will need to be practiced and reinforced in the general and special education classrooms. Additionally, it is important to recognize the value the related-service providers bring to the student's educational experience. Related-service providers are an important resource. Learn what each related-service provider offers to the student as well as the supports they can provide to the other team members who work with the student, including parents.

General Tips for Working with Related Service Providers

Support and Introduction

Often, related-service providers travel from school to school (sometimes from district to district). It is important to welcome them to your school and invite them to school activities, as they are a valuable part of the student's education. Work to make them feel like they are supported and included.

Recognize Them as Professional Related-service providers often have extensive training and background to be certified for their job. They are professionals and also are a great resource, and they often have suggestions for students with disabilities that may actually help you with many other students in your classroom.

Observe Their Practices If possible, observe the person providing the related services to get a better understanding of the skills they are addressing with the students, but also see if there is a chance for them to observe the student in your classroom to determine if there are tips or strategies you can reinforce on a regular basis.

Share Discuss with the related-service providers about the student's schedule, their preferred activities, and any aspect of the curriculum that may be causing problems. Talk with them about issues and concerns you may notice. Teachers are often working with the student more hours per week than a related-service provider. Talk with the provider about skills or strategies you should implement or any other follow-through activities you can provide for the student.

Respond Promptly Respond promptly to any questions and concerns and requests from the provider for more information about how the student is doing. Related-service providers, like many educators, have heavy schedules and must work with multiple students every day. Respect this reality and arrange meetings to talk with them about issues at times convenient for them.

Specially Designed Instruction: Supplementary Aids and Services

According to Tatgenhorst et. al. (2014), the deceptively simple definition of supplementary aids and services in the IDEA vastly understates its importance, and when

IEP teams fail to adequately consider them, a school district will likely be violating a student's right to a FAPE. The IDEA definition is

> Supplementary aids and services means aids, services, and other supports that are provided in general education classes, other education-related settings, and in extracurricular and nonacademic settings, to enable children with disabilities to be educated with nondisabled children to the maximum extent appropriate. (IDEA Regulations, 34 CFR § 300.42, 2006)

The purpose of providing supplementary aids and services is to support students with disabilities as active participants with nondisabled peers, as well as to enable their access to the general curriculum. To that end, supplementary aids and services include modifications to the general curriculum to ensure that "a child with a disability is not removed from education in age-appropriate regular classrooms solely because of needed modification in the general curriculum" (IDEA Regulations, 34 CFR § 300.116 [e], 2006). The regulations further require that

> Special classes, separate schooling, or other removal of children with disabilities from the regular educational environment occurs only if the nature or severity of the disability is such that education in regular classes with the use of supplementary aids and services cannot be achieved satisfactorily. (IDEA Regulations, 34 CFR § 300.114 [e], 2006)

Providing appropriate supplementary aids and services is extremely important; they may be necessary to ensure a student receives a FAPE and is educated in the least restrictive environment (see chapter 8 on placement).

Although officials in the US Department of Education have not defined the term "supplementary aids and services," the following examples were provided in the 1999 regulations:

> Certain changes may need to be made in the regular education classroom to make it possible for a child with a disability to participate more fully and effectively in general curricular activities that may take place in that room. These changes could involve (for example) providing a special seating arrangement for a child; using professional or student "tutors" to help the child; raising the level of the child's desk; allowing the child more time to complete a given assignment; working with the parents to help the child at home; and providing extra help to the child before or after the beginning of the school day. "Modifications" or "accommodations" could involve providing a particular assistive technology device for the child, or modifying the child's desk in some manner that facilitates the child's ability to write or hold books, etc. (*Federal Register*, v. 64, p. 12,595, 1999)

In the same document, officials also made it clear that supplementary aids and supports could include specific training and professional development for school personnel. Moreover, a student's IEP team would be the appropriate forum for determining if training is needed, deciding what the content should be, who should provide the training, and when and where the training should take place. In the commentary to the 1999 regulations, officials also noted that such training would "normally be targeted directly on assisting the teacher to meet a unique and specific need of the child and not simply to participate in an in-service training program that is generally available within a public agency" (*Federal Register*, v. 64,

p. 12,592, 1999a). Furthermore, such training would be provided to teachers or parents on behalf of the student to help them work more effectively with a student (*Federal Register*, v. 64, p. 12,593, 1999).

What Does This Mean?

As you can see from the federal definitions and guidance, supplementary aids and services are used to create a system of support(s) enabling students with disabilities to participate and learn in general education classrooms or at least in general education buildings. Supplementary aids and services make it possible for students with disabilities to be included in general education classrooms, in addition to nonacademic and extracurricular activities.

The determination of the necessary supplementary aids and services for the student must be given serious attention. There should be a systematic approach to considering all the necessary aids and services that might be of assistance for a student, and then also a structured method to evaluate their effectiveness. IEP team members should gather and analyze information about a student in relation to environmental and instructional demands of the general education classroom(s) and work to determine the needs of the student that must be addressed to allow them to participate meaningfully. Supplementary aids and services that would allow the student to participate are then delineated. The steps in the process for determining for supplementary aids and services are described next.

Step 1: Observe the Needs of the Student in the General Education Classroom

The first step is to make an environmental profile, which is a compilation of information about the methods, materials, practices, and physical requirements of a general education setting. If possible, a member of the team should observe the student in the general education classroom(s) in which a student would participate if they did not have a disability. This observation should occur across the day considering the needs of the student during structured and unstructured parts of the day, including lunch, class changes, and recess for elementary students. If a full-scale observation is not a possibility, the team should consider requirements similar to potential choices. After the specific classroom is selected, members of the IEP team can revisit the setting analysis, as necessary, adding more specific information to ensure the student has the supports necessary to participate in the classroom. This information is typically provided by a general education teacher in conjunction with the special education teacher, as they talk about the needs of the student and how they align with the demands of the classroom(s).

Step 2: Identify Barriers

To be able to determine whether a student can be effective in the general education classroom, it is necessary to identify the student's skills, learning characteristics, and needs necessary to consider the instructional and social demands, as well as the classroom routines for this individual student. Information about the student can come from the PLAAFP statements about the student, but also from discussions between the general and special education teachers.

This information provides the list of what is needed by the student to access the general education classroom. The purpose of this list is to be proactive in determining mismatches between a student and the instructional environment before actual problems occur. Selecting appropriate supports can then help to eliminate or minimize the instructional impact of any mismatch between what and how a student learns.

The team must identify the appropriate supplementary aids and services needed to support the student's learning and participation in the general education setting(s) based on a careful consideration of the interaction between general education classroom characteristics and practices, the individual student's learning needs and behavioral characteristics, and potential strategies available to serve as an instructional scaffold for the student. The team also should identify the supports necessary for the education staff to effectively implement the supports included in the student's IEP.

There are also needs to be time for the team to meet and discuss their observations and data about what supports are working and what needs to be modified. Too often, we provide strategies for the teachers to use without providing opportunities for the team to reflect upon and refine strategies for the student. A useful five-step procedure to enable IEP teams in such collaborative planning is to (a) scheduled time for team meetings and planning sessions, (b) ensure there are instructional supports that foster collaboration, be it co-teaching or shared paraprofessional support, (c) provide professional development for the teachers related to collaboration with a focus on teacher-to-teacher coaching about what they find helpful in particular situations and what they wish they would have done differently, (d) provide assistance in working with the student's assistive technology devices by checking assumptions about what the student knows what to do and how the device works, and (e) work with the parents to address their views and concerns about what is working and not working for their student.

In fully evaluating the effectiveness of the assigned supports, regular progress monitoring is required. The team must use the information provided by the progress monitoring to make adaptations and changes as needed. It is inappropriate to find out a student is not making progress and yet fail to make changes to the supports in place. When progress monitoring data indicate a lack of improvement, making the necessary adaptions so the student can be successful in the general education curriculum and with the demands of the classrooms is the central task of the team. In some cases, the IEP team may implement a support strategy, evaluate its effectiveness over time, and determine that it is not having the desired effect. The important part of the process is that the team keeps trying to make changes and improve the program for the child.

Specially Designed Instruction: Program Modifications and Support for School Personnel

The content of the IEP must include a "statement of the special education and related services and supplementary aids and services, based on peer-reviewed research to the extent practicable, to be provided to the child, or on behalf of the child, **and a** *statement of the program modifications or supports for school personnel that will be provided*" (emphasis added) (IDEA Regulations, 34 CFR § 300.320[a][4], 2006). Most educators are familiar with the concepts of "special education" and "related services" because these are directed toward student interventions. The latter part of this statement reminds us that it is the IEP team which has the responsibility of determining if supports and program modifications are necessary to help staff who are working with a student better understand and make modifications to programming that may be needed to meet the student's needs. Program modifications and supports for school personnel are focused on helping the staff who are working to implement the IEP. It is also important that such supports or modifications are targeted for the needs of that child and found in the IEP.

Pre-planned generic professional development or trainings that all teachers might use in their overall instruction, while perhaps beneficial, are not the intent of this requirement. Rather, there must be a clear, logical connection across (a) the needs of the individual student identified in the PLAAFP, (b) the student's annual goals, and (c) planned supports or modifications that are to be provided. The general education teacher and special educators serving on the child's IEP team may be helpful in identifying what knowledge, skills, and tools would be needed to educate their students as effectively as possible. Having such information and resources usually increases the likelihood that the student will meet the goals outlined in the IEP.

Supports for school personnel may include (a) training on the use of specialized equipment to assist the student and (b) training on instructional or behavior management methods needed to best implement the IEP to help the student meet goals and objectives in academic and/or behavioral domains. For example, trainings for teachers and/or support staff on how to use a student's assistive technology device or software applications or guidance for school lunchroom, recess, or bus assistants on the use of strategies to respond safely to a student's outbursts detailed in a behavior plan might be reasonable supports for school personnel.

Neither the IDEA nor regulations to the IDEA include a list of these supports and modifications because again—like all other aspects of the IEP—such decisions are individualized to the student. Other examples of supports might include:

(1) arranging for an autism specialist to provide direct training to teachers and staff about a specific intervention strategy (e.g., discrete trial training),
(2) having an outside consultant offer direct training and support to teachers and other staff members on the use of a specific data collection system in community settings, and
(3) having a pediatrician familiar with the unique medical needs of a child offer training and guidance to school staff working with a particular child.

A key point to stress is that the supports for school personnel provided are necessary components of the child's IEP; they are not "add-on" requirements to advantage a student. Training must be followed by monitoring to assure that needed supports are being provided—and that they are offered in an appropriate manner. It is essential to proactively encourage their acceptance and understanding of their use by all staff involved with the student.

Transition Services

What Is Transition?

The purpose of transition is to help students become prepared for post-school life. Post-school outcomes are an important part of the secondary education for all students. For eligible students with disabilities, it is vital we use the last few years of K-12 education to help get them as ready as possible for their post-school lives. Transition is intended to be a coordinated set of activities provided by the school and other agencies from outside the school, designed to promote a successful transition from high school to post-secondary education or employment, and independent living. Transition services must be based on a transition assessment in which a student's strengths, preferences, and interests are identified (see chapter 5). These assessments focus on a student's strengths; the ability and interests of the student - and not their limitations - are afforded much more attention. Such a strength-oriented approach had not been used prior to the inclusion of these requirements in the IDEA (Flexer, 2007).

What Is Included in Transition Planning?

There are some commonalities in transition-planning processes, but the goal of transition planning is as individual as the needs of the student. The federal regulations state:

> Beginning not later than the first IEP to be in effect when the student turns 16, or younger if determined appropriate by the IEP team, and updated annually thereafter, the IEP must include:

- Appropriate measurable postsecondary goals based upon age-appropriate transition assessments related to training, education, employment and, where appropriate, independent living skills;
- The transition services (including courses of study) needed to assist the student in reaching those goals. (Individuals with Disabilities Education Act, 20 USC § 1415[m], 2004)

As noted in other chapters, the program developed for the student is based on the student's individual needs, and for transition it is also based on the student's interests, strengths, and preferences. The IEP team should meet to talk about these aspects of the student's life and future goals and desires. The IEP team should ensure there are specific goals and objectives of the IEP designed to help the student prepare for post-school life while still addressing their current needs. For example, if a student with a learning disability is interested in college, time in high school that would help them develop skills to support their success in college, such as writing, time management, and note-taking should figure prominently in their transition plans. Students not planning on going to college could be provided opportunities to do job shadowing to help determine the specific skills necessary for different lines of work. All courses provided for the student and experiences during the transition period would relate to ensure the student graduates from school and builds the skills they need to be successful in the next step in their life after high school, whether that be continued education, vocation, and/or independent living.

To facilitate IEP development, the team needs to help students make decisions about possible future career choices. This process may include interest inventories, talking with the student, and specific skills assessments. The input of parents is another source of information that should be integral to this process. Assessment tools that can be used to help identify a student's specific strengths are typically conducted by the school counselors or the special education teacher(s). The goal of transition planning is to develop a statement of the transition services, including courses of study needed to assist the student in reaching those goals. The statement of transition services should relate directly to the student's post-secondary goals.

Who Should Participate in Transition Planning?

As students plan to transition into adult roles, two groups of service providers will be involved. In high school, the IEP team is primarily responsible for transition planning. After high school, the student begins receiving support from adult service providers. Oftentimes, the parent and student are the only consistent members of the team through the transition from high school to adult services, so it is extremely important for the IEP team members to educate families to help prepare them to advocate for their student.

An important member of the team is the student. Students are often not included in the IEP development when they are in elementary school, with many students receiving special education but not knowing why or for how long. However, as we start transition planning, we need to ensure students are involved. The purpose of transition planning is to prepare the student for their future. In order to be effective, we need to ask about their preferences and develop goals and programming in response to their answers. We also need to realize the student's interests will change over time, so ongoing transition assessment is important to ensure goals stay relevant (see chapter 5).

When we address the interests of the student, our task is to help students develop ambitious, yet achievable goals. Very few students ever become professional athletes or stunt-car drivers. Although goals should be student-centered, it is important that students understand activities required to accomplish those goals and develop back-up plans and strategies to ensure the student progresses toward successful adult roles. IEP teams are not trying to stifle a student's dream, but to help with the decision-making process and the reality of what is required.

Parents should also be involved in the transition planning process, as they are often the only consistent support between high school and adult services. We need to ensure that parents are heavily involved in transition planning and that their viewpoints are represented in the decision-making process for the student.

The Domains of Adulthood to Consider

The definition of transition services mentions specific domains of adulthood to be addressed during transition planning. They are:

- post-secondary education
- vocational education
- integrated employment (including supported employment)
- continuing and adult education
- adult services
- independent living
- community participation

Developing Post-School Goals

Once a goal has been identified, the IEP team must develop a legally compliant post-school goal. Post-school goals indicate what the student will accomplish up to twelve months following high school. Each goal has a condition statement; an observable, measurable behavior; a location; and a time frame. For example:

> *After high school, Brian will study concert piano at Cleveland State University within 12 months of graduation.*

The condition defines when the goal will occur—after high school. Then, the goal states Brian will study concert piano as a major, while attending Cleveland State University. Finally, the goal sets a clear time frame of twelve months after graduation. Thus, in order to meet this goal, Brian must enroll at Cleveland State and begin a concert piano major within twelve months.

Once the goal is established, the IEP team must define the transition services or activities the school will provide to support the student on the path to achieving those goals. Transition services or activities may involve additional assessment, such as career inventories, or more structured programs, like vocational training in the community. Goals focusing on post-secondary education may focus on taking advanced placement courses, the ACT, or the SAT to help prepare for college.

Planning for Transition Services or Activities

The IEP team is responsible for identifying transition services or activities logically related to the student's post-school goals. For example, if the student's goal is to attend the local community college to study welding, then the team should identify any activities or experience that will help them accomplish that goal. For example, they would need to continue taking academic high school courses so they would be eligible for community college, but they might also attend a half-day vocational program to get some experience with welding safety procedures. The team could also help them develop college applications or develop college admissions essays. However, each of these services or activities should be necessary to help the student accomplish the post-school goal.

Transition in Practice

After the IEP team has developed post-school goals, services should be developed to support the student's progress toward accomplishing those goals. For example, if Brian plans to attend Cleveland State to study concert piano, his IEP team should identify skills and activities that would help support these goals. For example, once Brian receives his high school credit, the team might allow him to take independent studies as music electives, so he is able to work on practicing piano or recording his performances. The team might explore whether he could take college-level music theory through a dual enrollment program as part of his high school experience. They may also help Brian prepare his piano resume to help him prepare to apply for colleges. Each of these activities directly align with his post-school goal and help him move closer to accomplishing that goal.

Goals can focus on post-secondary education, as well as independent living or employment. For example, if Yasmine's goal is: *After high school, Yasmine will work fifteen hours per week at Carissa's Crazy Cupcakes within twelve months of graduation*, the team can prepare a course of study promoting Yasmine's job skill development, specifically related to the food services industry. For example, she might take family and consumer sciences courses to help her develop kitchen safety skills. She might also work at the school café, to learn how to run a register or fill student orders. The IEP team also may work with the transition coordinator to get her a vocational training placement at a local bakery or coffee shop to help her further develop employment skills, making her more likely to accomplish her post-school goal of working at the bakery.

Summary of Transition Services

IDEA requires transition planning be integrated within legally compliant IEPs by the time a student turns 16. The purpose of transition planning is to set and achieve meaningful post-secondary goals for adult living. To accomplish these goals, the IEP must include a current transition assessment, individualized and student-centered post-school goals, and activities to support those goals. Team members should work with the student and family to identify ambitious, achievable post-school goals, ensuring family members are actively involved to ensure a successful transition for the student.

Extended School Year Services

ESY services are special education services provided to students with disabilities beyond the 180-day school year. IDEA requires that school districts provide ESY services if a student needs these services to receive FAPE. The reason for providing ESY services is that some eligible students will regress on skills and abilities so much during a break and take so long to recoup what they have lost that it threatens FAPE. In such cases, ESY services are then provided during breaks in the educational schedule to prevent this loss. Importantly, ESY services are not day care or respite services, and even though students may benefit from summer programming, not all students are eligible to receive such services. The determination about ESY eligibility is a decision of a student's IEP team, of which all members of the team should participate.

The regulations to the IDEA require that school districts ensure that ESY services are available as necessary to provide FAPE; however, they should be provided only if a student's IEP team determines the services are needed for the student to receive a FAPE (IDEA Regulations, 34 CFR § 300.106[a][1-2]). Moreover, the regulations prohibit school districts from limiting ESY services to particular categories of disabilities or unilaterally limiting the type, amount, or duration of those services (IDEA Regulations, 34 CFR § 300106[a][3][i-ii], 2006).

ESY services are not the same thing as summer school. Nonetheless, school districts may not deny summer ESY services to students with disabilities even if the district does not provide summer services to other students. ESY services can also be provided during extended breaks that occur during the school year, not just during the summer. Like the other special education services students receive, they are provided at no cost to the parents.

Requirements of ESY Services

All students who are eligible for special education should be considered to determine if ESY services are appropriate for them. It is understood most students will lose some educational progress they have made during the school year, but there are specific questions that can help the team address the necessity of services for eligible students. The questions the team considers are as follows: (a) Will a student lose critical skills during an extended break in instruction? and (b) Will the student take an inordinate amount of time for them to recoup those skills?

Teachers should take data during the school year about the progress a student is making. It is important that progress monitoring data be taken just before a break in programming and then just after the return to determine if the student has failed to retain previously learned material. This aids in determining a need for ESY services. If a student has a history of regressing and struggling to relearn, that must be taken into account. Without such data, it will be difficult to make an informed decision. The IEP team may ask the following questions to predict the likelihood of a student regressing and then failing to recoup in a reasonable amount of time.

* Does the student have difficulty retaining skills over shorter breaks?
* Does the student need continual reinforcement to keep skills during the regular school year?
* Does the student have behavior issues that get in the way of learning during the school year?
* Is the student making steady progress toward meeting the IEP goals? And will a break in services threaten that progress?
* Is the student about to master a critical skill?
* Does it take the student an inordinate amount of time to recoup lost skills?

Limits to ESY Services

Not every student is eligible for ESY services. Additionally, states have different rules and regulations relating to eligibility. All students receiving special education need to be considered every year for the ESY services. Being found eligible one year does not guarantee eligibility the following year.

Summary of ESY Services

The services provided must be individualized to the needs of a student. This does not necessarily mean that all of a student's IEP will be addressed during ESY programming: It may just be one or two goals. Important points to understand about providing ESY services are as follows:

1) Parents are not obligated to send their child to ESY if they choose not to. There is no obligation that students participate in ESY programming. If a student needs ESY services, the services must be offered, but parents can choose not to participate.
2) The purpose of ESY is to ensure that the student does not fall too far behind what would have happened if there had not been an extended break in their programming. The purpose of ESY services is to maintain skills and not to accelerate skill development.
3) The determination of ESY eligibility is to be made on an annual basis.
4) The determination of ESY eligibility is only for students eligible for special education and related services - not all students in the school.
5) The determination of eligibility is an individual determination, not based on the student's disability but based on the needs they present during the course of the school year.
6) All decisions related to ESY are IEP team decisions. These decisions should be documented with clear reasons why or why not ESY determinations were made.

Ensuring That Services Are Delivered with Fidelity

Failing to implement the services, related services, supplementary aids and services, and program modifications included in a student's IEP can lead to a denial of FAPE. In fact, Zirkel has asserted (2017) that implementation of the IEP is the third dimension of FAPE, along with the first dimensions, procedural and substantive. Parents have asserted that school districts have failed to provide FAPE because the school district failed to implement even when their children's IEPs were procedurally correct and substantially appropriate.

By the end of an IEP meeting, all participants should understand exactly what they need to do in order to correctly implement the student's program. In many cases, the teachers who developed a student's IEP will not be the only teachers implementing it. In such situations, fidelity or accuracy of implementing a student's IEP will be facilitated by creating a checklist that describes (a) who is responsible for executing parts of the IEP and (b) what that person should do in simple and concrete language. In essence, an implementation checklist can translate the IEP into the tasks that enable teachers and other involved service providers to implement their particular components of the student's IEP. For example, if a student's IEP requires that each of the student's teachers complete a behavior point chart at the end of class, and the same IEP requires that at the end of the school day a counselor picks up the student from class to briefly discuss his or her day and add up the points on his or her point chart, the teachers and the counselors would be given their individual implementation checklists. Table 7.4 represents the implementation checklist given to each teacher, and table 7.5 represents the implementation checklist provided to the counselor. In both cases, the implementation checklists should be explained them, and they and the LEA representative on the IEP team should sign the document.

TABLE 7.4   Implementation Checklist Example—Teacher

IEP Checklist—Mr. Shriner, Social Studies Teacher

Date _____   Student's name

                                                                     Nick _____

Implementation Procedures   **Yes**   **No**

1. Greet Nick when he enters the classroom and ask him for his behavior point chart.
2. Remind Nick of how he may earn his behavior points.
3. Provide frequent positive acknowledgments to Nick and the rest of the class.
4. Give Nick his point chart at the end of class.

                                                    Signatures

Teacher: _____

LEA Representative: _____

TABLE 7.5   Implementation Checklist Example—Counselor

IEP Checklist—Mr. Bateman, Counselor

                                                                     Student's name

Date _____   **Nick** _____

Implementation Procedures   **Yes**   **No**

1. Meet Nick at his last hour class at the end of school day.
2. Get Nick's point chart and ask him about his day.
3. Provide frequent positive acknowledgments to Nick about his day.
4. Sign the behavior point chart and give it to Nick to bring to his parents.

                                                    Signatures

Teacher: _____

LEA Representative: _____

TABLE 7.6   Practices to Follow and Practices to Avoid

Practices to Follow	Practices to Avoid
Services must be based on needs identified in the PLAAFP statement.	Do not base services on the availability of the service in the school district.
Services should be based on PRR.	Do not use lack of funds, administrative convenience, or cost as an excuse not to provide services.
Services must be so clearly specified that at the end of the IEP meeting all parties understand what will be provided to a student or on behalf of a student.	Do not use vague or overly general language in describing the services to be provided to a student.
Determine supplementary aids and services and program modifications that a student will need to participate in general education, which may include training of teachers or parents.	Do not provide services based on a student's category (e.g., only students with emotional and behavioral disorders received behavioral programming).
Ensure that all services are implemented as agreed upon in the IEP.	

Summary

Students' IEPs must include statements of the specific services to be provided by the school, including special education services, related services, supplementary aids and services, and program modifications. The purpose of service statements are to outline the programming that will be provided to students with disabilities so they may attain their IEP goals. The statement of services must be unambiguous and specific in order that the school's commitment of resources is clear to parents and other members of the team. Moreover, the services arrived at through the collaborative IEP process must be implemented. In the words of the US Supreme Court, the services developed and implemented must enable a student to make progress appropriate in light of his or her circumstances (*Endrew F. v. Douglas County School District*, 2017). Table 7.6 summarizes the procedures to follow and procedures to avoid in developing service statements in students' IEPs.

CHAPTER 8

Determining Placement

When making a placement decision, "a group of persons, including the parents, and other persons knowledgeable about the child, the meaning of the evaluation data, and the placement options" (IDEA Regulations, 34 CFR § 300.116[a][1], 2006) determine where and how a student's IEP will be implemented. The following requirements guide the team in making the placement decision: First, the least restrictive environment (LRE) mandate governs the placement decision (IDEA Regulations, 34 CFR § 300.116[a][2], 2006). Second, a student's placement must be based on his or her IEP (IDEA Regulations, 34 CFR § 300.116[b][2], 2006). Third, the team must determine the placement for a student at least annually (IDEA Regulations, 34 CFR § 300.116[b][1], 2006). Fourth, a student should be educated in the school he or she would normally attend unless the student's IEP requires otherwise (IDEA Regulations, 34 CFR § 300.116[b][3], 2006). Fifth, the student should be educated as close as possible to his or her home school (IDEA Regulations, 34 CFR § 300.116[c], 2006). Sixth, a student should not be removed from an age-appropriate regular classroom solely because of needed modifications in the general education classroom (IDEA Regulations, 34 CFR § 300.116[e], 2006).

In December 2017, the Office of Special Education and Rehabilitative Services (OSERS) in the US Department of Education released a document titled "*Questions and Answers (Q&A) on U. S. Supreme Court Case Decision, Endrew F. v. Douglas County School District Re-1*" (US Department of Education, 2017). The 17th question answered in the document was: "How does the *Endrew F.* decision impact placement decisions?" The answer provided by officials in OSERS was an excellent summary of the placement determination process. In their answer, officials at OSERS noted that:

> Consistent with the decision in *Endrew F.*, the Department (of Education) continues to recognize that it is essential to make individualized determinations about what constitutes appropriate instruction and services for each child with a disability and the placement in which that instruction and those services can be provided

for the child. There is no 'one-size-fits all' approach to educating children with disabilities. Rather, placement decisions must be individualized and made consistent with a child's IEP. (US Department of Education, Question and Answers, 2017)

In this chapter we (a) review the placement requirements of the IDEA, including the importance of individualization, parental participation, LRE, and the continuum of alternative placements; (b) describe the placement requirements to which IEP teams must adhere; and (c) offer principles to guide an IEP team's placement decisions. We included this chapter as the final chapter in the book for an important reason: The placement decision we make for a student in special education must be based on his or her IEP.

What Is a Placement Decision and Who Makes It?

Placement decisions are usually made by a student's IEP team, although the law does not specifically compel the IEP team to determine a student's placement. Neither is the placement decision technically part of the IEP process; nonetheless, the placement decision is almost always made by the IEP team and included in the IEP. This practice is acceptable because the IEP team meets the IDEA's personnel requirements for a placement team (i.e., the student's parents, persons knowledgeable about the child, the meaning of the evaluation data, and the placement options). Moreover, because the placement decision follows completion of the IEP and must be based on it, it is logical to complete the student's program of special education and related services and then turn to determining a student's placement. For the remainder of this chapter, we will refer to the placement decision as one that is made by a student's IEP team.

Placement determination is not just making a decision about the specific location where a student will receive their special education services. Rather, placement refers to the overall program, such as the classes and services a student will receive, not the particular school where a student will be provided the services (*T.Y. v. New York City Department of* Education, 2009). The placement is a point along the continuum of alternative placements, which we will describe later in this chapter. In fact, OSEP has made the distinction between special education placements from the location of special education services:

> Historically we have referred to "placement" as points along the continuum of placement options available for a child with a disability, and "location" as the physical surrounding, such as the classroom, in which a child with a disability receives special education and related services. Public agencies are strongly encouraged to place a child with a disability in the school and classroom the child would attend if the child did not have a disability. However, a (school district) may have two or more equally appropriate locations that meet the child's special education and related services needs and school administrators should have the flexibility to assign the child to a particular school or classroom, provided that determination is consistent with the decision of the group determining placement. (*Federal Register*, Vol. 71, No. 156, P. 46,588, 2006a)

If a school official were to contemplate moving a student to a different school or classroom that met the student's needs, they would have to issue the parents prior written notice in a reasonable amount of time before they implemented the change. Additionally, if a student were moved to a school other than their home school, the student would need to be provided transportation as a related service.

We next turn to an examination of the factors that school personnel must consider in making a placement decision. Of course, it goes without saying that a student's parents must be part of the team that makes the placement decision. When a team fails to involve parents in the placement decision, the team opens the school district up to charges of predetermination, a serious placement error that could lead to a decision that the school district denied a student a free appropriate public education (FAPE; Slater, 2010). Nonetheless, according to OSERS in the US Department of Education, the placement decision is a team decision and parental preference can neither be the sole nor predominant factor in determining a student's placement (*Letter to Burton*, 1991). This means the IEP team must strongly consider parental preference for a particular placement, but parental preference alone cannot be the basis for the final decision.

If school personnel cannot find a student's parents or are unable to convince them to attend a meeting, the team should use other methods to enable them to provide their input such as participating via telephone calls, videoconferencing, conference via computer (IDEA Regulations, 34 CFR § 300.501 [c][3], 2006). If the team has unsuccessfully made good-faith efforts to contact a student's parents, the team may go ahead and hold the placement meeting, but they should have thorough documentation of their unsuccessful attempts (IDEA Regulations, 34 CFR § 300.501 [c][34], 2006).

Additionally, the decision about the programming and placement for a student absolutely needs to be made based on the needs of the student, and not solely on factors such as (a) the student's disability label, (b) the severity of a student's disability, (c) what services and placement options happen to be available in the district, or (d) administrative convenience. The team may certainly consider these factors; however, none of these factors can be the sole determinant in the placement decision (Tatgenhorst et al., 2014). Teams may consider any harmful effects on a student or on the quality of services when selecting the LRE (IDEA Regulations, 34 CFR § 300.116[d], 2006).

Placement and Least Restrictive Environment

Students eligible for special education and related services are to receive their education in the LRE. Certainly, LRE is a very important factor in making the placement decision.

Federal regulations to the IDEA direct the IEP team to ensure that:

> To the maximum extent appropriate, children with disabilities, including children in public or private institutions or other care facilities, are educated with children who are non-disabled; and special classes, separate schooling, or other removal of children with disabilities from the regular educational environment occurs only if the nature or severity of the disability is such that education in regular classes with the use of supplementary aids and services cannot be achieved satisfactorily. (IDEA Regulations, 34 CFR § 300.114[a][2], 2006)

Clearly, students eligible for special education are to be educated in the least restrictive setting. What does this mean? To understand this concept, we need to discuss the different components of the requirement for providing services in the LRE. The first major component under the law is the presumption in favor of placements in the general education classroom. This preference is emphasized by the following IDEA regulation: "a student with a disability may not be removed from an age-appropriate general education classroom solely because of modifications needed to the general curriculum" (IDEA Regulations, 34 CFR § 300.116[e]). The regulations require that students eligible for special education are to be educated with their nondisabled peers to the maximum extent possible. IEP teams must make serious efforts to place and maintain students with disabilities in the general education classroom. This principle does not mean, however, that all students eligible for special education are to be placed in general education classrooms for their entire education. As Bateman & Linden (2012) asserted, "There is not now, and never has been, a requirement in the IDEA that all children with disabilities be 'included' or 'mainstreamed' in the regular (general education) classroom" (p. 16).

The Congressional authors of the IDEA recognized that for some students, other options are necessary to help them receive an appropriate education. Senator Robert Stafford, one of the primary writers of the original IDEA in 1975, in an article in 1978 wrote the following:

> The law also provides for an "appropriate" education to take place in the least restrictive environment. Some call this "mainstreaming" but that is not, in my view, a good expression because it implies that all handicapped children must be educated in the regular classroom. That is not at all what we in the Congress sought or intended. Rather, we had a view to integration with nonhandicapped children as the governing principle, especially where there is clear evidence that just the opposite was what was occurring in the past. (Stafford, 1978, p. 76)

The second part of the LRE requirement recognizes that to receive a FAPE, some students will need to receive their education in a more restrictive or segregated setting. The IDEA, however, requires that these more restricted settings be reserved for situations in which education in the general education classroom—even with the use of supplementary aids and services—will not result in a student receiving an appropriate education. Thus, if the IEP team recommends an option more restrictive than the general education classroom, they should make sure they have made good-faith efforts to maintain the student in less restrictive environments with the use of supplementary aids and services (see the *Daniel R.R.* and *Roncker* cases below).

When a student is placed in a more restrictive setting, the IEP team needs to emphasize integration with nondisabled peers whenever possible. To ensure this occurs, teams should consider transportation, morning activities, any classwork, lunch, assemblies, classes such as art/music, and other opportunities that may be available. In other words, every activity should be considered as a potential option for meaningful integration. Moreover, when considering a move to a more restrictive placement, the IEP team must use the continuum of alternative placements.

Continuum of Alternative Placements

The IDEA requires all school districts to have a full range, or continuum, of alternative placement options to meet student's unique academic and functional needs. The regulations require:

(a) Each [school district] shall ensure that a continuum of alternative placements is available to meet the needs of children with disabilities for special education and related services.
(b) The continuum required must:
    (1) Include the alternative placements (instruction in regular classes, special classes, special schools, home instruction, and instruction in hospitals and institutions); and
    (2) Make provision for supplementary services (such as resource room or itinerant instruction) to be provided in conjunction with regular class placement. (IDEA Regulations, 34 CFR § 300.551, 2006)

The continuum means all students can be placed in environments where they are able to receive the services they need. Decisions about the programming and placement of the student always are based on the unique circumstances of the student, and not on what is available within the district. Since the passage of the original version of IDEA in 1975, the continuum of alternative placement requirement has not changed. The continuum provides the IEP team options about where to provide the special education and related services to a student. As noted above, this decision is based entirely on the needs of the student, and not on the services that are available within the district.

What exactly is the continuum? States use different terms to describe the special education programming they have for eligible students. Basically, it is a stepwise progression from the general education classroom to programs where only students with disabilities are served. It begins with the general education classroom, including supplementary aids and services such as resource rooms to provide an appropriate education, and then lists more restrictive settings, such as self-contained settings and special schools. Placements are deemed more restrictive the less they resemble the general classroom environment (Champaign, 1993; Tatgenhorst et al., 2014; Yell et al., 2020). In all cases, the IEP considers the needs of the student, determines the extent of support the student requires to address those needs, and then determines where those services are to be provided. Textbox 8.1 is a depiction of the continuum.

> ### Textbox 8.1 The Continuum of Alternative Placements (IDEA Regulations, 34 CFR § 300.115, 2006)
>
> Each school district must ensure that a continuum of alternative placements is available to meet the needs of children with disabilities for special education and related services (IDEA Regulations, 34 CFR § 300.115[a], 2006).
>
> The continuum must include instruction in the:
>
> * Regular classroom
> * Special classes

* Special schools
* Home instruction
* Instruction in hospitals and institutions (IDEA Regulations, 34 CFR § 300.38, 2006).

Each school district must make provision for supplementary services (such as resource room or itinerant instruction) to be provided in conjunction with regular class placement (IDEA Regulations, 34 CFR § 300.115[a], 2006).

What Are Supplementary Aids and Services?

A key to maintaining students with disabilities in the general education classroom often lies in the implementation of supplementary aids and services. Thus, the first question that IEP team members must answer when considering a student's placement in a more restrictive setting is: "If we provide supplementary aids and services in the general education classroom, will that setting be appropriate?" When there is a reasonable likelihood a student can receive an appropriate education in the general education classroom with the use of supplementary aids and services, then the general education placement should be attempted (Yell et al., 2020). When the general education classroom is clearly inappropriate for a student, however, it is not required that a student be placed in the general education classroom to fail prior to being moved to an appropriate, but more restrictive placement (*D.F. v. Western School Corporation*, 1996). Nonetheless, IEP teams must consider placement in the general education classroom with supplementary aids and services before moving to a more restrictive environment.

Supplementary aids and services refer to specially designed instruction, adaptations, modifications, accommodations, and other supports that are provided in regular education classes, other education-related settings, and in extracurricular and nonacademic settings to enable children with disabilities to be educated with nondisabled children to the maximum extent appropriate (IDEA Regulations, 34 CFR § 300.42, 2006). Examples of supplementary aids and services include resource rooms, specialized teaching methodology, collaborative teaching, adapted learning materials and curriculum, para-educator assistance, specialized equipment, assistive technology services or devices, modified tests, and parallel curriculum.

Schools are responsible for providing the supplementary aids and services that are listed in the student's IEP. Because supplementary aids and services play an important role in maintaining students in less restrictive settings and ensuring that a student's placement addresses his or her needs, meeting this requirement is a critical responsibility of school and district personnel.

Case Law and Least Restrictive Environment

The actions that school district personnel take with respect to developing a student's IEP are clearly set forth in federal law and regulations (e.g., IDEA) and in state law and regulations. Moreover, the US Supreme Court rulings in two cases (i.e., *Board of Education v. Rowley*, 1982; *Endrew F. v Douglas County School District*) provided guidance on the degree of educational benefit that a student's IEP should likely or actually confer. Although the IDEA and state laws provide information on placing students in the LRE, there is no unifying Supreme Court ruling on LRE to provide guidance to hearing officers, judges, and school district officials. There are, however, a number of rulings from the US Courts of Appeals on LRE. Because these courts, often referred to as circuit courts or appellate courts, are below only the US Supreme Court with respect to the importance of their rulings, these court cases provide guidance for IEP teams in determining students' placement. The decisions in these cases we will discuss outline the considerations to be used in determining placements (often in more restrictive settings). Three different circuits of the US courts have established the dominant standards or tests that judges or hearing officers use in determining whether a student's placement was in the LRE. There are thirteen federal courts in the United States that sit below the US Supreme Court. As of this year, all but three of the circuit courts have adopted one of the three LRE tests from the following circuit court rulings: *Roncker v. Walter*, 1983; *Daniel R.R. v. State Board of Education*, 1989; *Sacramento City Unified School District v. Rachel H.*, 1994. We next review these standards.

The *Roncker* Test

Roncker v. Walter (1983) involved a nine-year-old boy with moderate intellectual disabilities, Neill Roncker. School personnel believed that a special school was the most appropriate placement for Neill. The parents objected because they believed Neill should be in his home school where he would be with his peers. The school personnel and Neill's parents agreed that he required special education, but they differed on where Neill should receive his services. The judges on the Sixth Circuit Court noted that the IDEA does not require mainstreaming in every case, but its requirement that mainstreaming be provided to the maximum extent appropriate indicates a very strong Congressional preference. However, if the benefits of mainstreaming were far outweighed by the benefits of the segregated setting and the student was a disruptive force in the classroom, mainstreaming was not required. The court found for the Ronckers.

The court developed a standard which required that when judges in lower courts (or hearing offers) in the Sixth Circuit heard an LRE test where a segregated facility was considered superior, the hearing officer or judge had to determine if those services could be feasibly provided in a nonsegregated setting. If they could, the placement in the segregated school would be inappropriate under the IDEA. This test, which has become known as the portability or feasibility test, was developed in the Sixth Circuit, which includes Kentucky, Michigan, Ohio, and Tennessee. The *Roncker* feasibility test has also been adopted by the

- US Court of Appeals for the Fourth Circuit, which includes the states of Maryland, North Carolina, South Carolina, Virginia, and West Virginia, and the
- US Court of Appeals for the Eighth Circuit, which includes Arkansas, Iowa, Nebraska, North Dakota, Minnesota, Missouri, and South Dakota.

The *Daniel* Test

Daniel R.R. v. State Board of Education (1989) involved Daniel, a six-year-old child with Down syndrome. When he entered school, his parents asked that Daniel be included in a prekindergarten for half of the school day and a special education class for the other half of the school day. A few months into the school year, school personnel decided that Daniel needed a full-time special education placement because he was not participating in class and was failing to master any of the skills that were being taught, despite having almost-constant attention and instruction from the teacher and aide. The parents requested a due process hearing, and the case was eventually heard by the US Court of Appeals for the Fifth Circuit.

The circuit court ruled in favor of the Board of Education. According to the court opinion, Congress had created a preference for mainstreaming but also created a tension between the appropriate education and mainstreaming provisions of the act. Congress recognized the general education environment would not be suitable for all students with disabilities, and a special setting may be necessary to provide an appropriate education. Thus, the FAPE mandate took precedent over the LRE mandate. The circuit court found that the *Roncker* test required too intrusive an inquiry into a school district's actions, so the court created a two-pronged test for hearing offices and judges to use in deciding LRE cases. The first question asked is, Has the school attempted to accommodate the student by providing sufficient supplementary aids, services, and program modifications in the general education setting? If the answer is no, the LRE mandate of the IDEA has been violated. The second question is, If the student cannot receive sufficient accommodations to be successful in the general education classroom, has the school mainstreamed the student to the maximum extent appropriate to ensure integration with nondisabled students? Again, if the answer is no, the LRE mandate of the IDEA has been violated. When the circuit court applied the two-pronged test, the judges found in favor of the school district.

The *Daniel* two-pronged test was subsequently adopted by the following circuit courts:

- US Court of Appeals for the Second Circuit, which includes the states of Connecticut, New York, and Rhode Island
- US Court of Appeals for the Third Circuit, which includes the states of Delaware, New Jersey, and Pennsylvania
- US Court of Appeals for the Fifth Circuit, which includes the states of Louisiana, Mississippi, and Texas
- US Court of Appeals for the Tenth Circuit, which includes the states of Colorado, Kansas, New Mexico, Oklahoma, Utah, and Wyoming
- US Court of Appeals for the Eleventh Circuit, which includes the states of Alabama, Georgia, and Florida.

The *Rachel H.* Test

Sacramento City Unified School District v. Rachel H. (1994) involved a young girl, Rachel Holland, with intellectual disabilities and speech and language impairments. In this case, heard by the US Court of Appeals for the Ninth Circuit, Rachel's parents believed she should be placed in a general education classroom for the entire school day. School district officials contended that Rachel's disability was too severe for her to benefit from being in a general education classroom and proposed she be placed in special education for academic subjects, attending the general education class only for nonacademic activities (e.g., art, music, lunch, recess). The circuit court ruled that Rachel could be successfully educated in a general education classroom with modifications to the curriculum and the assistance of a part-time para-educator.

The circuit court adopted the following four-factor test to balance the benefits of general education placement with supplementary aids and services. First, what were the educational benefits of full-time general education placement with supplementary aids and services, and how did these benefits compare to those of a special class placement? Second, what were the nonacademic benefits of full-time general education placement with supplementary aids and services? Third, what effect did the student have on the general education classroom teacher and children? Fourth, what was the cost of mainstreaming the student and did this cost significantly affect the education of other students? The circuit court found the four factors to be in favor of Rachel H., thus ruling against the school district and for Rachel H.

Although this test has not been adopted by any other circuit court, it is significant because of the number of states in the Ninth Circuit. The US Court of Appeals for the Ninth Circuit includes the states of Alaska, Arizona, California, Hawaii, Idaho, Montana, Nevada, Oregon, Utah, Oregon, and Washington.

Summary of the Judicial Tests

What are we to make of these judicial LRE tests? There are 44 states in the jurisdictions of the circuit courts that issued rulings in accordance with the *Roncker*, *Daniel R.R.*, and *Rachel H.* cases (e.g., Second, Third, Fourth, Fifth, Sixth, Eighth, Ninth, Tenth, and Eleventh), so LRE cases in these states will involve the tests used in their respective circuits. Three judicial circuits (i.e., the First, Seventh, and the District of Columbia) have not adopted a clear LRE test. We advise school district officials in the states with an LRE ruling to consider these tests when assessing how their IEP teams make decisions regarding student's placement in the LRE. We also believe school district officials in states without LRE rulings would be well-advised to follow the practices listed in the *Daniel R.R. v. State Board of Education* (1989) ruling, which has been the LRE ruling most frequently adopted in the various circuit courts. In any case, school district officials should note the importance all these rulings placed on (a) making decisions based on the individual needs of a student, (b) using supplementary aids and services to maintain students in the LRE, and (c) finding opportunities for students with disabilities to interact with their nondisabled peers to the maximum extent possible when they are placed in more restrictive settings.

General Education Class vs. General Education Curriculum

When thinking about placement for students, it is also important to consider the education the student will receive as a part of their special education services. It is important to understand the difference between a general education classroom and the general education curriculum. A general education classroom references the educational environments where non-eligible students participate in activities and are provided instruction. The general education curriculum is the content of the instruction that is to be taught to students in each grade and subject area. Not all students who are in the general education classroom receive education in the exact general education curriculum as other students. Some students may be educated in a general education classroom but be instructed using adaptations or modifications to the general education curriculum. The goal is for all students to receive as much instruction and exposure to the general education curriculum as possible. Not all content standards in any given subject area (e.g., English/language arts, mathematics, science) may be priorities for the instructional services a student needs. The state content standards and accountability tests are tied to the general education curriculum. Some students, as noted above, may require more assistance in addressing those standards in meaningful ways.

Determining Student Placement

Placement decision for students in special education must be made on an individual basis. Teams need to recognize, therefore, that all students with a certain disability do not necessarily receive (a) the same set of services, (b) the same level of service, or (c) placement in the same type of classroom. The determination about the level of support a student is to receive is based completely upon the needs of the student. Federal guidelines require that when determining the educational placement of an IDEA-eligible student with a disability, including a preschool child with a disability, each IEP team must ensure that the student's placement is (a) determined at least annually, (b) based on the student's IEP, and (c) as close as possible to the student's home. Unless the eligible student requires more intensive services than are provided in their home school, the child is educated in the school that he or she would attend if nondisabled. Furthermore, in selecting the LRE, consideration is given to any potential harmful effect on the child or on the quality of services needed. In all cases, the child is not to be removed from education in age-appropriate regular classrooms solely because of needed modifications in the general education curriculum (IDEA Regulations, 34 CFR § 300.116, 2006). Textbox 8.2 is a list of important concerns when determining a student's placement.

Textbox 8.2 Factors to Consider in Determining Student Placement

- Students with disabilities must be educated with nondisabled students to the maximum extent appropriate (IDEA Regulations, 34 CFR § 300.114[a][2][i], 2006).
- In addition to a general education placement, and general education placement with supplementary aids and services, a school district must be able to offer placement in the following settings: special classes, special schools, home instruction, and instruction in hospitals and institutions (IDEA Regulations, 34 CFR § 300.115[b][2], 2006).
- A student's placement is based on his or her IEP (IDEA Regulations, 34 CFR § 300.116[b][2], 2006).
- A student's placement must be determined at least annually (IDEA Regulations, 34 CFR § 300.116[b][1], 2006).
- A student must be educated in the school as close to home as possible (IDEA Regulations, 34 CFR § 300.116[b][3], 2006).

- A student should be educated in the school they would attend if not disabled unless the IEP requires some other arrangement (IDEA Regulations, 34 CFR § 300.116[b][3][C], 2006).
- Consider any potential harmful effects a placement may have on the student or on the quality of services that he or she needs (IDEA Regulations, 34 CFR § 300.116[d], 2006).
- Consider any potential harmful effects on the student's peers (*Federal Register*, v. 71, p. 46,589, 2006).
- Ensure a student is not removed from education in age-appropriate general classrooms solely because of needed modifications in the general education curriculum (IDEA Regulations, 34 CFR § 300.116[e] 2006).
- Ensure that each student with a disability participates with nondisabled students in nonacademic and extracurricular services and activities (e.g., counseling services, athletics, transportation, health services, recreational activities) to the maximum extent appropriate to the needs of the student (IDEA Regulations, 34 CFR § 300.107 and § 300.117, 2006).

Practices to Follow When Determining Student Placement

In a comment to the 2006 regulations to the IDEA, officials in the US Department of Education explained how placement decisions should be made for IDEA-eligible students with disabilities. We have added emphasis to this important statement from the department.

> the overriding rule . . . is that placement decisions for all children with disabilities must be made on an *individual basis* and ensure that each child with a disability is educated in the *school the child would attend* if not disabled *unless the child's IEP requires some other* arrangement. However, the act *does not require* that every child with a disability be placed in the regular classroom regardless of individual abilities and needs. This recognition that regular class placement may not be appropriate for every child with a disability is reflected in the requirement that LEAs make available a range of placement options, known as a *continuum of alternative placements*, to meet the *unique educational needs* of children with disabilities. This requirement for the continuum reinforces the importance of the *individualized inquiry, not a "one size fits all"* approach, in determining what placement is the LRE for each child with a disability. These options *must be available* to the extent necessary to implement the IEP of each child with a disability. The group determining the placement must select the placement option on the continuum in which it determines *that the child's IEP can be implemented* in the LRE. Any alternative placement selected for the child outside of the regular educational environment must include appropriate *opportunities for the child to interact* with nondisabled peers, to the extent appropriate to the needs of the children. (*Federal Register*, Vol. 71, No. 156, p. 46,587, 2006a)

This statement, along with the LRE court decisions, reinforces the important decision points to which an IEP team must attend when deciding on a student's placement. The statement and the court rulings also point to the practices we must avoid in placement determination.

Rule 1: Ensure Individualization and Program Appropriateness The principal rule of making placement decisions is that IEP teams must base a student's placement on his or her unique individual needs, and the placement must enable him or her to receive an appropriate education that meets those needs. Whereas the presumption is that all students should be educated in the general education classroom, the needs of a student and the appropriateness of the placement must be the foremost considerations of the IEP team. The judges in the ruling of the US Court of Appeals for the Fifth Circuit in *Daniel R.R. v. State Board of Education* (1989) wrote that "the (IDEA's) mandate to provide a free appropriate public education qualifies and limits its mandate for education in the regular classroom. Schools must provide a free appropriate public education and must do so, to the maximum extent appropriate, in regular education classrooms" (p. 1048). As Barbara Bateman noted in 2017, program appropriateness is the primary IDEA mandate (Bateman, 2017). This leads us to the second rule to follow in making placement decisions.

Rule 2: Provide Supplementary Aid, Services, and Program Modifications In chapter 7, we addressed the importance of including supplementary aids and service and program modifications in a student's IEP when necessary to ensure that his or her IEP meets the FAPE standards of the IDEA and meets the *Endrew F.* standard of enabling students to make progress in light of their circumstances. The IDEA is clear about the absolute importance of determining placements in the LRE <u>appropriate</u> for a student's needs. The IEP team is to determine the setting with the greatest degree of integration in which an appropriate education is available, and a key to ensuring that this occurs is by including supplementary aids and services and program modifications in a student's IEP and confirming that they are implemented as intended. If such efforts are not made, school district officials may find their district accused of violating the placement requirements of the IDEA. As judges on the US Court of Appeals for the Fifth Circuit asserted, the IDEA does not permit school districts to "make mere token gestures" to accommodate the needs of students with disabilities, and "its requirement for modifying and supplementing regular education is broad" (*Daniel R.R. v. State Board of Education*, 1989, p. 1048). It is important, therefore, that IEP team members thoroughly document their consideration of supplementary aids and services.

Rule 3: Adhere to the Continuum of Alternative Placements The preference in determining student placement is to assume the default position of educating students in the general education setting to the maximum extent appropriate. As we have previously discussed, however, Congressional authors of the IDEA understood that the general education setting, even with the use of supplementary aids and services, would not be appropriate for all students. As a district court judge in Pennsylvania wrote, "Nowhere in the (IDEA) is a handicapped child required to sink or swim in a (general education) classroom . . . Congress certainly did not intend to place handicapped children in a least restrictive environment and thereby deny them an appropriate education" (*Viscio v. School District of Pittsburgh*, 1988). To ensure that this problem would not occur, placement teams were allowed to move students along a continuum of alternative placements ranging to the least restrictive (i.e., the general education classroom or the general education classroom with supplementary aids and services) to the most restrictive (i.e., instruction in hospitals or institutions) based on a student's needs. The importance of using the continuum was included in the IDEA's definition of LRE: "special classes, separate schooling, or other removal of children with disabilities from the regular educational environment occurs only if the nature or severity of the disability is such that education in regular classes with the use of supplementary aids and services cannot be achieved satisfactorily" (IDEA Regulations, 34 CFR § 300.114[a][2], 2006).

To ensure that school districts' personnel had a variety of placements available to them, Congress and the US Department of Education mandated that "each (school district) must ensure that a continuum of alternative placements is available to meet the needs of children with disabilities for special education and related services" (IDEA Regulations, 34 CFR § 300.114 [a]), 2006). We need to ensure that a continuum is available so that students with disabilities can learn in the environment that is appropriate for them and based on their individual needs (Bateman & Linden, 2012). Moreover, when using this continuum, teams must go through in a stepwise progression, one step at a time, and give careful thought to the placement that is most appropriate for a student. As always, it is important that IEP team members thoroughly document their consideration of supplementary aids and services.

Rule 4: Provide Opportunities for Integration A broad mandate in the IDEA is that placement teams must ensure that to the maximum extent appropriate, students with disabilities, including children in public or private institutions or other care facilities, should be educated with students who are not disabled (IDEA Regulations, 34 CFR § 300.114[a][2], 2006). Because the Congressional authors of the IDEA recognized that for some students more restrictive settings would be necessary, they mandated that whenever possible students with disabilities be educated alongside their peers without disabilities. This could include nonacademic settings (e.g., lunch, recess, counseling groups, and extracurricular activities like clubs, sports).

Practices to Avoid When Determining Student Placement

Yell et al. (2020) identified five common errors made by school personnel when determining the placement of students with disabilities and concluded that when these errors are made, there may be sufficient grounds for a hearing officer or judge to rule that the school district has denied the child a FAPE or violated the LRE mandate of the IDEA. The errors included (a) failing to individualize a student's placement, (b) predetermining a student's placement, (c) placing a student prior to developing his or her IEP, (d) failing to adhere to the continuum of alternative placements, and (e) failing to use supplementary aids and services before moving a student to a more restrictive setting. Additionally, IEP teams should not adopt a placement policy for "all" students (e.g., all students with autism will attend a special school, all students with disabilities will be educated in general education classrooms). This would be a violation of the hallmark of the IDEA, individualization.

Additionally, IEP teams should never exclude a student's parents from collaborating in the placement decision. If a student's parent cannot be located or refuses to attend a meeting in which a placement decision will be made, the team may move forward with a placement determination but should have thorough documentation that they have made good-faith efforts to reach the parents or convince them to attend.

Steps in Determining Student Placement

The following steps for determining LRE are intended as guidance only; they are not absolute rules. However, the steps and information from the IDEA, the regulations, and case law provide guidance that should help IEP teams in making placement determinations. This guidance assumes that a student has already determined to be eligible for special education services under the IDEA. IEP teams must continuously monitor the programming for the student to determine if the various placements are resulting in a student making progress on his or her IEP goals and objectives. We also offer a flowchart to guide IEP teams through placement determination.

Step 1: The team develops a student's IEP, which is the blueprint of his or her FAPE. A student's placement decision must be based on a student's IEP (IDEA Regulations, 34 CFR § 300.116 [b][2], 2006). When teams decide on the placement prior to completing a student's IEP, they are engaging in an illegal practice referred to as "shoehorning," in which a student's program is shoehorned to fit a particular placement (Tatgenhorst et al., 2014).

Step 2: The IEP team determines if the student's needs can be addressed in the general education classroom. As part of this decision, the team must consider strategies that were taken to include the student in the general education classroom (e.g., Were there multiple strategies? Were they implemented with fidelity? Was there documentation regarding the strategies used?). If the student's needs are greater than those that can be provided in the general education classroom, the team moves to Step 3.

Step 3: The team considers whether there are supplemental aids and services, or program modifications, that can make the general education classroom an appropriate placement for a student and allow him or her to receive their education in the general education classroom. If the student can make progress on their goals and objectives with supplemental aides and services in the general education classroom, then that is likely the primary location for their services. We should note that resource rooms are not considered to be a more restrictive setting, but rather a service to help to ensure that students are educated in the LRE. If students cannot be educated in the general education setting with supplemental aids and services, go to Step 4.

Step 4: If the student cannot make progress on their goals and objectives in the general education classroom even with supplemental aides and services, what are the needs that are to be addressed in order to support progress? Determine the location where those needs can be addressed and the frequency of the services using the continuum of alternative placements. When moving to more restrictive placements, the IEP team must consider every opportunity for the student to participate with their nondisabled peers. This discussion should include transportation, before-school programs, lunch, specials, home room, after-school programming, and extracurricular activities.

Step 5: At a minimum, annually review the student's placement and ask the following questions: (a) What is unique about the programming in the more restrictive placement? and (b) Can the components that make the program unique be reasonably replicated in the general education classroom with supplementary aids and services? If the program cannot be replicated, then maintain the student's programming in their current setting while ensuring every opportunity for student to participate with their nondisabled peers.

Figure 8.1 is a graphic representation of a placement determination flowchart.

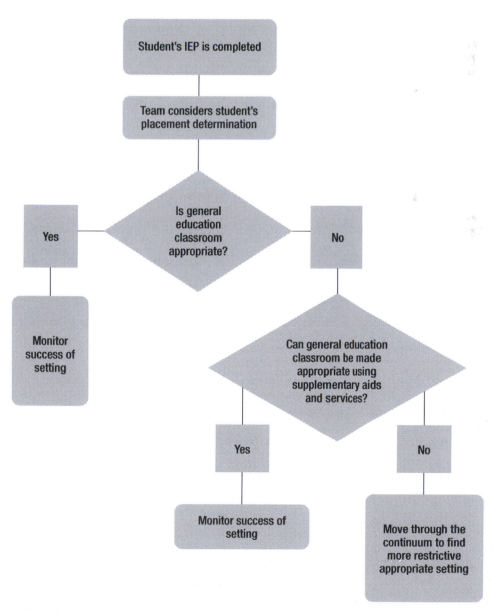

Figure 8.1 Placement Determination Flowchart.

Summary of Determining Placements

A placement determination involves a decision regarding where and how a student's IEP will be implemented. Placement decisions are to be made by a team of individuals including a student's parents. Typically, a student's IEP team makes the decision, which must follow the completion of the student's IEP. The placement decision must be made annually and be in conformity with the LRE and other requirements of the IDEA. When making placement and LRE determinations, there are general guidelines as to the appropriateness of considerations that IEP teams must take into account. Using inappropriate considerations such as the following may lead to improper decisions and poor instructional results for the student.

When making placement decisions, students' IEP teams need to understand that LRE is not synonymous with general education setting. It is the setting closest to the general education setting in which FAPE can be delivered. Placement decisions must be individualized. Blanket policies regarding students' placement violate the IDEA. Placement decisions, like all special education, must be based on the unique circumstances and needs of students. Table 8.1 depicts practices to follow and practices to avoid that we have addressed in this chapter.

TABLE 8.1   Practices to Follow and Practices to Avoid

Practices to Follow	Practices to Avoid
The placement decision must be made by a group of persons including a student's parents.	Do not make placement decisions without parental input.
A student's placement decision must be individualized and based on his or her IEP.	Do not make placement decisions prior to developing a student's IEP.
Consider any potential harmful effects on the student, other students without disabilities, or the quality of services when determining placement.	Do not remove a student from the general education environment unless education with the use of supplementary aids and services, including resource room, cannot provide FAPE.
Consider supplementary aids and services to maintain a student in the general education setting.	Do not base placement on the availability of the placement or personnel in the school district.
Ensure that the student has as many opportunities as possible to be integrated and participate with his or her nondisabled peers.	Do not use lack of funds, administrative convenience, or cost as an excuse not to provide the appropriate placement.
Follow the continuum of placements in a stepwise manner when considering a more restrictive placement.	Do not substitute a policy of full inclusion or make decisions based on a student's category instead of using the continuum of placements in making the placement decision.
Remember that providing a FAPE is the primary IDEA mandate.	Do not provide services based on a student's category (e.g., only students with emotional and behavioral disorders receive behavioral programming).

EPILOGUE

The IEP, which is the heart and soul of the IDEA, is approaching 50 years old as a federally required document outlining a student program of special education and related services. We agree with Dr. Barbara Bateman who in 1995 wrote the following:

> Most IEPs are useless or slightly worse, and too many teachers experience the IEP process as always time consuming, sometimes threatening, and, too often, a pointless bureaucratic requirement. The result is a quasi-legal document to be filed away with the expectation it won't be seen again except, heaven forbid, by a monitor or compliance officer--Parents too often experience the IEP process as an overgrown parent-teacher conference in which the school personnel present some previously prepared papers and request a signature. (Bateman, 1995, p. 1)

Dr. Bateman did not present an optimistic picture of the state of IEP development and implementation. She ended, however, by expressing her hope and belief that the IEP could be an extraordinarily useful tool in building the future of our students.

We too believe in the promise of the IEP as the means by which we design special education programs that, when implemented correctly and as agreed upon, can improve the lives of students with disabilities. We agree with the US Supreme Court that the "the essential function of an IEP is to set out a plan for pursuing academic and functional advancement" (*Endrew F.*, 2017, p. 992). We have posed the following four questions throughout this book, and we believe that these questions should drive our efforts to focus on the individual needs of our students and ensure that special educators design meaningful programming that is "reasonably calculated to enable a child to make progress appropriate in light of the child's circumstances" (*Endrew F.*, 2017, p. 999).

1. What are students' unique academic and functional needs that must be addressed in their IEPs?
2. What are the annual goals that must be included in students' IEPs to address their needs identified in the PLAAFP statements?
3. How will students' progress toward their annual goals be monitored?
4. What services will be provided to students so they may reach their goals?

The IEP is a complex and detailed document; however, the essence of the IEP is the individual student, the answers to these four questions, and the academic and functional progress that a student makes. The questions are answered in (a) the PLAAFP statements, (b) the measurable annual goals, (c) the methods to measure and report on a student's progress, and (d) the special education services, related services, and supplementary aids and services we will provide to the student.

It is crucial in IEP development that the process involves meaningful parental participation. We also need to appreciate that for administrators and special educators it is **another** IEP meeting, while for a student's parents it is **the** IEP meeting. We must always make good-faith efforts to collaborate.

Our IEPs must be developed in a manner that is procedurally sound and substantively meaningful. Throughout this book we have offered checklists and forms that we hope will be useful to you. We offer this final checklist to assist you in the adoption of better practices in IEP development (textbox 9.1).

Textbox 9.1 IEP Process and Content Checklist

Parental Involvement
- The parents were invited to all meetings involving decisions regarding their child's special education.
- The parents were meaningfully involved in the IEP meeting and school personnel elicited and considered their contributions.
- No final decisions were made regarding assessment, programming, or placement without the parents' involvement.
- If the parents chose not to be or could not be involved, were good-faith efforts made and documented to involve a student's parents?

Assessment
- Parent permission was obtained before conducting the assessment for special education.
- The assessment addressed all areas of need.
- Were procedures followed in conducting the assessment?
- The assessment leads to instructional implications for programming.
- If transition services are needed, the student's IEP includes an age-appropriate transition assessment.

Statements of Present Levels of Academic and Functional Performance
- The PLAAFP includes a statement regarding the student's academic and functional strengths.
- The PLAAFP statement addresses all of a student's academic and functional needs as identified in his or her assessment.
- The PLAAFP statement includes an impact statement (i.e., how the student's disability affects his or her participation in the general education curriculum).
- The PLAAFP statement is written in language understandable to a layperson.
- The IEP includes a student's parents' input into the PLAAFP statements.
- Each need identified in a PLAAFP statement leads to a goal, a service, or both a goal and a service.
- The IEP includes a statement that five special factors of student need have been considered: behavior, limited English proficiency, blind or visually impaired, communication needs, and assistive technology.

Measurable Annual Goals

- The measurable annual goals address a student's needs that are identified in the PLAAFP statements.
- Each measurable annual goal includes a target behavior.
- Each measurable annual goal includes information on how it will be measured.
- Each measurable annual goal includes a criterion for acceptable performance.
- If a student is taking an alternate achievement test, his or her IEP includes benchmarks or short-term objectives.

Measurement of Annual Goals (Progress Monitoring)

- The IEP describes how the student's progress toward meeting the goals will be measured.
- The method of measurement collects data that the teacher can use to analyze student progress.
- The IEP describes how and when the student's progress toward meeting the goals will be reported.

Statements of Special Education, Related Services, Supplementary Aids Services, and Program Modifications

- The IEP includes specific information on when services will begin.
- The IEP includes specific information on the frequency, duration, and locations of all services to be provided.
- The IEP includes specific information on supplementary aids and services, and accommodations and modifications are provided to the student in special education and general education settings.
- The services provided to the student are based on peer-reviewed research.
- If transition services are needed, has the student been invited to the transition planning meeting?
- If transition services are needed, does the IEP include an age-appropriate transition assessment?
- If transition services are needed, does the IEP include age-appropriate measurable postsecondary goals related to the training, education, employment, and, when appropriate, independent living skills?
- If transition services are needed, does the IEP include transition services, including courses of study, which are needed to assist the student in meeting the postsecondary goals?

Placement

- The IEP team (or placement team) determines the student's placement along with his or her parents.
- The IEP team (or placement team) ensures that to the maximum extent appropriate students with disabilities are being educated in the general education setting with their nondisabled peers.
- The IEP team (or placement team) ensures that prior to removing a student to a more restrictive setting, supplementary aids and services are considered.
- The IEP team (or placement team) uses the continuum of alternative placements in a stepwise manner when choosing a more restrictive placement.
- The IEP describes the extent to which the student will not participate with nondisabled students in the regular classroom.
- The IEP includes an explanation of why the student will not participate with nondisabled students in the regular classroom.

In the introduction, we quoted a ruling in *Rutland South Supervisory Union* (2000) in which the IEP was described as an intricate puzzle that is collaboratively put together by a student's parents and school-based personnel. It was our purpose to help administrators, parents, and teachers assemble IEPs in an educationally meaningful and legally correct manner. Our efforts do not constitute legal advice; rather we advocate for using better practices in IEP development. As educators we need to adhere to the evidence in crafting special education programs. We believe the use of the better practices we recommend will result in IEPs that meet the requirements of the law and will result in programming that enables students to make progress appropriate in light of their circumstances.

Resources

with Amelia Blanton

Appendix A: FAQs on IEPs

Appendix B: Schedules for IEP Development

Appendix C: Tips for Virtual IEP Meetings

Appendix D: Determining if an Aide Is Needed

Appendix E: Behavioral Aide Levels of Supports Form

Appendix F: Instructional Aide Levels of Support Form

Appendix G: Health Aide Levels of Support Form

Appendix H: Questions Related to Transportation for Students

1. Who Develops the Actual IEPs?

A school district is typically charged with developing and implementing an IEP for all eligible students that are within its jurisdiction. The law does not state who within a school district is the one ultimately responsible for the development of the IEP. School districts can assign the responsibility to whomever they feel has the necessary skills to develop the IEP.

Typically, it is a special education teacher who might be working with the student. This could be the student's current special education teacher or one who might be working with the student in the future. Prior to the IEP meeting, do not state a certain teacher will be the student's future teacher, as this is an indication that programming and placement decisions have been made prior to the meeting. Say a teacher might be the child's teacher, but be careful about the specific assignment.

Some districts also have case managers who are responsible for developing and leading IEPs.

2. Do Public Charter Schools Have to Comply with the IDEA's IEP Requirements?

Typically, yes. There may be state and local laws that might change the answer to this question. However, charter schools are public schools. They have the same requirements for the provision of special education services as public schools under the IDEA. Importantly, they cannot exclude students with disabilities from their services or from enrollment. Some charter schools are complete separate school systems or districts, while other charter schools are a subset or program within a district.

Best practice is to serve not only eligible students for special education, but also students eligible for accommodations under Section 504 of the Rehabilitation Act.

3. What Is an IEP Meeting?

By federal law, school districts are required to regularly meet with parents about the program being offered to students eligible for special education and related services. The purpose of the IEP meeting is to develop a program in conjunction with the parents. At the IEP meeting, the needs of the student are discussed, along with the suggested program, and the location where that program is to be implemented.

Best practice is to include the parents from the beginning of the process and ensure their suggestions are addressed. The important part of the meeting is that it is a team decision regarding the programming for the student. See chapter 4 for more guidance on conducting IEP meetings.

4. Is There a Required Format for an IEP Meeting?

There is nothing in the federal law stipulating the format of an IEP meeting. The structure of the IEP meeting varies from state to state, and even from district to district. There are some commonalities that need to be addressed as a part of the meeting:

- Expected attendees
- Parents as equal participants

Best practice includes making sure not only that the correct people are at the meeting, but that we base all of the programs and services for the student on his or her needs as identified in the PLAAFP section of the IEP. Teams often clarify the specific needs of the student and then make sure the goals and services directly relate to the identified needs. For more information on suggested meeting formats, see chapter 4, especially the section on agendas.

5. Is the IEP a Contract?

IDEA requires school districts to provide all of the special education and related services that are delineated in a student's IEP. Therefore, if an IEP is written and the student is to receive 90 minutes of language arts instruction on a daily basis, the student should receive 90 minutes of language arts instruction related to their IEP goals.

However, it is not a contract in that there is no guarantee a student will achieve a certain level of achievement and meet all of the IEP goals. A district's responsibilities are to ensure it makes a good faith attempt to have the student meet the goals, with necessary changes during the course of the year.

Best practice is to closely monitor the students throughout the year with regular progress monitoring and to make changes when it is clear the goals are either too easy or the student is not making enough progress. Also, there should be periodic reminders to the staff to ensure they are implementing the IEP as it is written, and if there are problems or concerns to alert others and to modify the IEP as necessary.

6. Does a Verbal IEP Comply with the IDEA?

Simple answer is no. An IEP is a written document (34 CFR § 300.320(a)). Districts have been held accountable for verbal offers to parents; therefore, make sure all offers for programming for the student are made at a team meeting where there is a representative of the local education agency (LEA) in attendance who can ensure the funds necessary for the student's program are provided.

Best practice is, if teachers or staff members are asked outside of a team meeting about services, to make sure they say it is a team decision and they cannot say yes or no to services. All requests for services need to be fully considered by the team with nothing ever dismissed without considering if it is necessary for the student to receive FAPE.

7. What Information Must Be Included in an IEP?

There is little federal guidance about what is specifically required, with states adding what they think is necessary. The list below may be different from what your state requires. This list contains the federal requirements, which serve as the minimum that should be required. Make sure you seek out information about what is specifically required in your state.

- Present levels of academic achievement and functional performance
- Measurable annual goals
- Short-term objectives or benchmarks for students who take alternative state assessments
- A description of the student's progress
- The specific special education services the student is to receive
- The supplementary aids and services the student is to receive
- The specific related services the student is to receive
- Any program modifications for school personnel
- The amount of time the student will be spending with their nondisabled peers
- Any accommodations that are to be provided to the student as a part of state or districtwide assessments
- The beginning date of the IEP
- The frequency of services to be provided to the student
- The duration of the services
- The location of the services

8. How Must the IEP Address Involvement in the General Education Curriculum?

One of the required components of the IEP is the determination of how each child's disability affects the child's involvement and progress in the general curriculum. For purposes of the regulations, general education curriculum is defined as the same curriculum as for nondisabled children. This does not mean the student has to be receiving their services or education in the general education environment; it just means the student is evaluated based on the content of the curriculum. As was noted in the discussion on placement in this book, the services a student receives should allow them to participate with their nondisabled peers to the maximum extent possible.

9. Must the IEP Describe the Total Education of the Student with a Disability?

An IEP is not a lesson plan, nor is it expected to detail the student's entire day. It is only expected to detail the special education programs and services along with any additional accommodations that are to be provided in general education settings. There is no expectation that the student's IEP will detail the general education services for the student. Only put in an IEP the information necessary to assist with the identified needs that are found in the PLAAFP section of the IEP.

10. Why Are Annual Goals Required in an IEP?

Annual goals are a requirement of the IDEA. The importance of measurable annual goals cannot be overstated: they are critical to the planning process of the team in the development of the IEP. IEPs are only to be written for one year and are expected to be reviewed and revised at least annually. Having the annual review of the IEP serves as an accountability device for the district to help determine if program adjustments are warranted. If a student is not making progress, the team could reasonably be expected to make changes to the IEP for the next year. The problem is when districts do not make changes and allow students to continually not make measurable progress on their IEP goals and objectives.

11. How Are Annual Goals Developed?

Annual goals are developed after the development of the PLAAFP statement. There should be an annual goal, a strategy for the general education classroom, a part of the transition plan, or a part of the behavioral intervention plan for every need identified in the PLAAFP. There should not be an annual goal for a student who does not have an identified need. Goals should be developed to help the child learn strategies for independence either in the general education classroom or as a part of their daily functioning. Goals should also be developed to minimize their areas of need.

Annual goals should be ambitious, with a real expectation of what the student should be able to learn or master within a year. Annual goals also should be developed in a manner so that they can be regularly monitored, with changes made as necessary over the year.

12. How Many Annual Goals Must Be Included in an IEP?

At a minimum, one. There are no specific guidelines indicating how many goals are necessary for a student. The goals are based on the needs in the PLAAFP statement. Every student eligible for special education and related services at a minimum should have at least one goal. If they do not have a need identified in the PLAAFP statement, then the student should not be identified as eligible for special education, as they fail the second part of the test for eligibility for services and should be exited from special education. For every identified need, there needs to be an annual goal, strategy for the general education classroom, part of the transition plan, or part of the behavioral intervention plan for every need identified in the PLAAFP. Goals may be able to address more than one need. However, be careful to ensure that all needs are being addressed appropriately.

13. What Is the Difference between a Short-term Objective and a Benchmark?

A short-term objective takes the annual goal and breaks it down into smaller, more manageable components, or steps toward the annual goal. Think of it as building blocks that move toward successful completion of the annual goal.

A benchmark is an expected level of achievement for the student that indicates whether process is being made toward an annual goal. These are indicators of progress.

Some states require short-term objectives, while others require benchmarks. Both are valid ways of helping a teacher determine if progress is being made toward the student's annual goal(s), as long as they are regularly used.

14. Should the IEP Include Goals for Related Services?

Only if the student has needs identified in the PLAAFP statement. If the student does not have an identified need in the PLAAFP statement, then there should not be related services goals. Related services, as covered in this book, are only required to the extent that such services are necessary for a child to benefit from special education. All determinations about the need for related services have to be made annually and on an individual basis.

15. Must the IEP Describe How a Child's Progress Will Be Measured?

The IEP must contain a description of how progress will be measured. What is important is that the measurement of the student's' progress on their IEP goals be objective, clearly describable, and clearly measurable.

A best practice tip is that if it cannot be measured, there needs to be change so that the goal and the means for determining progress can be measured.

16. What Is "Peer-Reviewed" Research?

The regulations at 34 CFR § 300.320 clearly state:

> (4) A statement of the special education and related services and supplementary aids and services, based on peer-reviewed research to the extent practicable, to be provided to the child, or on behalf of the child, and a statement of the program modifications or supports for school personnel that will be provided to enable the child -

> (i)   To advance appropriately toward attaining the annual goals;
> (ii) To be involved in and make progress in the general education curriculum in accordance with paragraph (a)(1) of this section, and to participate in extracurricular and other nonacademic activities; and
> (iii) To be educated and participate with other children with disabilities and nondisabled children in the activities described in this section.

Best practice questions:

- Is there reliable evidence that the program or services work?
- Has the program been tried with students with like needs and been shown to be successful?
- Is the research more than just anecdotal statements?
- Is there peer-reviewed research on the program that is being considered?
- If research does not exist in this area, what programs were rejected and why?

17. Must an IEP Identify a Student's Teachers or Other Service Providers by Name? By Qualifications?

Districts should NOT write the name of a teacher, aide, paraprofessional, bus driver, administrator, school counselor, or related services provider into the IEP as the provider of services. This may be a contentious issue at IEP meeting; however, districts have the discretion to determine who they will hire to fill the specific roles. If a teacher's name is written into the IEP as the provider of services and the teacher is absent, removed, or otherwise not there, then the district is in violation of the implementation of the IEP.

Qualifications? It is expected to have individuals who meet applicable state standards to hold the role of the job for which they are employed. Teachers need to have state certifications, as do related service providers. That is what is expected for qualifications.

18. *Must the IEP Indicate the Amount of Time a Student Will Not Be Educated in the General Education Classroom?*

States have various formats for how the level of services are to be reported in the IEP. Make sure you pay attention to the specific format, as there are not federal guidelines on how time should be reported in the IEP.

Best practice is to be clear enough so that the team members clearly understand what is expected for the student, and if the student were to move, the new team would also have an understanding of what to do.

19. *Is a Modification of an Assessment the Same as an Accommodation for an Assessment?*

Accommodations and modifications are not the same thing.

Accommodations change how a student learns the material. An accommodation allows a student to complete the same assignment or test as other students, but with a change in the timing, formatting, setting, scheduling, response, presentation, or a combination of these. The accommodation does not alter in any significant way what the test or assignment measures. For example, accommodations for presentation affect the way directions and content are delivered to students, helping students with different learning needs and abilities to engage in the content (e.g., a student with an anxiety takes a test in a different location). Accommodations for response offer different ways for students to respond to assessment questions. Accommodations for setting typically affect where work or specific tasks are completed; a change of setting may be particularly helpful to students who are easily distracted. Accommodations for timing and scheduling of assignments and assessments can be helpful for students who may need more processing time or frequent breaks.

Modifications change what a student is taught or expected to learn. Notably, they are adjustments to an assignment or a test that changes the standard of what the assignment or test is supposed to measure. The curriculum can be modified to retain specific standards that the student must meet to progress in the curriculum, while allowing for less depth of understanding of the concept.

20. *Can an IEP Meeting Be Combined and Held Concurrently with a Meeting to Determine Eligibility?*

States may allow this; however, check the specific regulations. If this is occurring, make sure the team addresses the eligibility question first, fully covering the needs of the student. If it is paired with an IEP team meeting, then the team needs to make sure there are comments related to needs included as a part of the evaluation that are reflected in the IEP. The problem in holding an IEP meeting with an eligibility meeting is that the student is not yet eligible for services, and any IEP developed will look like predetermination of services.

21. *How Often Must a School District Review and/or Revise an IEP?*

At a minimum annually. However, it is best practice to review the IEP more frequently, at least at the end of each marking period. There may be a need to review the IEP when there is new evaluation data provided, the child is making more than expected progress in their classes, the child is making less than expected progress in their classes, there is a discipline problem, or there is an indication from the parents that there are problems with the program. The IEP should be reviewed throughout the year to fully represent the needs of the student and to adapt to the changing educational environment.

22. May Revisions to an IEP Be Made without Convening a Meeting?

The IEP is a team document and should be changed through a team decision. However, the regulations allow the district and the parent to meet to make changes without the entire team present once there has been an annual meeting. Depending on the state, there are specifics that need to be documented, for example, who discussed what and who was present. It is not recommended if you are changing the level of placement for the student (e.g., going from about 20% of special education series per day to about 40% per day). For any change, make sure the parents are provided a copy of your state's procedural safeguards notice.

23. Must the School District Implement an Agreed-Upon IEP in Its Entirety?

Yes. Once the team, including the parents, has agreed to the IEP, the district should be expected to implement the IEP as written. If the team determines certain aspects are no longer necessary or the services listed are too intense for the student, then the IEP team should have another meeting where the program is amended or altered. In no way should the district unilaterally make changes to the IEP without agreement of the parents. Make sure the parents are aware of and consent to any changes to the program and placement for the student. If the parents do not agree to changes to the IEP, then the last agreed-upon IEP is the one that is to be implemented. This is done until there is either agreement or a statement from a hearing officer or judge saying the program should be changed.

24. How Soon after an IEP Is Formulated Must It Be Implemented?

There is no specific guidance from the federal regulations regarding when the IEP should be implemented after the meeting. States have different timelines about when the IEP should be implemented for the student after there is agreement. Pay attention to your specific state guidelines related to timelines. However, a good practice is there should not be a delay, but there is an understanding that it may take a few days to arrange transportation or hire aides to support a student. Those factors cannot be used to excessively delay the commencement of a student's instruction, as the district needs to figure out the services so the student can receive an education.

25. Must an IEP Be in Effect at the Beginning of Each School Year?

The IEP must be in effect at the beginning of the school year. Not only should the IEP be in effect but the student should be expected to be receiving services at the beginning of the school year. Teachers should not spend their time during the first two weeks of school determining a child's schedule or planning their own schedule. The student should start receiving services at the beginning of the school year. Finally, problems with administration or scheduling are not to be used as a way to deny a student services from the beginning of the year. A student missing services at the beginning of the year could be a reason that parents to sue for compensatory education, when the district knew or should have known services should have been provided; if this is the case, then parents could demand that either the services be made up or a monetary award given that then could be used for the missed services.

26. Can a School Start to Provide Special Education Services Prior to the Completion of the Evaluation? The IEP?

No. The delivery of special education and related services is to come after a complete evaluation, and then the development of an IEP that the parents and team members agreed to. Special education services are provided after a process where there are checks and balances and the need to keep parents informed about the process and secure their permission prior to changing a student's placement and providing service. A better way to think about this is, what service is the team providing to the student and how will the teacher know what to teach or focus on if there is not a complete evaluation or an IEP to guide the service? Imagine the scenario where the school district starts providing special education to the student prior to the completion of the evaluation and the student ends up not qualifying. The process may seem like it sometimes takes a long time, but it is a process to preserve the rights of the student and the parent to be fully informed about the education provided.

27. Are IEP Meetings Required to Be in Person?

The COVID-19 crisis affirmed that the IEP meeting does not need to be held in person. Please see the section where we cover tips for virtual IEP meetings.

28. If the Parents' Primary Language Is Other than English, What Are the Requirements Related to Hiring an Interpreter for the Meeting?

We want the parents to be fully informed and aware of the contents of the program for their child. There are ways of obtaining interpreters, where the interpreter is not physically present but participates by phone. There is a cost, but we need to make sure the parents are aware of the program. Although the IDEA does not require all documents to be translated, it is important to try to do this, as it will allow the district to be able to say they worked to keep the parents fully informed of the program that is being offered to their child.

Interpreters for individuals who are deaf and hard of hearing is also important. There are services that make use of programs like Zoom, FaceTime, or other similar platforms that allow the interpreter to be able to communicate with the person who is deaf or hard of hearing, working to ensure they understand the components of the meeting regarding their child.

29. Does Every Member of the IEP Team Have to Attend Every IEP Meeting?

It is good practice to try and get every member of the IEP team to attend each meeting. However, there is not a requirement that everyone does so. Members of the IEP team should attend for the part of the program specifically addressing their classes. It is also important for the IEP to get teachers and staff who actually know the student to participate in the meetings, instead of who happens to be free during that period. Have the teacher who is free go cover the class of the teacher who knows the student so that informed decisions about the student can be made. This is better for the student, better for the teacher who works with the student, and better for the overall development of a program that suits the student and their needs.

If a teacher is not going to be in attendance, it is best also to provide as much notice to the parents as possible about who will be participating in the meeting so the parents are not caught by surprise.

30. Who Is Authorized to Serve as a Representative of the School District at an IEP Meeting?

The IDEA at 34 CFR § 300.321 (a) (4) states:

(4) A representative of the public agency who -

(i) Is qualified to provide, or supervise the provision of, specially designed instruction to meet the unique needs of children with disabilities;
(ii) Is knowledgeable about the general education curriculum; and
(iii) Is knowledgeable about the availability of resources of the public agency.

What does this mean? Typically, this is thought of as a an individual who can authorize the expenditure of the funds necessary for the student's program. However, state and local officials may have differing interpretations of what is necessary as a representative of the LEA. The regulations leave it to the LEA to determine who will serve in this role. It could be a special education administrator, a special education director, a special education supervisor, a building-level principal, or even an assistant principal or another district-level administrator.

The purpose for not being specific about who can serve in this role is to give districts flexibility to be able to hold timely meetings with the parents.

Best practice is that it is not a teacher or school counselor, as they neither supervise the provision of special education services nor have the authority to commit funds for the provision of special education services.

Two Months before the IEP Meeting

- Give the family a Permission to Evaluate form (many months in advance, including re-evaluation once every three years).
- Obtain parents' written consent to evaluate for special education services (evaluation and re-evaluation).
- The evaluation process (60 school or calendar days): team members complete the necessary assessments outlined in IDEA.
- Triennial evaluation report: This is started 70 days prior to the IEP due date. The school psychologist is informed of this six weeks prior to sending the re-evaluation report home. The team uses this to determine continued eligibility for an IEP.
- Continue to collect data on the student and issue progress reports to parents.
- A team meeting needs to be held to make decisions as to whether a student is eligible or not for special education.
- Discuss assessment results and review them to consider determination for eligibility for services.
- Gather info from a variety of sources: aptitude/achievement tests, parent input, teacher recommendations, physical condition, social or cultural background, and adaptive behavior.
- Plan with family on a date for the IEP meeting; make several good faith attempts to contact the families, in different ways.
- Invite the LEA representative and other team members to attend the IEP meeting.
- Write a draft IEP (which is typically developed by the special education teacher or special education administrator).
- Review the current PLAAFP: Is there progress?
- Review the accommodations and modifications that have been put into place and what worked/did not work.
- Review the monitoring and reporting progress from the previous year's IEP goals.
- If student is 14 or older, they will also need to have transition input.

One Month before the IEP Meeting

- Contact family with notice of IEP meeting.
- Confirm parent attendance (three attempts).
- Contact the multidisciplinary team members to confirm attendance.
- Continue to collect data on the student.
- There is a continuation of assessment data collection, analysis, and consulting with the child's multidisciplinary team one month prior to the IEP meeting.

- Gather information from the student's teachers: academic, functional, and behavioral.
- Make sure all of the progress monitoring is up to date.
- Check their grades and assessments.
- If needed, do an assessment to collect more information on the progress of their previous goals.
- If the student is over the age of 14, they will need transition input.
- Obtain feedback from the family.

Two Weeks before the IEP Meeting

- Work with the parents and the LEA to schedule a date for the meeting.
- Work to develop an IEP draft based on the recent progress monitoring data.
- Work to get information from everyone who works with the student.
- Make sure that formal assessments have been completed and results are available.
- Consider what will need to be explained to the team in order for them to make appropriate educational decisions.
- Invite the LEA to the meeting.
- Reserve a room for the meeting.
- Possibly meet with parents to discuss questions, concerns, or ideas from the draft they received.
- Make sure to have all required documentation: some have already been listed, but also include attempted interventions and data reflecting how the student responded, observations, and work samples.
- Send out procedural safeguards with invitation.
- Parents should have at least a ten-calendar-day notice before the meeting; if not, attempts to reach out need to begin. Three documented attempts must be made for verification.
- If the parents need a translator, make sure one is available.
- Work with any related service providers that can attend the meeting.

One Week before the IEP Meeting

- Invite members to the meeting—Invites should have been sent out prior to one week out.
- Contact parents to remind them about the meeting.
- Send draft of IEP to the team.
- Make corrections to the IEP based off of feedback from the team.
- Send/email IEP draft to parents/family.
- Collect:
  1. Previous IEP for child if they had one,
  2. Important work samples and information from general education teachers,
  3. Any other observable data on the student,
  4. Any intervention strategies that were implemented,
  5. IEP draft to show the parents.
- Prepare questions.

- Reserve room for meeting.
- Make copies of draft IEP.
- Prepare a list of invited individuals and an attendance sheet of who is expected at the meeting, and make sure they are aware of the meeting's agenda, time, date, etc.
- Create graphs/charts to illustrate student's current supports.
- Review student's current supports.
- Make list of anticipated questions/concerns.
- Prepare examples of student work.

One Day before the IEP Meeting

- Check over IEP components and have professional peer edit.
- Print and make copies of drafted IEP for professional and parental reference.
- Print copies of parental consent forms, parental rights, and meeting schedule.
- Contact parents/guardians and remind them again of the meeting, including the time and, if applicable, where they ought to report.
- Send home parent survey to give them an overview of what will be discussed at the meeting, and have them write down concerns they may have as well as criteria they may want to address during the meeting.
- Create IEP meeting checklist to ensure all important information is covered and allow time for parents to ask questions and address concerns; make copies of the checklist for the other participants so that they can follow along and make notes as necessary.
- Reach out to other professionals such as general education teacher, specialists, etc. to once again confirm their attendance at the meeting.
- Create attendance sheet to document individuals that attend meeting.
- Ensure that all student data information (work samples, anecdotal notes, observations, interventions in place, progress made if applicable, etc.) has been collected and organized.
- Prepare materials such as a notebook to take notes regarding parent concerns, questions, etc., as well as folders, writing utensils, and previously written IEPs that were in place for that child.
- Ensure that the room previously reserved to hold the meeting (as that should be done further in advance) is still available to hold the meeting; if not, make other arrangements. Make certain there is enough seating for all attendees and that the setup of the room promotes discussion.

Day of the IEP Meeting

- Gather student's file (data regarding child work samples, anecdotal notes, observations, attempted interventions, etc.).
- Review student files prior to the meeting.
- Think of possible questions parents may have regarding students' files and be prepared to answer any question.
- Print IEP if not already done.
- Have draft watermark or "draft" written across the top.
- Signature pages without the draft watermark.

- Distribute copies to IEP team members if necessary.
- Check if all relevant members are attending the meeting such as parents, general education teachers, OT, etc. If not, it is important to acquire notes of the individual who will not be coming to share relevant and important information with the family.
- Create documentation of members absent for record of the meeting.
- Participants were invited a minimum of ten days in advance; clarify with parents if they are still able to attend - if someone cannot attend, offer attendance through phone call or video call.
- If someone cannot attend, offer additional information to them that they miss that is important. Keep them updated on information.
- Have space arranged prior to the start time of the meeting - make accommodations for accessibility if needed.
- Dress professionally.
- Print required documents - parental consent forms, parental rights, extra copies of documentation/data, meeting schedule (introductions of the team and statement of the purpose/overview of the meeting).
- Have a notebook or something to take notes on ready to note things such as parent concerns, questions, new accommodations, etc.
- Document questions parents may have or questions you may have. Keep copies of any questions that may be asked.
- Prepare folder to collect any forms/documentation from the meeting.
- Take notes during the meeting of things to potentially follow up on.
- Have student's current schedule, grades, and progress monitoring on hand.
- Gather student's cumulative file/portfolio.
- If a team member cannot make it to the meeting, make sure to get that member's input about the student's progress.
- Send message to all attendees with a reminder of the meeting (possibly a calendar invite sent in advance with a reminder on the day of).
- Take the time to answer questions during and after the IEP meeting as families develop them.
- Thank the IEP team (including the family) for their time and dedication to this meeting.

Day after the IEP Meeting

- Begin implementation of final IEP as soon as possible.
- If another meeting is needed to help complete the IEP, make plans for that.
- Print out final IEP and place into student's file.
- Call parents to check in and see if they have any questions.
- Thank them for their time.
- Another option for this is to write a letter.
- If the family could not attend, be sure they have the appropriate paperwork to understand what was discussed during the meeting. Then, obtain their informed consent to evaluate/begin recommended interventions by signing the consent form.
- Make copies of final IEP for anyone who works with the child.

- Remember confidentiality.
- Make any necessary corrections to IEP, including updates to goals or present levels as discussed and agreed upon in the meeting.
- Send parents a final copy of the IEP.
- Touch base with IEP team, making sure that each member's responsibility in terms of the IEP is understood.
- Relay the information gained from the meeting with anyone else necessary, including any member of the IEP team who was unable to attend the meeting.
- Begin constant communication with the parent(s)/guardian(s) of the student with the IEP regarding progress.
- Make a list of everything that was discussed at the IEP meeting; this information may be important to refer back to.
- Teacher sends email to say that all the IEP documents have been completed.
- May need to schedule a second meeting if the IEP was not completed.

Week after the IEP Meeting

- If IEP has not yet been implemented, begin (accommodations and specifically designed instruction) now to be in accordance with the timeline in place: no later than 10 school days!
- Each member of the team needs to be notified and prepared to start implementing once parents agree and sign.
- Send out an IEP overview to team members: ensure they are collecting data and monitoring student's progress to meeting benchmark/annual goals.
- Maintain constant communication with the parent(s)/guardian(s) of the student with the IEP regarding progress.
- Record/collect progress monitoring data toward benchmark/annual goals.
- Collect data from varying sources (a portfolio or physical file with this information included/gathered), not just from one type of assessment, assignment, or environment.
- Notify or update teachers of any new data tracking methods (such as progress monitoring).
- Check in on the student's progress since the IEP meeting occurred.
- Mail any original documents to the LEA and a copy to the parents.

Appendix C

Tips for Virtual IEP Meetings

Not every parent can make it into the district building for an IEP meeting. This may be due to work, family, or other responsibilities. Even though parents cannot physically come to the meeting, districts should still do everything they can to get parents to participate in the process. Ways to get parents involved can include Zoom, FaceTime, Skype, or just use of a phone. Widespread use of these became necessary as a result of the recent COVID-19 pandemic. The following are tips for school districts to pay attention to as a part of using alternative formats for IEP meetings. Please emphasize to your school team the need to keep the parent informed and get their meaningful participation. The following tips are provided to facilitate that participation, not to reduce it.

(1) As done for other IEP meetings, work to make sure the parents have a draft of the document(s) that are to be discussed prior to the meeting. Not only does this ensure they have a chance to read them ahead of time, it is good practice so they can digest the information prior to the meeting and come ready to discuss the program and placement.

(2) Make sure the documents you provide to the parents (and others) are clearly marked about what they are, and that each document also has clear page numbers. Both of these will be of great assistance when referencing documents in a virtual meeting. Use the names and page numbers of the documents when referencing the specific documents.

(3) If you are using some form of technology for live broadcasting the meeting, make sure parents (and others) have the necessary equipment and WIFI signal to participate. A trial test is a good way to checking on whether this works. Some participants' signals are better in one part of the house than others. Some parents may also need a different or newer laptop or tablet in order to participate. Strongly consider loaning them a laptop or tablet for the meeting. Even if you do find you have good technology, including a good WIFI signal, make sure there is an all-in number for the parents (and others) in case they are having problems with participating in the meeting, get removed from the live stream, or their WIFI signal does not work. Think about the backup plan before you need it.

(4) If people are sitting around a table, ensure the microphone works for everyone in the room and does not just work in one direction.

(5) If using presentation software, make sure the room is arranged so that the individuals who are not in the room can see everyone else, i.e., that the camera is not just focused on one person. An important part of participating in meetings is body language. If the remote participant cannot see what is occurring in the room, their participation is reduced. Remind the participants in the room that they are being watched at all times and to act accordingly: this is good advice for face-to-face meetings as well.

(6) Like any IEP meeting, make sure there are introductions of everyone who is in attendance. If you are using the phone for the meeting, make sure everyone identifies who they are prior to speaking.

(7) Many of the virtual forms also have a recording function. If you are going to be recording the meeting, make sure everyone knows this is occurring.

(8) Group rules for talking. Discuss the fact that since you are using technology that participants will have to wait while others are talking because it makes it very difficult to hear what is being said. Take turns. Give everyone a chance to communicate and share their information with others.

(9) Work to ensure the method that is being used has screen-sharing technology. This makes it easier for everyone to see what is happening and reference the same document at the same time.

(10) If screen sharing of a computer or tablet is going to be used, ensure the images that others will see when you are transferring to the screen share are appropriate. Check to make sure there is not open emails from students, parents, or other documents on your desktop that may release identifiable information to others.

(11) Work with the parents throughout the process to make sure they have a say in the agenda items, and that they also know what to expect as a part of the meeting. One of the big difficulties is that parents often feel overwhelmed at these meetings; make sure they are as comfortable as possible and that there are no surprises for them.

(12) Like other IEP meetings, make sure the parents know they can invite others to be a part of the meeting.

(13) For parents who are English language learners, make sure an interpreter is available who can translate and help the parents with understanding what is being discussed.

(14) For parents who are deaf or hard of hearing, use closed captions or ensure there is an interpreter who can help the parents understand what is being discussed.

(15) Periodically remind meeting attendees to cite specific page numbers on the documents to ensure everyone knows what is being discussed.

(16) Since the meeting is occurring virtually, there will be a loss of awareness that you would get if the individuals are in the room due to body language. Therefore, much more than in a face-to-face meeting, ask the parents if they have any questions, concerns, or issues that need to be addressed. Be careful how you ask the question; make sure they are open-ended and not just yes/no.

(17) Make sure all the staff are engaging in professional behavior at all times. If you are using some of the videoconferencing tools, you do not know what the parents are focusing on. They may be focusing on just one individual, or they may be paying attention to a group of individuals in the corner. Make sure all staff know they are being watched, and that they are expected to engage in professional behavior at all times. This includes what they are looking at, background sounds, background images, and what they are wearing. Tell everyone to assume they are the one that is being watched at all times.

(18) Some IEP meetings can become very emotional. Allow for this to happen and allow the parents to take a break and compose themselves. They are being watched too, and sometimes they are not comfortable with the situation.

(19) Like other IEP meetings, make sure the parents know they can ask for another meeting and that they do not have to finish everything in this one meeting.

(20) Like other IEP meetings, provide the parents with a point person who will follow up after the meeting to make sure any additional questions or concerns are addressed.

(21) Use the sample agenda items found in the other sections of this book for this meeting as well. Make sure the parents have a say in the items for the agenda, and that you listen to any concerns they may have.

(22) Review the meeting minutes. Go over the minutes of the virtual meeting with everyone at the end and ensure everyone is in agreement. Get copies to the parents as soon as possible.

Appendix D

Determining if an Aide Is Needed

The purpose of this section is to explain the components of the aide assessment and clarify the use of the form. Similar to the section on transportation support, this section will walk through the aide assessment form, explaining questions and why they are important, along with providing guidance and additional information that will help an IEP team in determining aide needs for eligible students with disabilities. It is recommended IEP teams consider every eligible student's needs for an aide at the minimum on an annual basis, or more frequently if there are changes to the students medical, behavioral, or instructional needs.

The purpose of this form is fairly straightforward: to assist IEP teams in making appropriate aide determinations. As noted in other sections, all decisions about a student need to be made related to the student's individual needs, and not based on the student's disability label. Do not assume all students with a certain disability need supports, and also do not assume that students with other disabilities DO NOT need supports. It depends on the individual needs of the student.

The purpose of special education is for the student to make progress. Keep this in mind when making aide determinations. Is the student making progress? If not, an aide may be necessary. However, also keep in mind that our goal in working with students is to have them become as independent as possible. The team should constantly think about whether there is a way the aide can be weaned from the student, focusing on getting the students to be independent. For some students, this may not be the case, but it should be a focus.

There may be additional questions raised not covered by this form: please add whatever questions or comments that are necessary. This form is not intended to provide legal guidance related to aide, just questions that IEP teams should ask to ensure students receive the aide supports necessary to attend the programs that are provided.

Two other important points. First, the individuals who are provided the information on this form are on a need-to-know basis. Work with the staff on the importance of confidentiality and not unnecessarily disclosing information to others. Second, the answers from this form may need to be modified on a regular basis. Work to make sure those who need to know about the changes are provided the information so they can provide a safe and appropriate learning environment for the student.

A non-annotated copy of the form is included at the end of the section.

I.

Type of Aide Required and Purpose of Support

Name:_____

Age:_____

Grade Level:_____

Disability(ies):_____

Primary Support:_____

Related Services:_____

School:_____

Date of Last IEP Revision:_____

Level of Support:_____

(Check the type of aide needed to support the student. Once the team has selected the type of aide that is needed, use specific aide need form to define specific needs.)

- Instructional Support: The student *needs* this type of aide to assist with instruction in the classroom setting. The instructional assistant's support is necessary for the student to complete instructional tasks. Without the support of this person, the student would be unable to complete the requirements and/or meet expectations within the classroom.
- Behavioral Support: The student *needs* this type of aide, in accordance with a behavior support plan, to support behavioral needs in the school setting. The behavioral assistant's support is necessary for the student to participate safely with others. Without the support of this person, the student would be unable to complete the requirements and/or meet expectations within the classroom.
- Health Support: The student *needs* this type of aide, in accordance with a health services plan, to monitor health needs in the school setting. The health assistant's support is necessary for the student to complete tasks involving health concerns. Without the support of this person, the student would be unable to complete the requirements and/or meet expectations within the classroom.

Comments

(1) The purpose of this part of the form is to determine what type of aide is necessary (if any) for the student. Some students may need aides in multiple settings. Ensure they receive the support necessary to make progress on their goals and objectives.

(2) Instructional support can be broadly defined as a variety of tasks, including implementing instructional programs, assisting with assessing student performance, and other tasks as needed by the instructor.

(3) Behavioral support can be broadly defined as assistance for students who exhibit angry, aggressive, withdrawn, or other correctable behaviors while at school or at school activities. Behavioral support could also create positive behavior strategies for children while promoting positive reinforcement.

(4) Health support can be broadly defined as assistance for a student who needs to be provided direct care, or personal assistance related to their disability. Assistance can be with activities such as bathing, grooming, dressing, and toileting. Students may need help with feeding or exercise. In some settings, students may need help with monitoring of vital signs or with taking their medications.

(5) The needs of the student may change over time. Regularly review the needs of the student to see if they are being appropriately addressed.

II.

Type of Aide Required and Purpose of Support

Name:_____

Age:_____

Grade Level:_____

Disability(ies):_____

Primary Support:_____

Related Services:_____

School:_____

Date of Last IEP Revision:_____

Level of Support:_____

(Check the type of aide needed to support the student. Once the team has selected the type of aide that is needed, use specific aide need form to define specific needs.)

- Instructional Support: The student needs this type of aide to assist with instruction in the classroom setting. The instructional assistant's support is necessary for the student to complete instructional tasks. Without the support of this person, the student would be unable to complete the requirements and/or meet expectations within the classroom.
- Behavioral Support: The student needs this type of aide, in accordance with a behavior support plan, to support behavioral needs in the school setting. The behavioral assistant's support is necessary for the student to participate safely with others. Without the support of this person, the student would be unable to complete the requirements and/or meet expectations within the classroom.
- Health Support: The student needs this type of aide, in accordance with a health services plan, to monitor health needs in the school setting. The health assistant's support is necessary for the student to complete tasks involving health concerns. Without the support of this person, the student would be unable to complete the requirements and/or meet expectations within the classroom.

The purpose of this section is to explain the components of the aide assessment related to behavioral needs and clarify the use of the form. This form should be used after the aide assessment form is used determining the type of aide a student might need. This section will walk through the aide assessment behavioral form, explaining questions and why they are important, providing guidance and additional information that will help an IEP team in determining behavioral aide needs for eligible students with disabilities. It is recommended IEP teams consider every eligible student's needs for an aide at the minimum on an annual basis, or more frequently if there are changes to the student's medical, behavioral, or instructional needs.

The purpose of this form is fairly straightforward: to assist IEP teams in making appropriate behavioral aide determinations. As noted in other sections, all decisions about a student need to be made related to the student's individual needs, and not based on the student's disability label. Do not assume all students with a certain disability need supports, and also do not assume students with other disabilities DO NOT need supports. It depends on the individual needs of the student.

The purpose of special education is for the student to make progress. Keep this in mind when making behavioral aide determinations. Does the student engage in behaviors that may inhibit their learning or that of others? If so, a behavioral aide may be necessary. However, also keep in mind that our goal in working with students is to have them become as independent as possible. The team should constantly think about whether there is a way that the aide can be weaned from the student, focusing on getting the students to be independent. For some students, this may not be the case, but it should be a focus.

There may be additional questions raised not covered by this form: Please add whatever questions or comments that are necessary. This form is not intended to provide legal guidance related to behavioral aides, just questions that IEP teams should ask to ensure students receive the aide supports necessary to attend the programs that are provided.

Two other important points. First, the individuals who are provided the information on this form are on a need-to-know basis. Work with the staff on the importance of confidentiality and not unnecessarily disclosing information to others. Second, the answers from this form may need to be modified on a regular basis. Work to make sure those who need to know about the changes are provided the information so they can provide a safe and appropriate learning environment for the student.

A non-annotated copy of the form is included at the end of the section.

II.

Behavior aide level of supports

Name:_____

Age:_____

Grade Level:_____

Disability(ies): _____

Primary Support:_____

Related Services: _____

School:_____

Date of Last IEP Revision:_____

Level of Support:_____

(Check all that apply to the student's needs in the school setting.)

Comments

1) This part of the form is fairly self-explanatory. Keep in mind the form may need to be updated on a regular basis.
   - **Behavioral Support: The student *needs* this type of aide, in accordance with a behavior support plan, to:**
     ◦ Prompt or cue through verbal, visual, or physical signals, or combinations thereof, the application of learned coping or adaptive responses.
     ◦ Interpret for the student then-occurring life events, social interactions, and verbal and nonverbal communication in a manner that identifies the emotional and social signals being used and explains their meaning in context.
     ◦ Prompt or facilitate appropriate peer or adult interaction.
     ◦ Implement a crisis management plan.
     ◦ Reinforce appropriate or replacement behavior or provide scheduled reinforcement.
     ◦ Collect and record or chart behavioral data.
     ◦ Rehearse or role-play anticipated situations and appropriate behaviors and responses related to previously identified areas of difficulty.
     ◦ Model, review, or discuss appropriate or replacement behavior or alternative behaviors.
     ◦ Disengage the student from an activity or environment to which the student is responding with inappropriate behaviors.
     ◦ Review after-the-fact appropriate or inappropriate behaviors and either deliver reinforcement or discuss and plan future responses to similar situations.
     ◦ Apply principles of functional behavior analysis to promote systematic development of communication and social skills and appropriate on-task behaviors.

- ○ Demonstrate successful strategies to significant adults who will apply those strategies to transfer previously acquired skills from one environment, activity, or person to another.
- ○ Interrupt, block, or restrain aggressive or self-injurious behavior and redirect to appropriate replacement behaviors. Please describe:

1. The types of aggressive or self-injurious behavior observed:

_____

_____

_____

_____

_____

_____

_____

2. The frequency of behaviors:

_____

_____

_____

3. The conditions under which such behavior occurs:

_____

_____

_____

Comments

(1) This list is not comprehensive. There may other components necessary depending upon the student's behavioral needs. Make sure they are addressed.

(2) Any program for the student should be addressed through the use of quantifiable data from observations regarding the student's progress (or lack thereof). Train staff to take regular behavioral data reflecting the needs of the student, which they also relate to the needs of the others in the classroom, in addition to the needs of the general school population.

(3) Ensure there is appropriate training, along with follow-up for implementation, on the information and use of this form.

(4) Ensure everyone responsible for the implementation of this form understands their responsibilities.

(5) Ensure there can be a meeting, if necessary, if there are changes needed or problems noted with the use of this plan.

(6) If aides or teachers feel they need more support, work to quickly determine the level of support necessary so that they can adequately perform their jobs.

Behavior:

A (Antecedent)	B (Behavior)	C (Consequence)

Behavior:

A (Antecedent)	B (Behavior)	C (Consequence)

Comments

(1) This is where the team would place information related to any A-B-C chart that has been completed on the student. It is important to highlight any antecedents that may be causing the behaviors to occur. The team can have multiple sections of this chart if there are multiple behaviors that are serving as an antecedent.

(2) Have the team also be aware of the consequences of the behaviors to help determine if the they are reinforcing the behaviors.

Specific training needed:

Next steps and who is responsible:

Step to be taken:	Responsible party:

Comments

(1) Not everyone will be aware of the specifics of behavior management. There may need to be training to demonstrate not only how to observe and document the behaviors, but also how to not reinforce the behaviors.

(2) Document the specific steps that are to be taken, along with who will be providing the training. Make sure the training is tailored to the specifics of the student's needs.

(3) Like the other sections of this form, there may be a need to revisit this section of the form periodically as the behaviors either change or adapt over time.

School Day Needs Assessment

Directions: Review the student's entire school day and determine specifically what the student can or cannot do and the extent he/she needs assistance.

Activity	What student can do without assistance	What student cannot do and needs accommodations to complete	What student cannot do and needs assistance with	Identify areas to promote social acceptance and how peers will be utilized	Identify areas you will target for independence (should be identified in IEP)

Comments

(1) As much as possible, go through the student's day highlighting where they specifically may need assistance. This can help as the team makes determinations about whether the aide needs to be with the student the full day or part of the day, and where there may be times to consider whether the supports are really necessary.

(2) This chart can also help with determining when there is a need for a substitute aide about where they specifically need to provide support.

(3) Ensure there is appropriate training for any and all teachers and aides who need to know about working with the student.

(4) Like other sections, this may need to be modified on a regular basis. Keep the team aware of any changes.

II.

Behavior Aide Level of Supports

Name:_____

Age:_____

Grade Level:_____

Disability(ies):_____

Primary Support:_____

Related Services: _____

School:_____

Date of Last IEP Revision:_____

Level of Support:_____

(Check all that apply to the student's needs in the school setting.)

- **Behavioral Support: The student *needs* this type of aide, in accordance with a behavior support plan, to:**
  - Prompt or cue through verbal, visual, or physical signals, or combinations thereof, the application of learned coping or adaptive responses.
  - Interpret for the student then-occurring life events, social interactions, and verbal and nonverbal communication in a manner that identifies the emotional and social signals being used and explains their meaning in context.
  - Prompt or facilitate appropriate peer or adult interaction.
  - Implement a crisis management plan.
  - Reinforce appropriate or replacement behavior or provide scheduled reinforcement.
  - Collect and record or chart behavioral data.
  - Rehearse or role-play anticipated situations and appropriate behaviors and responses related to previously identified areas of difficulty.
  - Model, review, or discuss appropriate or replacement behavior or alternative behaviors.
  - Disengage the student from an activity or environment to which the student is responding with inappropriate behaviors.

- Review after-the-fact appropriate or inappropriate behaviors and either deliver reinforcement or discuss and plan future responses to similar situations.
- Apply principles of functional behavior analysis to promote systematic development of communication and social skills and appropriate on-task behaviors.
- Demonstrate successful strategies to significant adults who will apply those strategies to transfer previously acquired skills from one environment, activity, or person to another.
- Interrupt, block, or restrain aggressive or self-injurious behavior and redirect to appropriate replacement behaviors. Please describe:

1. The types of aggressive or self-injurious behavior observed:

_____

_____

_____

_____

_____

_____

_____

2. The frequency of behaviors:

_____

_____

_____

3. The conditions under which such behavior occurs:

_____

_____

_____

_____

Behavior:

A (Antecedent)	B (Behavior)	C (Consequence)

Behavior:

A (Antecedent)	B (Behavior)	C (Consequence)

Specific training needed:

_____

_____

_____

_____

_____

_____

Next steps and who is responsible:

Step to be taken:	Responsible party:

School Day Needs Assessment

Directions: Review the student's entire school day and determine specifically what the student can or cannot do and the extent to which he/she needs assistance.

Activity	What student can do without assistance	What student cannot do and needs accommodations to complete	What student cannot do and needs assistance with	Identify areas to promote social acceptance and how peers will be utilized	Identify areas you will target for independence (should be identified in IEP)

Appendix F

Instructional Aide Levels of Supports Form

The purpose of this section is to explain the components of the aide assessment related to instructional needs and clarify the use of the form. This form should be used after the aide assessment form is used determining the type of aide a student might need. This section will walk through the aide assessment instructional form, explaining questions and why they are important, providing guidance and additional information that will help an IEP team in determining instructional aide needs for eligible students with disabilities. It is recommended that IEP teams consider every eligible student's needs for an aide at the minimum on an annual basis, or more frequently if there are changes to the students medical, behavioral, or instructional needs.

The purpose of this form is fairly straightforward: to assist IEP teams in making appropriate instructional aide determinations. As noted in other sections, all decisions about a student need to be made related to the student's individual needs, and not based on the student's disability label. Do not assume that all students with a certain disability need supports, and also do not assume that students with other disabilities DO NOT need supports. It depends on the individual needs of the student.

The purpose of special education is for the student to make progress. Keep this in mind when making instructional aide determinations. Does the student need someone to provide support to help maximize instructional time? If so, an instructional aide may be necessary. However, also keep in mind that our goal in working with students is to have them become as independent as possible. The team should constantly think about whether there is a way that the aide can be weaned from the student, focusing on getting the students to be independent. For some students, this may not be the case, but it should be a focus.

There may be additional questions raised not covered by this form: Please add whatever questions or comments that are necessary. This form is not intended to provide legal guidance related to instructional aides, just questions that IEP teams should ask to ensure students receive the aide supports necessary to attend the programs that are provided.

Two other important points. First, the individuals who are provided the information on this form are on a need to know basis. Work with the staff on the importance of confidentiality and not unnecessarily disclosing information to others. Second, the answers from this form may need to be modified on a regular basis. Work to make sure those who need to know about the changes are provided the information so they can provide a safe and appropriate learning environment for the student.

A non-annotated copy of the form is included at the end of the section.

I.

Instructional Aide Level of Supports

Name:_____

Age:_____

Grade Level:_____

Disability(ies):_____

Primary Support:_____

Related services: _____

School:_____

Date of last IEP revision:_____

Level of Support:_____

(Check all that apply to the student's needs in the school setting.)

Comments

(1) This part of the form is fairly self-explanatory. Keep in mind the form may need to be updated on a regular basis.
  * **Instructional Support. The student** *needs* **this type of aide to:**
    ◦ Preview or review instruction.
    ◦ Prompt or cue application of learning strategies.
    ◦ Prompt or redirect attention.
    ◦ Clarify, simplify, restate, or repeat instructions.
    ◦ Drill for fluency.
    ◦ Assist with writing process.
    ◦ Highlight key terms or concepts in texts and other reading materials.
    ◦ Assist with note taking.
    ◦ Serve as a reader of text written at levels above instructional or independent reading level of the student.
    ◦ Prompt or cue language or other communication in natural or functional contexts.
    ◦ Other (describe):

    _____

    _____

    _____

Comments

(1) This is not an all-inclusive list. There may be other tasks an instructional aide may have when working with a student. Consider the needs of the student in the present level statement of the IEP and ensure they are being addressed in the goals and that the student is being supported.

(2) Any program for the student should be addressed through the use of quantifiable data from observations regarding the student's progress (or lack thereof).

Train staff to take regular data reflecting the needs of the student and who they relate to the needs of the others in the classroom, in addition to the needs of the general school population.

(3) Ensure there is appropriate training, along with follow-up for implementation, on the information and use of this form.

(4) Ensure that everyone responsible for the implementation of this form understands their responsibilities.

(5) Ensure that there can be a meeting, if necessary, if there are changes needed or problems noted with the use of this plan.

(6) If aides or teachers feel they need more support, work to quickly determine the level of support necessary so that they can adequately perform their job.

Specific training
needed:_____

_____

_____

Next steps and who is responsible:

Step to be taken:	Responsible party:

Comments

(1) Not everyone will be aware of the specifics of working with students with disabilities. There may need to be training to demonstrate how to not only observe and document any needs but also to not reinforce the incorrect behaviors.

(2) Document the specific steps that are to be taken, along with who will be providing the training. Make sure the training is tailored to the specifics of the student's needs.

(3) Like the other sections of this form, there may be a need to revisit this section of the form periodically as the needs either change or adapt over time.

School Day Needs Assessment

Directions: Review the student's entire school day and determine specifically what the student can or cannot do and the extent he/she needs assistance.

Activity	What student can do without assistance	What student cannot do and needs accommodations to complete	What student cannot do and needs assistance with	Identify areas to promote social acceptance and how peers will be utilized	Identify areas you will target for independence (should be identified in IEP)

Comments

(1) As much as possible, go through the student's day highlighting where they specifically may need assistance. This can help as the team makes determinations about whether the aide needs to be with the student full day, part of the day, and where there may be times to consider whether the supports are really necessary.

(2) This chart can also help with determining when there is a need for a substitute aide about where they specifically need to provide support.

(3) Ensure there is appropriate training for any and all teachers and aides who need to know about working with the student.

(4) Like other sections, this may need to be modified on a regular basis. Keep the team aware of any changes.

II.
Instructional Aide Level of Supports

Name:_____

Age:_____

Grade Level:_____

Disability(ies):_____

Primary Support:_____

Related services: _____

School:_____

Date of last IEP revision:_____

Level of Support:_____

(Check all that apply to the student's needs in the school setting.)

- **Instructional Support. The student *needs* this type of aide to:**
  - Preview or review instruction.
  - Prompt or cue application of learning strategies.
  - Prompt or redirect attention.
  - Clarify, simplify, restate, or repeat instructions.
  - Drill for fluency.
  - Assist with writing process.
  - Highlight key terms or concepts in texts and other reading materials.
  - Assist with note taking.
  - Serve as a reader of text written at levels above instructional or independent reading level of the student.
  - Prompt or cue language or other communication in natural or functional contexts.
  - Other (describe):

  _____

  _____

  _____

Specific training needed:

_____

_____

_____

Next steps and who is responsible:

_____

Step to be taken:	**Responsible Party:**

School Day Needs Assessment

Directions: Review the student's entire school day and determine specifically what the student can or cannot do and the extent he/she needs assistance.

Activity	What student can do without assistance	What student cannot do and needs accommodations to complete	What student cannot do and needs assistance with	Identify areas to promote social acceptance and how peers will be utilized	Identify areas you will target for independence (should be identified in IEP)

Appendix G
Health Aide Levels of Supports Form

The purpose of this section is to explain the components of the aide assessment related to health needs and clarify the use of the form. This form should be used after the aide assessment form is used determining the type of aide a student might need. This section will walk through the aide assessment health form, explaining questions and why they are important, providing guidance and additional information that will help an IEP team in determining health aide needs for eligible students with disabilities. It is recommended that IEP teams consider every eligible student's needs for an aide at the minimum on an annual basis, or more frequently if there are changes to the students medical, behavioral, or instructional needs.

The purpose of this form is fairly straightforward: to assist IEP teams in making appropriate health aide determinations. As noted in other sections, all decisions about a student need to be made related to the student's individual needs, and not based on the student's disability label. Do not assume that all students with a certain disability need supports, and also do not assume that students with other disabilities DO NOT need supports. It depends on the individual needs of the student.

The purpose of special education is for the student to make progress. Keep this in mind when making health aide determinations. Does the student have health or medical needs requiring support? However, also keep in mind that our goal in working with students is to have them become as independent as possible. The team should constantly think about whether there is a way that the aide can be weaned from the student, focusing on getting the students to be independent. For some students, this may not be the case, but it should be a focus.

There may be additional questions raised not covered by this form: Please add whatever questions or comments that are necessary. This form is not intended to provide legal guidance related to health aides, just questions that IEP teams should ask to ensure students receive the aide supports necessary to attend the programs that are provided.

Two other important points. First, the individuals who are provided the information on this form are on a need-to-know basis. Work with the staff on the importance of confidentiality and not unnecessarily disclosing information to others. Second, the answers from this form may need to be modified on a regular basis. Work to make sure those who need to know about the changes are provided the information so they can provide a safe and appropriate learning environment for the student.

A non-annotated copy of the form is included at the end of the section.

I.

Health Level of Supports

Name:_____

Age:_____

Grade Level:_____

Disability(ies): _____

Primary Support:_____

Related Services: _____

School:_____

Date of Last IEP Revision:_____

Level of Support:_____

(Check all that apply to the student's needs in the school setting.)

- **Health Support: The student *needs* this type of aide, in accordance with a health services plan, to:**
  - ☐ Monitor for seizure activity, vital signs, other medical symptoms, or drug side effects. Describe the nature of the activity or symptom for which monitoring will be required and, if possible, the actual or expected frequency of such activity or symptoms:

  _____

  _____

  _____

  - ☐ Implement emergency medical procedures pending arrival of nurse.
  - ☐ Monitor or make routine adjustments to equipment. Describe the equipment in
    question: _____
  - ☐ Assist with toileting or self-care.
  - ☐ Assist with feeding.
  - ☐ Assist with mobility (wheelchair, walker, lift, positioning).
  - ☐ Other (describe):

  _____

  _____

  _____

Comments

(1) This list is not comprehensive. There may other components necessary depending upon the student's medical or health needs. Make sure they are addressed.

(2) Any program for the student should be addressed through the use of quantifiable data from observations regarding the student's progress (or lack thereof). Train staff to take regular data reflecting the needs of the student and who they

relate to the needs of the others in the classroom, in addition to the needs of the general school population.

(3) Ensure there is appropriate training, along with follow-up for implementation, on the information and use of this form.

(4) Ensure that everyone responsible for the implementation of this form understands their responsibilities.

(5) Ensure that there can be a meeting, if necessary, if there are changes needed or problems noted with the use of this plan.

(6) If aides or teachers feel they need more support, work to quickly determine the level of support necessary so that they can adequately perform their job.

Specific training needed:

_____

_____

_____

Next steps and who is responsible:

Steps to be taken:	Responsible party:

Comments

(1) Not everyone will be aware of the specifics of health management. There may need to be training to demonstrate not only how to observe and document any health needs, but also to ensure the student is safe and monitored appropriately.

(2) Document the specific steps that are to be taken, along with who will be providing the training. Make sure the training is tailored to the specifics of the student's needs.

(3) Like the other sections of this form, there may be a need to revisit this section of the form periodically as the health needs either change or adapt over time.

School Day Needs Assessment

Directions: Review the student's entire school day and determine specifically what the student can or cannot do and the extent he/she needs assistance.

Activity	What student can do without assistance	What student cannot do and needs accommodations to complete	What student cannot do and needs assistance with	Identify areas to promote social acceptance and how peers will be utilized	Identify areas you will target for independence (should be identified in IEP)

Comments

(1) As much as possible, go through the student's day highlighting where they specifically may need assistance. This can help as the team makes determinations about whether the aide needs to be with the student the full day, part of the day, and where there may be times to consider whether the supports are really necessary.

(2) This chart can also help with determining when there is a need for a substitute aide about where they specifically need to provide support.

(3) Ensure there is appropriate training for any and all teachers and aides who need to know about working with the student.

(4) Like other sections, this may need to be modified on a regular basis. Keep the team aware of any changes.

II.

Health Level of Supports

Name:_____

Age:_____

Grade Level:_____

Disability(ies): _____

Primary Support:_____

Related Services: _____

School:_____

Date of Last IEP Revision:_____

Level of Support:_____

(Check all that apply to the student's needs in the school setting.)

- • **Health Support: The student *needs* this type of aide, in accordance with a health services plan, to:**
  - ▢ Monitor for seizure activity, vital signs, other medical symptoms, or drug side effects. Describe the nature of the activity or symptom for which monitoring will be required and, if possible, the actual or expected frequency of such activity or symptoms:

    _____

    _____

    _____

  - ▢ Implement emergency medical procedures pending arrival of nurse.
  - ▢ Monitor or make routine adjustments to equipment. Describe the equipment in question:_____
  - ▢ Assist with toileting or self-care.
  - ▢ Assist with feeding.
  - ▢ Assist with mobility (wheelchair, walker, lift, positioning).
  - ▢ Other (describe):

    _____

    _____

    _____

Specific training needed:

_____

_____

_____

Next steps and who is responsible:

Steps to be taken:	Responsible party:

School Day Needs Assessment

Directions: Review the student's entire school day and determine specifically what the student can or cannot do and the extent he/she needs assistance.

Activity	What student can do without assistance	What student cannot do and needs accommodations to complete	What student cannot do and needs assistance with	Identify areas to promote social acceptance and how peers will be utilized	Identify areas you will target for independence (should be identified in IEP)

Meeting Date_____

Student Name:_____

Date of Birth:_____ Grade Level:_____

Disability(ies):_____

School Attending:_____

District: _____

Case Manager:_____

Related Services:_____

Level of Support:_____

Date of Last IEP Revision:_____

Transportation Information

Address: _____

City: _____ State: _____ Zip: __ Phone: _____

Guardian Name(s): _____

Who can get child off of the bus:_____

Guardian's Cell Phone Number(s): _____

Guardian's Email Address: _____

District of Residence:_____

Classroom Location: _____

District Resident? If not, clarify: _____

Length of Ride:_____

Can this student be transported with his or her peers?

- Yes, with no modifications or support
- Yes, with modifications specified below
- No, needs special transportation with modifications noted below

Route change considerations

  ○ To meet the student's medical/behavioral needs
  ○ Are there problems with certain locations that need to be avoided?

- ◦ Sounds/smells/problems with highways?
- ◦ To lessen exposure to traffic?
- ◦ Length of time on bus?
- ◦ Order of pick-up issues?
- ◦ Concern about others on the bus?
- ◦ Other: Clarify: _____

Weather factors

- ◦ Weather factors:

  - • Clarify: _____

  - • Protocol:

    _____

    _____

- ◦ Street/sidewalk conditions:

  - • Clarify: _____

  - • Protocol:

    _____

    _____

Pickup/Drop-off Notes

- ◦ Pull in drive to pick up/drop off
- ◦ Pick up/drop off on residence side
- ◦ Pick up required medicine/device from parents/guardians:
  Clarify: _____
- ◦ Pick up/drop off at school entrance that allows for less congestion or more supervision
- ◦ Supervision required when dropped off at school? Clarify: _____
- ◦ Other: Clarify: _____

Seating on Bus/Van

- ◦ Front of bus/van
- ◦ Back of bus/van
- ◦ Assigned seat
- ◦ Seating with limited access to other riders
- ◦ Away from door or window
- ◦ Window seat
- ◦ Seated with feet on floor or low floor bus
- ◦ Seated out of emergency exits
- ◦ Seated with seat belt on
- ◦ Seated with harness only

- ○ Seated with seat belt and harness
- ○ Seated with car seat/booster seat
- ○ Seated next to aide
- ○ Other devices necessary for travel. Clarify: _____
- ○ Other: Clarify: _____

Behaviors

- ○ Does the student have behaviors on the bus?
  - • Yes
  - • No

If yes, please give further details about behaviors:

_____

_____

_____

- ○ Who should the bus driver contact if there is a behavior issue?

_____

- ○ Add any relevant behaviors from the BIP.

_____

_____

Supervision Necessary?

- ○ **Discharge of Student** - Can this student be discharged from the bus/van without an adult waiting to receive him/her?
  - ○ Yes
  - ○ No

    - • If No and no adult is present, who should be called?

    _____

- ○ **Supervision/Assistance When Taking Transportation:**
  - ○ To board bus/on steps
  - ○ To remain safe in "danger zone" – from all sides of the bus
  - ○ To cross street or safely navigate into home/school
  - ○ To stay seated upright on the seat in the compartment
  - ○ To maintain appropriate/safe behavior
  - ○ To avoid contact with emergency exits
  - ○ To avoid putting anything out of the windows
  - ○ To navigate emergency exits
  - ○ To leave bus in the event of an emergency

- Person(s) responsible:

  _____

- Level of assistance:

  _____

Communication

- Verbal
- English language learner (specify native language): _____
- Sign language
- Communication board
  - Will communication board be on the bus?
    - Yes
    - No
- Picture exchange system
- Gestures
- Other:_____

Equipment

- Auditory equipment
- Special items for the student
  - special book
  - transitional item
  - access to music
  - screen device
- Step-stool access
- Safety vest/harness (can be used on traditional bus seat without lap belt or reinforced seat with lap belt) _____
  - Waist size with outer clothing _____
  - Waist size without outer clothing _____
  - Person(s) responsible for putting vest on/off _____
  - Person(s) responsible for connecting vest to mount/taking vest off of mount
    _____
  - Person(s) responsible for installing mount

    _____
- Child safety seat _____ Weight _____ Height _____
- Wheelchair
  - Person responsible for attaching chair

    _____
- Safety items on bus:
  - Transport of auxiliary equipment according to appropriate guidelines
  - Child safety belt cutter
  - Non-latex gloves
  - Evacuation blanket
  - Individual student bag

- Basic first aid kit and emergency numbers
- Belt extender
- Body fluid cleanup kit
- Oxygen
- Steps taken to carry oxygen:

_____

_____

- Other: Clarify: _____

Procedural Safeguards for Medical/Behavioral Concerns

- Medical crisis intervention plan (attached)
- Behavioral intervention plan (attached) with training
- Crisis management plan that can be implemented from the bus
- Do not resuscitate order
  - Person responsible:_____
  - Protocol:_____
- Oxygen or ventilator: Clarify: _____
  - Person responsible:_____
  - Protocol:_____
- Cardiac problems: Clarify: _____
  - Person responsible:_____
  - Protocol:_____
- Seizure precautions: Clarify:_____
  - Person responsible:_____
  - Protocol:_____
- Asthma or other respiratory conditions: Clarify: _____
  - Person responsible:_____
  - Protocol:_____
- Allergies: Clarify: _____
- Shunt precautions: Clarify: _____
  - Person responsible:_____
  - Protocol:_____
- Feeding tube or significant swallowing problems: Clarify: _____
  - Person responsible:_____
- Fragile bones or other orthopedic precautions: Clarify: _____
- Medication side effects: Clarify: _____
- Other: Clarify: _____

TRAINING AND SUPPORT

- Does the student need a test ride?
  - Yes – Date to be completed _____
  - No

- **OTHER**
  - Equipment use for field trip; will the sending district provide equipment?
    - Yes
      - If so, what equipment?   _____
    - No
    - Who is responsible for maintaining /cleaning equipment?_____
- Sending district has a weather-related delay; who is responsible for calling
  - (1) parents:_____
  - (2) bus driver:_____

- School district where classroom is has delay; who is responsible for calling
  - (1) parents:_____
  - (2) bus driver:_____

- If seating needs to be adjusted, who is responsible?_____

Summary of Transportation Plan

- Date provided to transportation_____

Next Steps Required

- Yes – Training required for staff, drivers, parents, caregivers
  - Type of training needed _____
  - Participants _____
  - Date of training _____
- No

Steps to be taken:	Responsible party:

Transportation Training for Student Necessary?

- Yes
  - Clarify: _____

- No

Notification to Parent/Guardian:

If there are any changes in your child's medical or behavioral status that you believe may affect transportation, please contact one of the following people to assist with the plan:

_____

_____

_____

IEP team participants:

Transportation personnel	Title	Date
Parent	Title	Date
Name	Title	Date
Name	Title	Date

References

A Nation at Risk (1983). Available at https://www2.ed.gov/pubs/NatAtRisk/risk.html.

Advance CTE. https://careertech.org/career-clusters.

Aguilar, J. (2018, February 12). Douglas County Schools must pay the private education costs of student who has autism, judge rules. *Denver Post*.

Amanda J. v. Clark County School District, 260 F.3d 1106 (9th Cir. 2001).

Anchorage School District, 51 IDELR 230 (SEA AK 2008).

B.P. and A.P. v. New York City Department of Education, 842 F. Supp. 2nd 605 (EDNY 2012).

Bangser, M. (2008). Preparing high school students for successful transitions to postsecondary education and employment. National High School Center. https://files.eric.ed.gov/fulltext/ED502596.pdf.

Bateman, B. D. (1995). Writing individualized education programs for success. *Learning Disabilities Association*. Available at https://www.wrightslaw.com/advoc/articles/iep.success.bateman.htm.

Bateman, B. D. (2017). Individual education programs for children with disabilities. In J. M. Kauffman, D. P. Hallahan, & P. C. Pullen (Eds.). *Handbook of Special Education* (2nd ed.). pp. 91–108). Routledge.

Bateman, B. D., & Herr, C. M. (2013). *Writing Measurable IEPs Goals and Objectives* (3rd ed). Attainment.

Bateman, B. D., & Linden, M. A. (2012). *Better IEPs: How to Develop Legally Correct and Educationally Useful Programs* (5th ed.). Attainment.

Beattie v. Board of Education, 169 Wis. 231 (1919).

Berney, D. J., & Gilsbach, T. (2017). Substantive vs. procedural violations under the IDEA. http://www.berneylaw.com/2017/11/12/substantive-vs-procedural-violations-idea/

Blakely, S. (1979). Judicial and legislative attitudes toward the right to an equal education of the handicapped. *Ohio State Law Journal, 40*(3), 603–636.

Board of Education of Monroe-Woodbury Central Sch. Dist., 31 IDELR 121 (SEA NY 1999).

Board of Education of the City School District of the City of New York, 24 IDELR 199 (SEA NY 1996).

Board of Education of the Rhinebeck Central School District, 103 LRP 25895 (SEA NY 2003).

Board of Education of the Wappingers Central School District, 43 IDELR 131 (SEA NY 2004).

Board of the Hendrick Hudson Central School District v. Rowley, 458 US 176 (1982).

Bolling v. Sharpe, 347 US 497 (1954).

Bradley, M. R., & Danielson, L. (2004). The office of special education LD initiative: A context for inquiry and consensus. *Journal for Learning Disabilities, 27*, 184–194.

Brand, B., & Valant, A. (2013). Improving college and career readiness for students with disabilities. College and Career Readiness Center at American Institutes for Research https://ccrscenter.org/sites/default/files/Improving%20College%20and%20Career%20Readiness%20for%20Students%20with%20Disabilities.pdf.

Briggs v. Elliott, 342 US 350 (1952).

Brown v. Board of Education, 347 US 483 (1954).

Carter v. Florence County School District Four, 950 F.2d 156 (4th Cir. 1991).

Chris D. v. Montgomery County Board of Education, 743 Supp. 1524 (MD AL 1990).

Coalition for Evidence-Based Policy. (2002). *Bringing Evidence-Based Policy to Education: A Recommended Strategy for the U.S. Department of Education*. Author. Available in PDF format at www.excelgov.org/usermedia/images/uploads/PDFs/CoalitionFinRpt.pdf.

Colker, R. (2013). *Disabled Education: A Critical Analysis of the Individuals with Disabilities Education Act*. New York University Press.

Common Core State Standards Initiative. (2012). Common Core State Standards Initiative: Preparing America's students for college and career. Retrieved from http://www.corestandards.org.

Congressional Record (1975). v. 121, p. 19485, remarks of Senator Williams. https://www.govinfo.gov/content/pkg/GPO-CRECB-1975-pt22/pdf/GPO-CRECB-1975-pt22-6-2.pdf.

Congressional Record (1977, April 26). p. 122, https://www.govinfo.gov/app/details/GPO-CRECB-1977-pt32/GPO-CRECB-1977-pt32-1.

Conroy, T., & Yell, M. L. (2019). Free appropriate public education after *Endrew F. v. Douglas County School District* (2017). *Touros Law Review, 35*(1), 100–169.

Couette, M. (Director and Writer) (2014). *Mr. Civil Rights: Thurgood Marshall and the NAACP*. [Film, educational DVD]. South Hills Films.

Council of Chief State School Officers, Assessing Special Education Students [ASES-SCASS] (2012). *Module 2: Standards-Based IEPs: Developing Present Levels of Academic Achievement and Functional Performance*. Authors. https://ccsso.org/resource-library/assessing-special-education-students-ases.

Council on Developmental Disabilities, Minnesota Department of Administration (2013). *The ADA Legacy Project: The Right to Education Based on Brown v. Board of Education*. Downloaded on 6/24/2018 from https://mn.gov/mnddc/ada-legacy/ada-legacy-moment6.html.

D.F. v. Western School Corporation, 921 F. Supp. 559 (SD Ind. 1996).

Dallas Independent School District, 29 IDELR 930 (SEA TX 1998).

Daniel R.R. v. State Board of Education, 874 F.2d 1036 (5th Cir. 1989).

Davis v. County School Board of Prince Edward County, 103 F. Supp. 337 (ED, VA, 1952).

Deal v. Hamilton County Board of Education, 392 F.3d 840 (6th Cir. 2004).

Deno, S. L. (1992). The nature and development of curriculum-based measurement. *Preventing School Failure, 36*(2), 5–10.

Department of Public Welfare v. Haas, 154 NE 2d 265 (IL 1958).

District of Columbia Public Schools, 109 LRP 25385 (SEA DC 2007).

Drasgow, E., Martin, C. A. O'Neill, R. E., & Yell, M. L. (2014). Functional behavioral assessments, behavior intervention plans, and collecting student data. In M. L. Yell, N. B. Meadows, Drasgow, E. & Shriner, J. G. (Eds.), *Evidence-Based Practices for Education Students with Emotional and Behavioral Disorders* (2nd ed.). Pearson.

Drasgow, E., Yell, M. L., & Robinson, T. R. (2001). Developing legally correct and educationally appropriate IEPs. *Remedial and Special Education, 22*(6), 353–373.

Endrew F. v. Douglas County School District, 580 U. S. ____ (2017), 798 F.3d 1329 (10th Cir. 2015), 137 S. Ct. 988 (2017), 290 F. Supp. 3d 1175 (D. Colo. 2018).

Escambia County Board of Education v. Benton, 358 F. Supp. 1112 (SD AL 2005).

Every Student Succeeds Act (2015). 20 USC §1111et seq.

Federal Register (1999). Vol. 64, p. 12, 428, p. 12, 473, p. 12,592.

Federal Register (2006). Vol. 71, p. 46, 568, p. 46, 587–46, 588, p. 46, 664, p. 46, 665, p. 46, 667, p. 46, 670, p. 46, 674, p. 46, 675.

Flexer, R. W. (2007). *Transition Planning for Secondary Students with Disabilities*. Pearson.

Gebhart v. Belton, 87 A.2d 862 (Del. Ch. 1952).

Gerstmyer v. Howard County Public Schools, 850 F. Supp. 361 (D. MD 1994).

Gilhool, T. K. (1976). Education: An inalienable right. In F. Weintraub, A. Abeson, J. Ballard, & M. LaVor (Eds.), *Public Policy and the Education of Exceptional Children* (pp. 14–21). The Council for Exceptional Children.

Gilhool, T. K. (2011). *Visionary Voices, Leaders, Lessons, and Legacy: An Interview with Thomas K. Gilhool.* Institute on Disability at Temple University. http://www.temple.edu/instituteondisabilities/voices/detailVideo.html?media=006-01.

H.B. v. Las Vegas Unified School District, 239 Fed Appx 342 (9th 2007).

Handel, R. C. (1975). The role of the advocate in securing the handicapped child's right to an effective minimal education. *Ohio State Law Journal, 36*(2), 349–375.

Harbaugh, W. H. (1973). *Lawyer's Lawyer: The Life of John W. Davis.* Oxford University Press.

Hedin, L., & DeSpain, S. (2018). SMART or not? Writing specific, measurable IEP goals. *Teaching Exceptional Children, 51*(2), 100–110. DOI: 10.1177/0040059918802587.

Herr, S. (1972a). Retarded children and the law: Enforcing the constitutional rights of the mentally retarded. *Syracuse Law Review, 23,* 995–1036.

Herr, S. (1972b). Rights into action: Protecting human rights of the mentally handicapped. *Catholic Urban Law Review, 26* (2), 204–318.

History.com (2009, October). Separate but equal. https://www.history.com/topics/black-history/brown-v-board-of-education-of-topeka.

Huefner, D. S. (2000). *Getting Comfortable with Special Education Law: A Framework for Working with Children with Disabilities.* Christopher-Gordon.

Illinois State Board of Education, *Alternate assessment participation guidelines* (2019). Available at https://www.isbe.net/Documents/dlm-partic-gdlns.pdf

In Re: Martin v. North Middlesex Regional School District (2020). https://www.specialedlaw.com/database/in-re-martin-v-north-middlesex-regional-school-district-bsea-20-03661/.

Individuals with Disabilities Education Act (IDEA), 20 USC § 1400 et seq.

Individuals with Disabilities Education Act (IDEA) Regulations (2006). 34 CFR § 300 et seq.

Jones, N. L. (1995). The Individuals with Disabilities Education Act: Congressional Intent. https://digital.library.unt.edu/ark:/67531/metacrs7997/m1/1/high_res_d/95-669A_1995May19.pdf.

Karvonen, M. (2009). Developing standards-based IEPs that promote effective instruction. In M. Perie (Ed.), *Considerations for Alternate Assessment Based on Modified Achievement Standards: Understanding the Eligible Population and Applying That Knowledge to Their Instruction and Assessment* (pp. 51–89). Retrieved December 12, 2015 from: http://www.cehd.umn.edu/nceo/AAMAS/AAMASwhitepaper.pdf.

King, D. G. (2009). Van Duyn v. Baker School District: A "material" improvement in evaluating a school district's failure to implement an individualized education program. *Northwestern Journal of Law and Social Policy, 4*(2), 457–486.

Kirby v. Cabell County Board of Education, 46 IDELR 149 (SD WV 2006).

Kochar-Bryant, C. A., Shaw, S., & Izzo, M. (2008). *What Every Teacher Should Know about Transition and IDEA 2004.* Pearson.

Kode, K. (2016). *Elizabeth Farrell and the History of Special Education.* The Council of Exceptional Children.

Lake, S. E. (2007). *Slippery Slope: The IEP Missteps Every Team Must Know-and How to Avoid Them.* LRP Publications.

Lennon, T. (2007). *The Supreme Court.* [Film; four-disc DVD]. Public Broadcasting System.

Letter to Anonymous, (OSEP 2008).

Letter to Cox, 54 IDELR 60, OSEP.

Letter to Gray, 50 IDELR 198 (OSEP 2008).

Letter to Hayden, 22 IDELR 501 (OSEP 1994).

Letter to Richards, 55 IDELR 107 (OSEP 2010).

Levine, E. L., & Wexler, E. (1981). *Pl-94142: An Act of Congress*. Collier Macmillan.

Lignugaris/Kraft, B., Marchand-Martella, N., & Martella, R. (2001). Writing better goals and short-term objectives or benchmarks. *Teaching Exceptional Children, 34*(1), 52–58.

M. C. v. Antelope Valley Union High, 858 F.3d 1189 (9th Cir. 2017).

M. L. v. Federal Way School District, 394 F.3d 634 (9th Cir. 2005).

Mager, R. F. (1962). *Preparing Instructional Objectives*. Center for Effective Performance.

Mager, R. F. (1997). *Preparing Instructional Objectives: A Critical Tool in the Development of Effective Instruction*. Center for Effective Performance.

Martin, E. W. (2013). *Breakthrough: Federal Special Education 1965-1981*. Bardolf & Company.

Martin, E. W., Martin, R., & Terman, D. L. (1996). The legislative and litigative history of special education. *The Future of Children: Special Education for Students with Disabilities, 6*(1), 25–39.

Mazzotti, V. L., Rowe, D. A., Kelley, K. R., Test, D. W., Fowler, C. H., Kohler, P. D., & Kortering, L. J. (2009). Linking transition assessment and post-secondary goals: Key elements in the secondary transition planning process. *Teaching Exceptional Children, 42*, 44–51.

Mehfoud, K. S. (2015). Determining LRE without engaging in predetermination. Presentation to the Tri-State Special Education Law Conference, Omaha, NE.

Mills v. Board of Education of the District of Columbia, 348 F. Supp. 866 (DDC 1972).

Musgrove, M. (2011). *A Response to Intervention (RTI) Process Cannot Be Used to Delay-Deny an Evaluation for Eligibility under the Individuals with Disabilities Education Act (IDEA)*. US Department of Education, the Office of Special Education Programs. Available at https://www2.ed.gov/policy/speced/guid/idea/memosdcltrs/osep 11-07rtimemo.doc.

National Assessment of Student Progress (n.d.). Available at https://nces.ed.gov/ nationsreportcard/.

National Center on Educational Outcomes at: https://nceo.info/state_policies/policy/parti cipationswd.

Neubert, D. A. (2003). The role of assessment in the transition to adult life process for students with disabilities. *Exceptionality, 11*(2), 63–75.

Neubert, D. A., & Leconte, P. J. (2013). Age-appropriate transition assessment: The position of the Division on Career Development and Transition. *Career Development and Transition for Exceptional Individuals, 36*, 72–83.

Norlin, J. W. (2011). *What School Districts Need to Know about IDEA Parental Rights*. LRP Publications.

Norlin, J. W., Slater, A. E., & Lake, S. E. (2010). *IEPs That Succeed: Developing Legally Compliant Programs*. LRP Publications.

Ohio Revised Code Annotated. http://codes.ohio.gov/orc/3321.

O'Neill, P. T. (2004). *No Child Left Behind Compliance Manual*. Brownstone Publications.

O'Neill, R. E., Horner, R. H., Albin, R. W., Story, K., & Sprague, J. R. (1997). *Functional Analysis of Problem Behavior: A Practical Assessment Guide* (2nd ed.). Brooks/Cole.

Osborne, A. (2004). To what extent can procedural violations of the IDEA render an IEP invalid? *West's Education Law Reporter, 185*, 15–29.

Pelka, F. (2012). *What We Have Done: An Oral History of the Disability Rights Movement*. University of Massachusetts Press.

Pennsylvania Association for Retarded Citizens (PARC) v. Commonwealth of Pennsylvania, 343 F. Supp. 279 (ED Pa. 1972).

Pierangelo, R. & Giuliani, G. (2007). *Understanding, Developing, and Writing Effective IEPs: A Step-by-Step Guide for Educators.* Corwin Press.

Plessy v. Ferguson, 163 US 537 (1896).

President's Commission on Excellence in Special Education (2002). *A New Era: Revitalizing Special Education for Children and Their Families.* Available at https://ectacenter.org/~pdfs/calls/2010/earlypartc/revitalizing_special_education.pdf

Prince, A. M. T., Plotner, A. J., & Gothberg, J. E. (2019). Current special education legal trends for transition-age youth. In D. F. Bateman & M. L. Yell (Eds.), *Current Trends and Legal Issues in Special Education* (pp. 72–91). Corwin.

Rehabilitation Act of 1973, Section 504, 29 USC § 794.

Rio Rancho Public Schools, 40 IDELR 140 (SEA NM 2003).

Roncker v. Walter, 700 F.2d 1058 (6th Cir. 1983).

Rowe, D. A., Kortering, L. J., & Test, D. W. (2012). Transition assessment for instruction. In D. W. Test (Eds.), *Teaching Secondary Transition Skills.* Brookes Publishing.

Rowe, D. A., Mazzotti, V. L., Hirano, K., & Alverson, C. Y. (2015). Transition assessment in the 21st century. *Teaching Exceptional Children, 47,* 301–309. doi: 10.1177/0040059915587670

Rowley, A. J. (2008). Rowley revisited: A personal narrative. *Journal of Law and Education, 37*(3), 311–328.

Rowley v. The Board of Education of the Hendrick Hudson Central School District, 493 F. Supp. (SDNY, 1980). 632 F.2d 945 (2nd Cir. 1980).

Rutland South Supervisory Union, 33 IDELR 140 (SEA VT 2000).

Sacramento City School District v. Rachel H., 14 F.3d 1398 (9th Cir. 1994).

Salvia, J., Ysseldyke, J. E., & Witmer, S. (2017). *Assessment in Special and Inclusive Education* (13th ed.). Cengage.

Shriner, J. G., & Thurlow, M. L. (2019). What educators need to know about accountability. In D. Bateman & M. Yell (Eds.), *Current Trends and Legal Issues in Special Education* (pp.126–138). Corwin Press.

Shriner, J. G., Carty, S. J., Rose, C. A., Shogren, K. A., Kim, M., & Trach, J. S. (2013). Effects of using a web-based individualized education program decision-making tutorial. *Journal of Special Education, 47,* 175–185.

Shriner, J. G., Carty, S. J., Thurlow, M. L., & Goldstone, L. (2017). Teacher perspectives on the impact of standards and professional development on Individualized Education Programs. *Journal of Special Education Leadership, 30,* 67–81.

Slater, A. E. (2010). *Placement under the IDEA: Avoiding Predetermination and Other Legal Pitfalls.* LRP Publications.

Smith, R. C. (1996). *A Case about Amy.* Temple University Press.

Solicitor General (2017). Brief for the United States as Amicus Curiae to US Supreme Court. In *Endrew F. v. Douglas City Schools.* Downloaded from https://www.scotusblog.com/wp-content/uploads/2016/08/15-827-US-Amicus.pdf.

Stafford, R. T. (1978). Education for the handicapped: A senator's perspective. *Vermont Law Review, 3,* 71–82.

T.B. v. Prince George's County Board of Education, 70 IDELR 40 (D. MD 2016).

T.Y. v. New York City Department of Education, 584 F.3d 412 (2nd Cir. 2009).

Tatgenhorst, A., Norlin, J. W., & Gorn, S. (2014a). *The Answer Book on Special Education Law* (5th ed.). LRP Publications.

Tatgenhorst, A., Norlin, J. W., & Gorn, S. (2014b). *The Answer Book on Special Education Law* (6th ed.). LRP Publications.

Tatgenhorst, A., Norlin, J. W., & Gorn, S. (2014c). *What Do I Do When...The Answer Book on Special Education Law* (6th ed.). LRP Publications.

Test, D. W., Aspel, N. P., & Everson, J. M. (2006). *Transition methods for youth with disabilities*. Pearson.

Tindal, G. A., & Marston, D. B. (1990). *Classroom-Based Assessment: Evaluating Instructional Outcomes*. Pearson.

US Department of Education (1994). Appendix C to Part 300. Available at https://www.wrightslaw.com/bks/aaiep/Appendix.C.1994.pdf.

US Department of Education (2015). *Dear Colleague Letter on Free and Appropriate Public Education (FAPE)*. Washington, DC: US Department of Education, Office of Special Education and Rehabilitation Services. Retrieved from: http://www2.ed.gov/policy/speced/guid/idea/memosdcltrs/guidance-on-fape-11-17-2015.pdf.

US Department of Education (2017). *Questions and Answers (Q&A) on U.S. Supreme Court Case Decision Endrew F. v. Douglas County School District Re-1*. Washington, DC: US Department of Education, Office of Special Education and Rehabilitation Services. Retrieved from: https://sites.ed.gov/idea/files/qa-endrewcase-12-07-2017.pdf.

Urban v. Jefferson County School District, 89 F.3d 720 (10th Cir. 1996).

Van Duyn v. Baker School District, 502 F.3d 811 (9th Cir. 2007).

Viscio v. School District of Pittsburgh, 684 F. Supp. 1310 (WD PA 1988).

Weatherly, J. (2015, March). *Keeping the "I" in IEP: Defensible IEP Practices*. Presentation to the Focus on Inclusion Conference. Indianapolis, IN.

Weber, M. C. (2008). *Special Education Law and Litigation Treatise* (3rd ed.). LRP Publications.

Weintraub, F. J., & Abeson, A. R. (1972). Appropriate education for all handicapped children: A growing issue. *Syracuse Law Review*, 23(4), 1037–1058.

Winzer, M. A. (1993). *History of Special Education from Isolation to Integration*. Gallaudet Press.

Yell, M. L. (2019). *The Law and Special Education* (5th ed.). Pearson.

Yell, M. L., & Bateman, D. F. (2017). Defining educational benefit. An update on the US Supreme Court's ruling in *Endrew F. v. Douglas County School District* (2017). *Teaching Exceptional Children*, 52(5), 283–290.

Yell, M. L., & Busch, T. W. (2012). Using curriculum-based measurement to develop educationally meaningful and legally sound individualized education programs (IEPs). In C. A. Espin, K. L. MacMaster, Rose, S., & M. M., Wayman (Eds.), *A Measure of Success: The Influence of Curriculum-Based Measurement on Education*. University of Minnesota Press.

Yell, M. L., & Rozalski, M. E. (2013). The peer-reviewed research requirement of the IDEA: An examination of law and policy. In B. G. Cook, M. Tankersley, & T. J. Landrum (Eds.). *Evidence-Based Practices* (pp. 1–26). Emerald.

Yell, M. L., Katsiyannis, A., & Shriner, J. G. (2006). *No Child Left Behind*, adequate yearly progress, and students with disabilities. *Teaching Exceptional Children*, 38(4), 32–39.

Yell, M. L., Katisiyannis, A., Ennis, R. P., Losinski, M., & Bateman, D. F. (2020). Making legally sound placement decisions. *Teaching Exceptional Children*, 52(5), 291–303.

Yell, M. L., Shriner, J. G., Thomas, S. S., & Katsiyannis, A. (2017). Special education law for leaders and administrators of special education. In J. B. Crockett, B. S. Billingsley, & M. L. Boscardin (Eds.). *Handbook of Leadership and Administration for Special Education* (2nd ed., pp. 69–96). Routledge.

Zettel, J. J., & Ballard, J. (1982). The Education for All Handicapped Children Act of 1975 (P.L. 94-142): Its history, origins, and concepts. In J. Ballard, B. Ramirez, & F. Weintraub (Eds.), *Special Education in America: Its Legal and Governmental Foundations* (pp. 11–22). Council for Exceptional Children.

Zirkel, P. A. (2015). The "red flags" for child find under the IDEA: Separating the law from the lore. *Exceptionality*, 23, 192–209. DOI: 10.1080/09362835.2014.986615.

Zirkel, P. A. (2017). Failure to implement the IEP: The third dimension of FAPE under the IDEA. *Journal of Disability Policy Studies*, 28(3), 174–179.

Zirkel, P. A., & Hetrick, A. (2017). Which parts of the IEP process are most procedurally vulnerable? *Exceptional Children*, 83(2), 219–235.

academic achievement. *See* present levels of academic achievement and functional performance
academic content standards, 75–76
achievement tests, 72, 77
administrative appeals officer, 37
adult service providers, 128
aide for student: behavioral support by, 178, 179, 181–85; behavioral support school day assessment for, 185–89; determination of, 177–79; health support by, 178, 179, 197–99; health support school day assessment for, 200–202; instructional support by, 178, 179, 191–93; instructional support school day assessment for, 194–96
Amanda J. v. Clark County School District, 32
ambition, 99, 104, 111
anger, *87*
ASRS. *See* Autism Spectrum Rating Scales
assessment: in IEP development, 73–74, *152*; for special education, 70–73. *See also* school day assessment
assessment for IEP accountability: alternate assessment in, 76; cognitive disability review for, 76; Every Student Succeeds Act on, 75; general assessment in, 76; IDEA on, 75–77; state academic content standards in, 75–76
assessment for IEP eligibility: achievement tests for, 72, 77; adaptive behavior scales for, 72; behavioral checklists for, 72; educational performance and, 71; eligibility determined by, 70–71, 77; eligibility limited by, 71, 71n5; initial requirements in, 68, *69*; intelligence tests for, 72, 77; legal requirements of, 68; parental consent in, 68, 70, 70n3; PLAAFP and, 67–68; purpose of, 68, 70; referral for, 70; tests for, 71–73
assessment for IEP planning: behavior problems in, 73–74; criterion-referenced tests for, 73; FBA in, 73–74; functional areas tests for, 73
assessment for IEP progress monitoring: accommodations in, 162; CBM in, 74, *75*; definition of, 74; formative assessment in, 74; frequency of, 74; goal referencing in, 74; IDEA on, 74; performance graphs in, 74, *75*
assessment for transition: definition of, 78–79, 127; formal assessments in, 80; informal assessments in, 80–81; PLAAFP in, 81–82; planning in, 79–80; selection of, 80–81; skills and, 81
assistive technology, 64
attendance laws, 5–7

autism: ASRS in, *90*; above average performance by, *89*; *Endrew F. v. Douglas County School District* on, 20–24; nonverbal communication lacking in, *89–90*; special education supplementary aids and services in, 126; in students with disabilities, 20–24, 63, 76
Autism Spectrum Rating Scales (ASRS), *90*

Bateman, Barbara, 59–60, 146, 151
Bateman, David F., 2, 32, 36, 100, 138
Beattie, Merritt, 6
Beattie v. Board of Education, 6
behavior, *102*; aide support in, 178, 179, 181–85, 185–89; anger in, *87*; assessment of, for IEP eligibility, 72; assessment of, for IEP planning, 73–74; IDEA on, 62–63; IEP development and, 62–63; lying in, *88*; measurable behavior statements in goals, of IEP, 95–96, 104, 106; on-task, *90*; PBIS in, 68; target, 95–96
Benton, Jarred, 94
blindness, 62, 63
Board of Education of the Hendrick Hudson Central School District v. Rowley: on deafness, 16–20, 23–24; on due process, 17; US Court of Appeals for the Second Circuit for, 17–18; US District Court for, 17; US Supreme Court for, 16, 18–20, 23–24, 25, 26
Board of Education of the Rhinebeck Central School District, 37, 110
Board of Education of Washington, DC, 9–10
Bolling v. Sharpe, 7
Bradley, M. R., 2
Braille, 62, 63
Brennan, William, 19
Briggs v. Elliott, 7
Brown v. Board of Education, 7–8, 13
Brown v. Board of Education of Topeka, 7

Carter, Shannon, 99
Carter v. Florence County Four, 99
CBM. *See* curriculum-based measures
charter schools, 157
child find, 26–27, *27*
Civil Rights Act of 1964, Title IV, 11
Coalition for Evidence-Based Policy, 114
cognitive disability, 76
Colker, R., 11
college, 127, 129–30
commercial progress monitoring programs, 97
Common Core State Standards, 79

communication needs: assistive technology for, 64; of student, 62, 63–64. *See also* nonverbal communication

Congress: on EAHCA, 1–2; on IEP, 1–2

Council for Exceptional Children, 7

counseling, 46, 133, *133*

courts: on EAHCA, 15; on FAPE, 15–24; on general education teacher, 60; on LRE, 141–43, 145–46; on parental participation in IEP process, 43, 58, 65; on student placement, 140–43, 145–46; US Court of Appeals, 17–18, 22, 32, 43, 49, 60; US District Court for, 17, 21–22, 23, 110. *See also* Supreme Court, US

curriculum-based measures (CBM), 74, *75*

Cuyahoga County Ohio Council for the Retarded Child, 7

Daniel R.R. v. State Board of Education, 141–42, 146

Danielson, L., 2

Daniel two-pronged test, 142

Davis v. County School Board of Prince Edward County, 7

deafness: *Board of Education of the Hendrick Hudson Central School District v. Rowley* ruling on, 16–20, 23–24; IEP development and, 62; in students with disabilities, 16–19, 23–24, 62

Deno, S. L., 74, 107–8

Department of Public Welfare v. Haas, 6

divorce, 44–45

Down syndrome, 141–42

Drasgow, E., 63

due process: for *Board of Education of the Hendrick Hudson Central School District v. Rowley*, 17; for *Endrew F. v. Douglas County School District*, 21

Dybwad, Gunnar, 8

educational performance, special education eligibility and, 71

Educational Sciences Reform Act, 114

Education for All Handicapped Children Act (EAHCA): Congress on, 1–2; courts on, 15; on FAPE, 12–13, 12n1, 14; on goals, 93–94; Martin on, 13; Stafford on, 1–2, 67; Supreme Court on, 18–19. *See also* Individuals with Disabilities Education Act

Education of the Handicapped Act (EHA), 10–11

EHA. *See* Education of the Handicapped Act

Eisenhower, Dwight, 8

Elementary and Secondary Education Act (ESEA), 10

Endrew F. v. Douglas County School District: on autism, 20–24; on due process, 21; US Court of Appeals for the Tenth Circuit for, 22; US Department of Education on, 81–82, 99; US District Court for, 21–22, 23; US Supreme Court for, 2, 20, 22–24, 25, 35, 99, 135–36

Escambia County Board of Education v. Benton, 94

ESEA. *See* Elementary and Secondary Education Act

ESY. *See* special education extended school year services

Every Student Succeeds Act, 75

F., Endrew (Drew), 20–23

failure: of general education, 114; of implementation dimension of IEP, 40–41

Family Educational Rights and Privacy Act (FERPA): parental right and child educational records, IDEA and, 49–50; on student educational records, 49

FAPE. *See* free appropriate public education

FBA. *See* functional behavioral assessment

federal government, in special education, 10–13

FERPA. *See* Family Educational Rights and Privacy Act

Firefly Autism House, 20

Ford, Gerald, 12

foster parents, 44

14th Amendment, 8

Frankfurter, Felix, 8

free appropriate public education (FAPE), 1; courts on, 15–24; definition of, 12–13; EAHCA on, 12–13, 12n1, 14; IDEIA on, 26; procedural dimension of, 26, 34; Rehnquist on, 18; Supreme Court on, 18–19. *See also* history, of FAPE

functional behavioral assessment (FBA), 73–74

Gebhart v. Belton, 7

general education: definition of, 144–45; failure of, 114; goal development and, 100; IEP development and, 159; NCLB on, 114–15; scientifically-based research in, 114–15; student placement in, 140, 143–44, *144*, 148, 159, 162; students in, 124; US Department of Education on, 100

general education curriculum: goals of IEP and, 100; math in, *87, 88*, 98; NCLB on, 114–15; SBR in, 114–15; student in, 124; US Department of Education on IEP on, 100

general education teacher: courts on, 60; in IEP team, 59–60, 60n1; student placement and, 60

General Outcomes Measures (GOM) in goals of IEP, 105

Gilhool, Thomas, 8–9

goals, of IEP, *153*; ambition in, 99, 104, 111; avoidance and, 104, 110–11, *111, 134,*

147–48, *150*; benchmarks in, 160; commercial progress monitoring programs in, 97; condition identification in, 96; criterion statement for, 96–98; EAHCA on, 93–94; *Endrew F. v. Douglas County School District* on, 99; *Escambia County Board of Education v. Benton* on, 94; general education curriculum and, 100; GOM in, 105; high-quality measurable annual, 100–106, *101–4*; IDEA on, 93–94, 159–60; IEP Quality Project on, 97, 100–101, *102–4*; Mager on, 94–95, 111; measurable behavior statements in, 95–96, 104, 106; methods for measurable annual, 94–100, *98*; PLAAFP in, 95, 99, 100, 104, 160; in progress monitoring assessment, 74, *153*; quality test questions for, 100–101, *101*, *102–4*; requirements in, 93–94, 95–98, *98*; short-term objectives for, 105–6, 105n2, 160; in special education related services, 121, 160–61; state requirements in, 98–99; student progress monitoring in, 107; substantive dimension identification of, 36–37; target identification in, 95–96; in transition planning, 128, 129–30; US Department of Education on, 99

GOM. *See* General Outcomes Measures

Handel, R. C., 2–3, 5–6
hard of hearing. *See* deafness
health: aide support for, 178, 179; school day assessment in, 200–202; support levels for, 197–99
Hehir, Thomas, 63
Herr, Stanley, 8
history, of FAPE: advocacy after *Brown* ruling in, 8–10; *Brown v. Board of Education* in, 7–8, 13; compulsory attendance laws, children with disabilities and, 5–7; EAHCA in, 12–13, 12n1, 14; federal involvement in, 10–13; *Mills v. Board of Education* in, 9–10; *Pennsylvania Association for Retarded Children v. Commonwealth of Pennsylvania* in, 9; Rehabilitation Act, Section 504 in, 11, 13–14; segregation in, 7–8, 11; state developments for, 10
Holland, Rachel, 142–43
Huefner, D. S., 93
Humphry, Hubert, 11

IDEA. *See* Individuals with Disabilities Education Act
IDEIA. *See* Individuals with Disabilities Education Improvement Act
IEP. *See* Individualized Education Program
IEP development, 2–3, 25–26, 67, 151; assessment in, 73–74, *152*; behavioral concerns and, 62–63; blindness and, 62, 63; deafness and, 62; final stage of, 57; general education and, 159; parental involvement in, 152, *152–53*; PLAAFP in, 35–36, 38, 39, 53–54, 60, 83–85, *152*; school district and, 157, 162–63, 165; service statements for, 34, *134*; in special education related services, 120–22, *153*; special factor accommodation in, 62–63. *See also* assessment for IEP accountability; goals, of IEP; implementation dimension, of IEP; meetings, for IEP; parental participation, in IEP process; procedural dimension, of IEP; substantive dimension, of IEP; team, for IEP

IEP Quality Project, 97, 100–101, *102–4*
implementation dimension, of IEP, 163–64; contract in, 40; definition of, 40, 41; failure of, 40–41; special education related services in, 132; special education services in, 132, 164; special education supplementary aids and services in, 132; special education teacher in, 59, 157; team in, 132–33, *133*
independent living, 130
Individualized Education Program (IEP): Bateman, D. on, 2; better practices in, 2; Congress on, 1–2; contract for, 158; history of, 5–14; Linden on, 2, 100, 138; Martin on, 13; problems with, 2; Roberts on, 2; Stafford on, 2, 13; Supreme Court on, 2, 15, 134, 151; verbal, 158. *See also* IEP development
Individuals with Disabilities Education Act (IDEA), 1, 22; Amendments (1997) on, 44, 63, 93; Amendments (2004) on, 30–31, 32, 77; Amendments (2006) on, 50, 58, 60; on assessment, 68, *69*, 73; on assessment for IEP accountability, 75–77; on assessment for progress monitoring, 74; on assistive technology, 64; on charter schools, 157; dispute regulation system of, 15–16; on divorce, 44–45; on eligibility, 70–71, 77; on ESY, 130; evaluation with, 28–29; on FBA, 74; on general education teachers in IEP and, 59–60, 60n1; on goals, 93–94, 159–60; IEP requirements by, 36, 38, 67, 157, 158; on LEA representatives, 58; LRE mandated by, 33–34; on mandatory team members, 57–58; on meetings, 50–51, 164–65; parental definition by, 44–45; parental procedural rights in, 45, *45*; parental right and child educational records, FERPA and, 49–50; parental right to attend meetings regarding child special education in, 50; parental right to related services in, 46, *47–48*, 49, 53–54; on person interpreting evaluation in IEP, 60; PRR in, 115; on special education services, 113–14, 117; on special education supplementary aids

and services, 122–23, 126; on special education teachers in IEP and, 59; special service definition by, 38–39; Stafford on, 138; on student behavioral concerns, 62–63; on student majority age, 61–62; on student placement, 33–34, 137–39, *139–40*, 146–47; on student progress monitoring, 110; on tests, 71–73. *See also* Individuals with Disabilities Education Act

Individuals with Disabilities Education Improvement Act (IDEIA), 26, 115. *See also* Individuals with Disabilities Education Act

instructional support: aide in, 178, 179; levels of, 191–93; school day assessment in, 194–96

intelligence tests, 72, 77

internal consistency, of IEP, *39*, 39–40

labels, 86

Lake, S. E., 30, 43

LEA. *See* local education agency representative

leader, *55–56*, 55–57

least restrictive environment (LRE): courts on, 141–43, 145–46; IDEA mandate of, 33–34; in student placement, 135, 137–38, 137–43, 141–43, 141–46, 144

Linden, M. A., 2, 100, 138

local education agency (LEA) representative: IDEA on, 58; in IEP meetings, 58–59, 165; qualifications of, 58–59; school principals as, 59; US Department of Education on, 58

LRE. *See* least restrictive environment

lying, *88*

Mager, Robert F., 94–95, 111

majority age, 46, 61–62

Marshall, Thurgood, 19

Martin, E. W., 7, 10, 13

math, *87*, *88*, 98

mediation, 58

meetings, for IEP, 157–58, 162; agenda for team, *55–56*, 55–57; day after, 170–71; day of, 169–70; documentation, IDEA and, 51; leader for, *55–56*, 55–57; LEA representative in, 58–59, 165; one day before, 169; one month before, 167–68; one week before, 168–69; parental involvement in, *47–48*, 50, 51–53, 54–55, 164; parental PLAAFP development in, 53–54; PRR in, 116; revisions and, 163; scheduling, IDEA and, 50–51, 164–65; student problem identification in, 56–57; Supreme Court on, 43, 58, 65; two months before, 167; two weeks before, 168; virtual, 173–75; week after, 171. *See also* team, for IEP

Mehfoud, Kathleen S., 106

members, of IEP team, *30*. *See also* team, for IEP

Mills v. Board of Education, 9–10

multi-tiered system of support (MTSS), *27*, 28n1, 68, *69*

Musgrove, Melody, 78

National Assessment of Student Progress (NASP), 114

National Association of Parents and Friends of Mentally Retarded Children, 8

National Center on Educational Outcomes, 76

NCLB. *See* No Child Left Behind Act

New York State Commissioner of Education, 17

Nixon, Richard, 11

No Child Left Behind Act (NCLB), 71, 114–15

nonverbal communication, *89–90*

Norlin, J. W., 46, 59

Office of Special Education and Rehabilitative Services (OSERS). *See* US Department of Education

Office of Special Education Programs (OSEP). *See* US Department of Education, on IEP

Paige, Rod, 115

PARC. *See* Pennsylvania Association for Retarded Children

parental participation, in IEP process: courts on, 43, 58, 65; IEP development by, 152, *152–53*; meaningful, 43, 46, *47–48*, 51–52, 54–55; parental definition, IDEA and, 44–45; parental procedural rights, IDEA and, 45, *45*; parental right and child educational records, IDEA, FERPA and, 49–50; parental right to attend meetings regarding child special education, IDEA and, 50; parental right to receive information on child progress, IDEA and, 49; parental right to related services, IDEA and, 46, *47–48*, 49, 53–54; in procedural dimension of IEP, 32; school personnel and, 51–52, 65; in transition planning, 128

parents, 8; consent from, 28, 52–53, 61, 68, 70, 70n3; in ESY, 132; foster, 44; Martin on, 7; meeting involvement by, *47–48*, 51–55, 58, 65, 164; meetings, Supreme Court on, 43, 58, 65; PLAAFP development with, 53–54; in student placement, 135–37, 147–48

PBIS. *See* positive behavior interventions and supports system

pediatrician, 126

peer-reviewed research (PRR), 161; in IDEA, 115; in meetings for IEP, 116; in special education services, 114–16, *116*; US Department of Education on, 115

Pennsylvania Association for Retarded Children (PARC), 9

Pennsylvania Association for Retarded Children v. Commonwealth of Pennsylvania, 9

PLAAFP. *See* present levels of academic achievement and functional performance statements

Plessy v. Ferguson, 8

positive behavior interventions and supports system (PBIS), 68

Preparing Instructional Objectives (Mager), 94–95, 111

present levels of academic achievement and functional performance (PLAAFP) statements: avoiding practices in, 86, *91*; in goals development, 95, 99, 100, 104, 160; in IEP assessment and, 67–68; in IEP development, 35–36, 38, 39, 53–54, 60, 83–85, *152*; parental development with, 53–54; progress evaluation and, 85; required components of, *82*, 82–83, *84*; in special education related services, 120; in special education services, 117; in special education supplementary aids and services, 125, 126; structure of, 83–85, *84*, 91, *91*; student needs in, 83; in student progress monitoring, 110; in substantive dimension, of IEP, 35–36, 38, 39; by team, for IEP, 83–84, 86; test questions for, *86–90*; in transition assessment, 81–82; US Department of Education on, 81

President's Commission on Excellence in Special Education, 77–78

procedural dimension, of IEP: child find in, 26–27, *27*; components of, 31–32, *31–32*; definition of, 26, 41; evaluation in, 28–29, *28–29*, 28n1; FAPE in, 26, 34; MTSS in, *27*, 28n1, 68, *69*; parental participation in, 32; placement, student and, 33–34; predetermination in, 32; procedural requirements of the initial evaluation and re-evaluation, *28–29*; team composition in, *30*, 30–31; timelines in, 29–30

PRR. *See* peer-reviewed research

Rachel H. test, 142–43

Reading Excellence Act, 114

reading proficiency, *88*, 98, *102*, *103*

regular education (teacher). *See* general education teacher

Rehabilitation Act, Section 504, 11, 13–14

Rehnquist, William, 6, 18

related service provider, 61, 122

response to intervention (RTI), 68, *69*, 78

Rio Rancho Public Schools, 37, 96

Roberts, John, 2, 106

Roncker, Neill, 141

Roncker feasibility test, 141, 142

Roncker v. Walter, 141

Rowley, Amy, 16–19, 23–24

Rozalski, M. E., 115–16

RTI. *See* response to intervention

Rutland South Supervisory Union, 3, 154

Sacramento City Unified School District v. Rachel H., 142–43

SBR. *See* scientifically-based research

school day assessment: behavioral support in, 185–89; health in, 200–202; instructional support in, 194–96

school district, 157, 162–63, 165

school personnel: educational methods by, 54–55; multidisciplinary team in, 70, 70n2; parental involvement encouraged by, 51–52, 65; related service provider as, 61, 122; special education supplementary aids and services in, 123–24, 126; student placement by, 137. *See also* general education teacher; LEA; special education teacher

school psychologist, 60

scientifically-based research (SBR), 114–15

segregation, 7–8, 11

special education: assessment process for, 70–73; eligibility tests for, 71–73, 77–78; President's Commission on Excellence in Special Education on, 77–78

special education extended school year services (ESY): definition of, 130, 132; eligibility in, 130–31, 132; IDEA on, 130; limits of, 131; parents in, 132; progress monitoring in, 131; team for IEP in, 131

special education related services: definition of, 120, *120*; eligibility for, 120–21; goals in, 121, 160–61; IEP development in, 120–22, *153*; IEP implementation of, 132; PLAAFP in, 120; related service provider in, 122; team for IEP in, 121; transportation in, 121; US Department of Education on, 121

special education services, *153*; date, duration, frequency, location and, 118, *118*; definition of, 117; delivery models of, 118–19; IDEA on, 113–14, 117; implementation of, 132, 164; indirect services in, 118–19; PLAAFP in, 117; PRR in, 114–16, *116*; pull-out services in, 119; push-in services in, 119; self-contained classrooms for, 119; specially designed instruction in, 117–19, *118*; team for IEP in, 117–18

special education supplementary aids and services, *153*; autism in, 126; barriers identified in, 124–25; definition of, 122–23; environmental profile in, 124; IDEA on, 122–23, 126; implementation of, 132; PLAAFP in, 125, 126; program modification in, 125–26; progress monitoring in, 125, 127; school personnel in, 123–24, 126; student placement in, 140, 146, 148; team for IEP in, 123–26; training for, 123–24, 126–27; US Department of Education on, 123

special education teacher, 161; IDEA on, 59; IEP implementation by, 59, 157; in IEP team, 59, 60n1, 132–33, *133*

speech impairment, 120

Stafford, Robert, 1–2, 13, 67, 138

student: behavioral concerns, IEP and, 62–63; communication needs of, 62, 63–64; in general education curriculum, 124; in IEP team, 61; majority age of, 46, 61–62; PLAAFP needs of, 83; in substantive dimension of IEP, 35–36; transition planning with, 61, 128; transportation for, 203–9. *See also* aide for student

student placement, *153*; continuum of alternative, 139, *139–40*, 146–47; courts on, 140–43, 145–46; *Daniel R.R. v. State Board of Education* on, 141–42, 146; *Daniel* two-pronged test in, 142; definition of, 136; determination of, *144–45*, 144–50, *149*, *150*; Down syndrome in, 141–42; in general education, 140, 143–44, *144*, 148, 159, 162; general education teacher and, 60; IDEA on, 33–34, 137–39, *139–40*, 146–47; integration in, 147; LRE in, 135, 137–43, 141–46; parents in, 135–37, 147–48; predetermination in, 137; in procedural dimension of IEP, 33–34; *Rachel H.* test in, 142–43; requirements of, 135; *Roncker* feasibility test in, 141; *Roncker v. Walter* in, 141; *Sacramento City Unified School District v. Rachel H.* in, 142–43; school personnel in, 137; steps for, 148–49, *149*; supplementary aids and services in, 140, 146, 148; team for IEP on, 135–40, 144, 145, 148–49, *149*, 150; US Department of Education on, 33, 60, 135–37, 145, 147; Yell on, 147

student progress monitoring, 114; analyzing data of, 108; characteristics of, 107, *108*; Deno on, 107–8; formative evaluation in, 107; goals of IEP and, 107; graphs for, 107–8, *108*; IDEA on, 110; in IEP planning, 106, 161; measurement strategy in, 110–11, *111*; Mehfoud on, 106; PLAAFP in, 110; progress monitoring form example of, *109*; purpose of, 106–7, 111; Roberts on, 106; by team for IEP, 106; US Department of Education on, 106, 107

students with disabilities, 159; accountability assessment for, 75–76; assistive technology for, 64; attendance laws, compulsory for, 5–7; autism in, 20–24, 63, 76; blindness in, 62, 63; after *Brown* ruling, 8–10; deafness in, 16–19, 23–24, 62; discrimination definition on, 11; educational performance of, 71; identification of, 77–78;

public school admission of, 1; special factors in IEP development for, 62–63; speech impairment in, 120

substantive dimension, of IEP: definition of, 34–35, 40, 41; goals identification in, 36–37; IDEA special service definition in, 38–39; internal consistency of, *39*, 39–40; PLAAFP statements in, 35–36, 38, 39; progress monitoring in, 36–37; services provided in, 38–39; student needs and, 35–36

Supreme Court, US: *Board of Education of the Hendrick Hudson Central School District v. Rowley* ruling by, 16, 18–20, 23–24, 25, 26; *Brown v. Board of Education* ruling by, 7–8, 13; on EAHCA, 18–19; *Endrew F. v. Douglas County School District* ruling by, 2, 20, 22–24, 25, 35, 99, 135–36; on FAPE, 18–19; on IEP, 2, 15, 134, 151; on parents, IEP meetings and, 43, 58, 65; on special education, 15

Tatgenhorst, A., 122–23

team, for IEP: assistive technology determination by, 64; avoidance, goals and, 104, 110–11, *111*, *134*, 147–48, *150*; behavioral aide determination by, 181–85; blindness accommodation by, 62, 63; decision making in, 58; English proficiency determination by, 64; in ESY, 131; general education teacher in, 59–60, 60n1; implementation by, 132–33, *133*; leader for, *55–56*, 55–57; LEA representative in, 58–59, 165; mandatory members, IDEA and, 57–58; mediation in, 58; meeting for, *55–56*, 55–57; members of, *30*, 30–31, 61; parents in, 58, 65; person interpreting evaluation in, 60, 73; PLAAFP by, 83–84, 86; related service provider in, 61, 122; school personnel in, 70, 70n2; special education related services in, 121; special education services in, 117–18; special education supplementary aids and services in, 123–26; special education teacher in, 59, 60n1, 132–33, *133*; special expertise individuals in, 61; special factor accommodation by, 62–63; student behavioral concerns and, 62–63; student communication needs in, 62, 63–64; student in, 61; student placement by, 135–40, 144, 145, 148–49, *149*, 150; student progress monitoring by, 106; student reaching age of majority and, 61–62; transition planning in, 127–30; transition services agency representative in, 61; US Department of Education on, 31

tests: achievement tests for IEP eligibility, 72, 77; criterion-referenced, 73; *Daniel* two-pronged, 142; functional areas, 73; goals and quality questions for, 100–101, *101*, *102–4*; IDEA on,

71–73; intelligence, 72, 77; PLAAFP questions for, *86–90*; *Rachel H.*, 142–43; *Roncker* feasibility, 141, 142; scores in, 86; special education eligibility, 71–73, 77–78; Woodcock Reading Mastery, 74

transition planning: adulthood domains in, 129; adult service providers in, 128; application of, 129–30; career planning in, 128, 130; college in, 127, 129–30; definition of, 127, 130; federal regulation on, 127; goal development in, 128, 129–30; independent living in, 130; parental consent in, 61; parental participation in, 128; student involvement in, 61, 128; team for IEP on, 127–30; transition services agency representative in, 61. *See also* assessment for transition

transportation: communication in, 206; equipment in, 206–7; planning for, 203–9; procedural safeguards in, 207–8; special education related services in, 121; supervision in, 205–6

US Department of Education, on IEP: on *Endrew F. v. Douglas County School District*, 81–82, 99; on general education curriculum, 100; on goals, 99; internal consistency in, 39; on LEA representatives, 58; parental rights in, 44–45; periodic reporting requirements in, 49; on PLAAFP, 81; on PRR, 115; on special education related services, 121; on special education supplementary aids and services, 123; on student placement, 33, 60, 135–37, 145, 147; on student progress monitoring, 106, 107; team composition in, 31

Vanik, Charles, 11
Vinson, Fred M., 8
visual impairment. *See* blindness

Waddy, Joseph, 10
Warren, Earl, 8
WCPM. *See* Words Correct per Minute
White, Byron, 19
Williams, Harrison, 12
Woodcock Reading Mastery Test, 74
Words Correct per Minute (WCPM), 85

Yell, M. L., 115–16, 147

Zirkel, P. A., 132

Mitchell L. Yell, Ph.D., is the Fred and Francis Lester Palmetto Chair in Teacher Education and a professor in special education at the University of South Carolina. He earned his Ph.D. in special education from the University of Minnesota. His professional interests include special education law, IEP development, progress monitoring, and parent involvement in special education. Dr. Yell has published 136 journal articles, 6 textbooks, and 38 book chapters and has conducted numerous workshops on various aspects of special education law, classroom management, and progress monitoring. His textbook, *The Law and Special Education,* is in its 5th edition. In 2020, he was awarded the Researcher of the Year from the Council for Exceptional Children. Dr. Yell also serves as a State-level due process review officer (SRO) in South Carolina and is on the Board of Directors of the Council for Exceptional Children. Prior to working in higher education, Dr. Yell was a special education teacher in Minnesota for 12 years.

David F. Bateman is a professor of special education at Shippensburg University of Pennsylvania. He was a special education classroom teacher and a due process hearing officer for the Commonwealth of Pennsylvania for hundreds of hearings. His latest area of research has been on the role of principals in special education. He has been a classroom teacher of students with learning disabilities, behavior disorders, intellectual disability, and hearing impairments and a building administrator for summer programs. Dr. Bateman earned a Ph.D. in special education from the University of Kansas. He has recently co-authored the following books: *A Principal's Guide to Special Education, A Teacher's Guide to Special Education, Charting the Course: Special Education in Charter Schools, Special Education Law Case Studies,* and *Current Trends and Legal Issues in Special Education.* He uses his knowledge of litigation relating to special education to assist school districts in providing appropriate supports for students with disabilities.

James G. Shriner is associate professor in the Department of Special Education at the University of Illinois Urbana-Champaign. His work includes research on the effects of federal and state policies on the educational services provided to students with disabilities. He is the creator and developer of the *IEP Quality Project Tutorial*—a web-based decision-making support tool for IEP teams (Institute of Education Sciences awards, R324J06002; R324A120081, and Illinois State Board of Education, *Part D* awards). Dr. Shriner serves as a member of the stakeholder advisory group of the National Center of Educational Outcomes (NCEO) at the University of Minnesota.